Introduction to

Controlled Vocabularies

Terminology for Art, Architecture,
and Other Cultural Works

First edition

Patricia Harpring

Murtha Baca, Series Editor

Published by the Getty Research Institute

The Getty Research Institute Publications Program
Thomas W. Gaehtgens, *Director, Getty Research Institute*
Gail Feigenbaum, *Associate Director*

Introduction to Controlled Vocabularies: Terminology for Art, Architecture, and Other Cultural Works
Lauren Edson, *Manuscript Editor*
Elizabeth Zozom, *Production Coordinator*
Designed by Hespenheide Design, Newbury Park, California
Printed and bound by Odyssey Press, Inc., Gonic, New Hampshire

Published by the Getty Research Institute, Los Angeles
Getty Publications
Gregory M. Britton, *Publisher*
1200 Getty Center Drive, Suite 500
Los Angeles, California 90049-1682
www.getty.edu

14 13 12 11 10 5 4 3 2 1

Library of Congress Cataloging-in-Publication Data
Harpring, Patricia.
Introduction to controlled vocabularies : terminology for art, architecture, and other cultural works / Patricia Harpring.
p. cm.
Includes bibliographical references.
ISBN 978-1-60606-018-6 (pbk.)
1. Subject headings—Cultural property. 2. Subject headings—Art. 3. Subject headings—Architecture. 4. Information retrieval. I. Title.
Z695.1.C85H37 2010
025.4'7—dc22

2009040848

Cover: The story of the Tower of Babel (Genesis 11) was an allegory to explain why different societies spoke different languages (in addition to the obvious warnings against pride toward the deity and urban evils). Babel was a city in Babylon, where after the great flood, humanity was united in one large urban center, speaking a single language. In their pride, the inhabitants began construction of the Tower of Babel, with the intention of reaching the clouds of heaven. Their arrogant plan was foiled by God, who scattered them across the earth and confused their language so they could no longer understand each other.

Draftsman: Lieven Cruyl (Flemish, ca. 1640–ca. 1720); etcher: Coenraet Decker (Dutch, 1651–1685); *Tower of Babel* (detail), etching; folio height 39 cm (15⅜ inches); in Athanasius Kircher (German, 1601/1602–1680); *Athanasii Kircheri e Soc. Jesu Turris Babel;* published: Amsterdam: Ex officina Janssonio-Waesbergianna, 1679; Research Library; The Getty Research Institute (Los Angeles, California); 85-B16716-pl.[2].

Back cover: Antoine Babuty Desgodets, after George Marshall, *The Temple of Vesta at Tivoli* (detail). See fig. 24.

Contents

Foreword

The Getty Vocabulary Program has devoted almost three decades to building thesauri that can be used as knowledge bases, cataloging and documentation tools, and online search assistants. In addition to building tools for use by art and cultural heritage professionals and the general public, we also provide training opportunities and educational materials on how to build and implement controlled vocabularies. Part of our mission as an institution devoted to research and education is to share our knowledge and expertise with the international art and cultural heritage communities in their broadest sense.

Elisa Lanzi's *Introduction to Vocabularies,* which appeared in print in 1998 and was updated in an online version in 2000, offers a general overview of vocabularies for art and material culture. *Introduction to Controlled Vocabularies* is a much more detailed "how-to" guide to building controlled vocabulary tools, cataloging and indexing cultural materials with terms and names from controlled vocabularies, and using vocabularies in search engines and databases to enhance discovery and retrieval in the online environment.

"How forceful are right words!" is written in Job 6:25. The King James Version of the Bible uses the word *forcible,* meaning "forceful" or "powerful," instead. In the online environment, words have the power to lead users to the information resources that they seek. But we should not force users to know what we consider to be the "right" word or name in order for them to be able to obtain the best search results.

We recognize that a single concept can be expressed by more than one word, and that a single word can express more than one concept. Words can change over time and take a variety of forms, and they can be translated into many languages. A carefully constructed controlled vocabulary provides catalogers and others who create descriptive metadata with the "right" or "preferred" name or term to use in describing collections and other resources, but it also clusters together all of the synonyms, orthographic and grammatical variations, historical forms, and even in some cases "wrong" names or terms in order to enhance access for a broad range of users without constraining them to the use of the "right" term. With millions of searches being conducted by millions of users each day via Web search engines and in proprietary databases, the power of words is a crucial factor in providing access to the wealth of information resources now available in electronic form. We hope that this book will provide organizations and individuals who wish to enhance access to their collections and other online resources with a practical tool for creating and implementing vocabularies as reference tools, sources of documentation, and powerful enhancements for online searching.

Murtha Baca, Getty Research Institute

Acknowledgments

I wish to thank Murtha Baca for her lasting support, thoughtful guidance, and expert editing. I am also grateful to Joan Cobb, Gregg Garcia, Marcia Zeng, and Karim Boughida, who provided invaluable advice on the technical aspects of this book. I extend sincere thanks to the indefatigable Getty Vocabulary Program editors Antonio Beecroft, Ming Chen, Robin Johnson, and Jonathan Ward, who proofed the manuscript and provided important feedback.

Finally, thanks go to the scores of earlier vocabulary editors and users of the Getty vocabularies, who have provided countless insights and advice over the last three decades.

Patricia Harpring

1. Controlled Vocabularies in Context

A controlled vocabulary is an information tool that contains standardized words and phrases used to refer to ideas, physical characteristics, people, places, events, subject matter, and many other concepts. Controlled vocabularies allow for the categorization, indexing, and retrieval of information. This book deals specifically with controlled vocabularies related to cultural works—products of human creativity that have visual aesthetic expression. Such vocabularies are employed with the ultimate goal of allowing cultural works, images of cultural works, and information about them to be discovered, brought together, and compared for study and appreciation.

The intended audience of this book includes students, academics, and professionals in art museums, art libraries, archives, visual resources collections, and other institutions that catalog the visual arts, architecture, and other cultural objects. The audience may include systems developers who support these communities as well as consortia or other groups attempting to compile or use vocabularies for cultural materials. The topics discussed here may also be applicable to disciplines outside the visual arts.

The art and cultural heritage communities have increasingly made use of vocabularies and other standards as they seek to provide access to information that was previously held in paper files or isolated in local systems. Inspired by the power of online databases and the World Wide Web, professionals in the various art and cultural heritage communities now see the value of efficiently exchanging information with each other. Practical concerns and limited resources have proven the value of shared cataloging. In addition, the mission of many cultural heritage institutions has changed over the years to include dissemination of information to the public and to other institutions. Institutions are gradually becoming adept at utilizing appropriate information standards, such as *Categories for the Description of Works of Art* (*CDWA*) and *Cataloging Cultural Objects* (*CCO*), as well as controlled vocabularies that are used or designed specifically for art and architecture, including the *Library of Congress Subject Headings* (*LCSH*) and the *Library of Congress Authorities,* the *Art & Architecture Thesaurus®* (*AAT*), the *Union List of Artist Names®* (*ULAN*), the *Getty Thesaurus of Geographic Names®* (*TGN*),

Robert Chenhall's *Revised Nomenclature for Museum Cataloging,* the *Thesaurus for Graphic Materials* (*TGM*), and the *Iconclass* system, among others.

Such data standards and controlled vocabularies take into account the unique nature of cultural information, which is characterized by conflicting opinions, changing interpretations, and information that must be expressed with nuance and indications of ambiguity and uncertainty. For example, scholars may disagree about the purpose of a given object or its date of creation, or a work may have been attributed to one artist in 1958 and then to a different artist in 2008 based on new analysis. Biographical information about an artist may be amended because of new research; the usage of a generic term such as *naive art* might differ over time. The history of these changing opinions is valuable in itself, so earlier opinions and original information must be preserved.

1.1. What Are Cultural Works?

In order to understand the context of the vocabularies discussed here, it is first necessary to define the types of materials for which the terminology is created.

In this book, objects representing visual arts and material culture are called *works. Material culture* refers to art, architecture, and also more broadly to the aggregate of physical objects produced by a society or culturally cohesive group. *Cultural works* are the physical artifacts of *cultural heritage,* which encompasses broadly the belief systems, values, philosophical systems, knowledge, behaviors, customs, arts, history, experience, languages, social relationships, institutions, and material goods and creations belonging to a group of people and transmitted from one generation to another. The group of people or society may be bound together by race, age, ethnicity, language, national origin, religion, or other social categories or groupings. The works discussed in this book are cultural works, but they are limited to fine arts, architecture, and other visual art as described below.

1.1.1. Fine Arts

Fine arts include physical objects—such as drawings, paintings, and sculpture—that are meant to be perceived primarily through the sense of sight, were created by the use of refined skill and imagination, and possess an aesthetic that is valued and of a quality and type that would be collected by art museums or private collectors. In this book, conceptual art and performance art are included in the visual arts, but the performing arts and literature are not.

1.1.2. Architecture

Architecture includes structures or parts of structures that are made by human beings. Generally, it refers only to structures that are large enough for human beings to enter, are of practical use, and are relatively stable and permanent. Works of architecture are often limited to the built environment that is generally considered to have aesthetic value, is designed by an architect, and is constructed with skilled labor.

1.1.3. Other Visual Arts

In addition to fine arts and architecture, cultural works may include crafts, decorative arts, textiles, clothing, ceramics, needlework, woodworking, furniture, metalwork, decorative documents, vehicles, and other works noted for their design or embellishments and used as utilitarian items or for decorative purposes.

1.2. Creators of Art Information

In addition to the complexity inherent in art information itself, the issues surrounding the development and maintenance of such information are further complicated by the diverse spectrum of information creators, including museum professionals, librarians, archivists, visual resources specialists, art and architectural historians, archaeologists, and conservators. Users of the information may include all of these groups as well as the general public. While these communities share a vast overlap of required information about works, they also have various requirements and different cataloging and indexing traditions, as described below.

1.2.1. Museums

Traditional museums house collections of works of art, antiquities, or other artifacts that are displayed for public benefit. Art museum professionals may include registrars, curators, conservators, and other scholars in the fields of art and architectural history and archaeology. These are the people who acquire, catalog, care for, and research the history and significance of the works in their collection. They are accustomed to dealing with unique objects, unlike librarians, who typically catalog an item in hand as a nonunique representation of an intellectual work.

Unlike the library and archival communities, museums have historically recorded information about works using long-established local practices rather than a shared, standard set of rules. Even so, there was always a certain amount of consistency in the way that museums recorded information because it was based on common practice in art-historical literature. However, consistency was uneven and unreliable, so the advent of data standards like *CDWA* and *CCO* provided much-needed written guidelines based on generally familiar practice in this community.

The standards and vocabularies required by the cultural heritage community must take into account the fact that the people who document the works typically derive much of the information directly from the objects themselves, rather than relying on other sources, as visual resources professionals must do. Therefore, rules must include instructions on, for example, not only how to record the dimensions of an object but also how to actually measure it. Unlike librarians, museum professionals usually deal with works that do not have the vital information printed or inscribed on the work itself. For instance, there is generally no title page or inscribed creator name on a museum object. It may be necessary for a museum to devise a title for the work, to establish the identity of the creator, or to estimate the date of creation through research and stylistic analysis.

Also in contrast to other communities, a museum actually houses and cares for valuable and unique works, requiring a great deal of administrative information, such as conservation and treatment history, exhibition history, provenance, and information concerning the specific circumstances of the excavation of an artifact. This community, as compared to librarians or visual resources specialists, requires more areas of the record in which to document detailed scholarly research, such as how a work fits into the evolution of an artist's style or details regarding why a work is dated to a particular year. Controlled vocabularies must provide names and terms to support these needs.

1.2.2. Visual Resources Collections

Visual resources collections maintain images that are typically collected to support the teaching and research requirements of universities, museums, or research institutions. Visual resources professionals are involved in the cataloging, classification, and indexing of images. They generally deal with slides, photographic prints, and digital images depicting art, architecture, or other subjects. They routinely catalog, manage, and store large numbers of images, often in the hundreds of thousands or even millions. Their work includes cataloging single items as well as sets of images.

Because their users will need to retrieve images based on the works depicted in them, the visual resources professional must catalog both the item in hand (slide, photograph, or digital image) as well as the art work or other cultural object depicted in it.

Fig. 1. Oil paintings such as this one are collected by art museums.
Vincent van Gogh (Dutch, 1853–1890); *Irises;* 1889; oil on canvas; 71.1 × 93 cm (28 × 36⅝ inches); J. Paul Getty Museum (Los Angeles, California); 90.PA.20.

Visual resources professionals were formerly called *slide librarians.* While the images they now deal with are of many media, these professionals are still often trained as librarians and may work in an image collection that is affiliated with or even located in a library. In addition, they are generally familiar with traditional museum cataloging. They have long been accustomed to using library standards and have been active in developing new standards and vocabularies that accommodate the unique requirements of image cataloging.

1.2.3. Libraries

Libraries are collections of documents or records that are made available for reference or borrowing. Librarians are professionals schooled in the cataloging and classification of books, journals, and other published textual materials. Since libraries may also collect rare books, prints, and art, librarians are often called upon to catalog these items as well. They are guided by principles and practices originating from national institutions, such as the United States Library of Congress and the British Library. Their approach is based primarily on the concept that the item in hand is one of many of the same thing, not a unique item in itself. For this reason, data sharing among libraries has long been seen as economically advantageous, because copy cataloging is more economical than original cataloging.

The librarian's model of the world is codified in the *Functional Requirements for Bibliographic Records* (*FRBR*) model. In *FRBR,* a *work* is defined as an abstract notion of an artistic or intellectual creation (not analogous to the art community's *work*). The *FRBR expression* is the intellectual or artistic realization of a work; a work may have many expressions, such as in different languages. The *FRBR manifestation* is the physical embodiment of an expression of a work, such as a particular print run of a book. The *FRBR item* is a single exemplar of the manifestation, such as a specific book in hand, which is a physical object that has paper pages and binding (comparable to a unique *work* in art standards, but considered by *FRBR* to be only one of many identical items). The corresponding model for authority information is found in the *Functional Requirements for Authority Data* (*FRAD*).

Librarians are accustomed to doing authority work and using controlled vocabularies. This community has a long tradition of following prescribed rules, striving for consistency, and using well-established standards such as the Machine Readable Cataloging (MARC) format and *Anglo-American Cataloguing Rules* (*AACR2*), currently evolving into *Resource Description and Access* (*RDA*).

1.2.4. Special Collections

Special collections contain rare or unique materials that are held by libraries or historical repositories but are typically not placed in public stacks. These materials may be available to the public only if special arrangements have been made in advance. The items may include rare books, manuscripts, personal papers, artworks such as prints, and other fragile or sensitive items. The people who work with special collections are often trained as librarians but occasionally as archivists, historians, or art historians.

1.2.5. Archival Collections

Archives are repositories for the noncurrent records of individuals, groups, institutions, and governments that contain information that is rare or of enduring historical value. Archival records are the products of everyday activity that are maintained to enable research. Documents represented in an archive may include administrative records, unpublished letters, diaries, manuscripts, architectural drawings, architectural models, photographs, films, videos, sound recordings, optical disks, computer tapes or digital files, and other items.

The archivist's job involves the arrangement and description of these documents with the goal of maintaining physical and intellectual control of the materials. The work is done in accordance with accepted standards, such as Encoded Archival Description (EAD), and following practices of national institutions such as the U.S. National Archives and Records Administration (NARA). Many archivists have been educated as librarians or historians.

The methodology of the archivist emphasizes the function and provenance of archival materials. The archivist typically documents large groups, subgroups, collections, and series of items rather than individual works, creating finding aids that briefly detail the physical location of groups and individual works in the archive.

1.2.6. Private Collections

Private collections are aggregations of objects gathered by or for one or more people but are not intended to be accessible to the general public. Individual collectors, families, architectural firms, corporations such as banks, or others develop private collections. The expertise of the people who maintain such collections varies widely.

Private collections may include a variety of objects of the types that would otherwise be located in museums, archives, or libraries. Materials from private collections may sometimes be seen in exhibitions at publicly accessible institutions.

1.2.7. Scholars

Art and cultural heritage information may also be created by scholars or academics—often art historians or architectural historians who are associated with teaching institutions or museums, but are not trained as librarians, archivists, visual resources professionals, or museum professionals. The information may be collected during the course of research—for example, for the purpose of teaching or writing books, articles, or other publications. Scholars are now beginning to capture information about art and architecture in electronic form in order to organize or aid in their research.

1.3. Standards for Art Information

There are several types of standards used to record art information. Standards for data values provide the actual values to be entered in fields, including the vocabulary terms and allowable character sets. Controlled vocabularies are standards for data values. They fit into the broader scheme of standards together with standards for data structure and for data content.

Standards for data structure dictate what constitutes a record. They define the names, length, repeatability, and other characteristics of fields and their relationships to each other. Examples are the MARC format and *CDWA*.

Standards for data content indicate how data should be entered, including cataloging rules and syntax for data. They may refer to standards for data values and standards for data structure. Examples of standards for data content are *AACR2* and *CCO*. For a typology of data standards, see the chapter by Anne Gilliland in *Introduction to Metadata,* edited by Murtha Baca.

1.3.1. Standards for the Creation of Vocabularies

While controlled vocabularies may function as standards for data values and be referenced in standards for data content, they themselves should ideally be constructed according to established standards for vocabulary creation. Institutions should use established vocabularies that are compliant with national and international standards. Furthermore, if a cataloging institution creates its own controlled vocabularies or adapts existing vocabularies to its local needs, it should consult these standards in order to make it easier to integrate its local vocabularies into a shared environment for search and retrieval.

The following standards for the creation of thesauri and other controlled vocabularies provide high-level guidelines regarding how a thesaurus should be structured, what kinds of relationships should be included, and how to identify preferred terms. The standards supplement each other in various areas, but where they overlap directly, they are generally in agreement. Thus, being compliant with one typically means being compliant with the others in most respects. More detailed rules for constructing vocabularies for art information may be found in **Chapter 7: Constructing a Vocabulary or Authority**, in *CCO* and *CDWA,* and in the more detailed rules of the *Editorial Guidelines* for the Getty vocabularies.

> ***ANSI/NISO Z39.19-2005: Guidelines for the Construction, Format, and Management of Monolingual Controlled Vocabularies***
> The National Information Standards Organization (NISO) is a nonprofit association accredited by the American National Standards Institute (ANSI). This publication discusses how to formulate preferred terms, establish relationships among terms,

and present the information in print and on a computer screen. It also discusses interoperability, methodologies for maintaining a thesaurus, and recommended features for thesaurus management systems.

BS 8723-1:2005, BS 8723-2:2005, BS 8723-3:2007, BS 8723-4:2007: Structured Vocabularies for Information Retrieval
This is a British Standards work published in four parts. Parts 1 and 2 include the basic principles of thesaurus construction, including facet analysis, presentation in electronic and printed media, thesaurus functions in electronic systems, and requirements for thesaurus management software. Parts 3 and 4 cover vocabularies other than thesauri and interoperability between vocabularies.

ISO 2788:1986: Documentation—Guidelines for the Establishment and Development of Monolingual Thesauri
This standard is an International Organization for Standardization (ISO) publication on the construction of monolingual thesauri. It includes guidelines for dealing with descriptors, compound terms, basic relationships, vocabulary control, indexing terms, display, and management of a thesaurus. Updates and additions to this standard are in development at the time of this writing, including *ISO/CD 25964-1: Information and Documentation—Thesauri and Interoperability with Other Vocabularies: Part 1: Thesauri for Information Retrieval.*

ISO 5964:1985: Documentation—Guidelines for the Establishment and Development of Multilingual Thesauri
This standard is intended as an extension of *ISO 2788,* the standard for monolingual thesauri. It includes guidelines for dealing with degrees of term equivalence and nonequivalence, single-to-multiple term equivalence, and thesaural displays.

1.3.2. Issues in Sharing Data

The various types of creators of information described above often wish to share data with each other or in a consortium. There are several steps involved with data sharing, including the extraction of data from a system, mapping data to another system or format, and delivering the data to the new environment.

Data standards and information systems are critical in data sharing. Standards are usually intended to be applicable independently of any particular automated system. However, in practical terms, the ability of an institution to apply a standard depends in part on the system used to collect and store data. It is easiest to accommodate standards when an institution is building a new system for which requirements of the standard may be planned. Building or implementing a new system allows an institution the opportunity to use the standard as a starting point for incorporating the core fields, planning requirements based on the data model and editorial demands suggested by the standard, and implementing authority files and vocabularies.

However, most institutions must use existing cataloging systems. Sharing data first requires that the different institutions (or multiple departments in one institution) map fields in their existing systems to each other or to a common set of data elements, such as *CDWA*. Data exchange or metadata harvesting standards, such as *Dublin Core* or *CDWA Lite,* may be utilized.

After deciding upon common core (required) fields, the collaborators must agree that, in shared files, there is a range of acceptable ways for different institutions to record display information. This is necessary because it is very unlikely that there will be absolute consensus regarding how to display information. For example, institutions may vary in the way they wish to publish a display date of creation or a creation statement—using different syntax or vocabulary. This is typically acceptable within the parameters of the standards, provided that the information is indexed in a consistent way that allows access across the databases. The distinction between information for display and indexed information is discussed in **Chapter 2: What Are Controlled Vocabularies?**

Following cataloging rules—such as *CDWA* and *CCO*—and indexing using common vocabularies—ideally thesauri that link synonyms—comprise the most efficient course to ultimately achieving good access to the data. The thesauri should also be applied using strategies and interfaces that accommodate the various ways users may try to access the data. The thesaurus should provide end users access via synonyms and relationships between concepts.

In summary: When information providers at a museum or other cultural heritage institution begin the process of making information accessible across departments, between institutions, and for the general public, they must consider the following issues:

- They must decide which data elements are important to share.
- They must identify the audience for the shared information.
- They must use a technical standard for data exchange between systems, such as *Dublin Core, CDWA Lite,* or the *Visual Resources Association Core Categories* (*VRA Core*).

- They must agree upon guidelines and rules for data content, such as *CCO* and *CDWA*.
- They must agree upon controlled vocabularies for ensuring consistency and coordination of data values.

This book deals primarily with the last issue: it seeks to explain what controlled vocabularies are and how to identify, use, and create controlled vocabularies for ensuring consistency and coordination in data values and for enhancing access for a wide range of users.

2. What Are Controlled Vocabularies?

A controlled vocabulary is an organized arrangement of words and phrases used to index content and/or to retrieve content through browsing or searching. It typically includes preferred and variant terms and has a defined scope or describes a specific domain.

2.1. Purpose of Controlled Vocabularies

The purpose of controlled vocabularies is to organize information and to provide terminology to catalog and retrieve information. While capturing the richness of variant terms, controlled vocabularies also promote consistency in preferred terms and the assignment of the same terms to similar content.

Given that a shared goal of the cultural heritage community is to improve access to visual arts and material culture information, controlled vocabularies are essential. They are necessary at the indexing phase because without them catalogers will not consistently use the same term to refer to the same person, place, or thing. In the retrieval process, various end users may use different synonyms or more generic terms to refer to a given concept. End users are often not specialists and thus need to be guided because they may not know the correct term.

The most important functions of a controlled vocabulary are to gather together variant terms and synonyms for concepts and to link concepts in a logical order or sort them into categories. Are a *rose window* and a *Catherine wheel* the same thing? How is *pot-metal glass* related to the more general term *stained glass?* The links and relationships in a controlled vocabulary ensure that these connections are defined and maintained, for both cataloging and retrieval.

2.2. Display Information and Controlled Information

Records for cultural objects typically contain both descriptive data and administrative data, which are outlined and defined in *CCO* and *CDWA*. Data elements record an identification of the type of object, creation information, dates of creation, place of origin and current location, subject matter, and physical description, as well as administrative information about provenance, history, acquisition, conservation, context related to other objects, and the published sources of this information.

Both descriptive and administrative data must be maintained in ways that will accommodate two categories of information: information intended for display to end users and information intended for retrieval. Information utilized for retrieval should be adapted for controlled vocabularies and controlled format.

Why are the display and indexing of information separate issues? Art and cultural heritage information provides unique challenges in display and retrieval. Information must be displayed to users in a way that allows expression of nuance, ambiguity, and uncertainty. The facts about cultural objects and their creators are not always known or straightforward, and it is misleading and contrary to the tenets of scholarship to fail to express this uncertainty. At the same time, efficient retrieval requires indexing according to consistent, well-defined rules and controlled terminology.

A successful catalog of art and cultural heritage information maintains a balance between flexible standards and consistent rules. On the one hand, it must be flexible in allowing the expression of uncertainty and ambiguity where the discipline requires it, while also accommodating nuance and differences in style between departments and institutions. On the other hand, it must apply rules consistently where it is most critical—namely, for information that is indexed for retrieval.

In the context of this book, the controlled fields in a record are specially formatted and often linked to controlled vocabularies (authorities), controlled lists, or ruled by formatting restrictions (e.g., formatting of numbers) to allow for successful retrieval.

For a full list of fields for art information and their requirements for free-text, controlled format, or controlled vocabulary, see *CDWA* (fields and rules) and *CCO* (detailed rules for a subset of the *CDWA* categories).

2.2.1. Display Information with Controlled Vocabularies

It is often necessary to allow fuzziness in the expression of information that at the same time must be retrievable via terminology from a controlled vocabulary; in certain key areas of a work record, this is accomplished by including separate display and indexing fields for the same information. For example, in the creation statement and in technique, medium, and support statements, the information may be complex and may include indications of uncertainty through the use of words such as *or* or *probably*.

The most effective way to express the nuances of such information is to use natural language in a display field and to index the same information separately, using controlled vocabulary (typically contained in an authority file). In the examples below, the creator's role is indexed with controlled terms, and the identity of the creator is indexed as well. The Creator Description field is free text, and authority files control the other fields. See **Chapter 6: Local Authorities** for a discussion of authority files and local authorities.

> **Creator Description:** Vincent van Gogh (Dutch, 1853–1890)
> **Role:** painter **Identity:** Gogh, Vincent van

> **Creator Description:** Marco Ricci (Venetian, 1676–1730), figures by Sebastiano Ricci (Venetian, 1659–1734)
> **Role:** painter **Extent:** landscape | architecture
> **Identity:** Ricci, Marco
> **Role:** painter **Extent:** figures **Identity:** Ricci, Sebastiano

> **Creator Description:** primary painter and calligrapher was Dai Xi (Chinese, 1801–1860), with additional inscriptions and colophons added by other officials; commissioned by Wu Zhongzhun
> **Roles:** painter | calligrapher **Identity:** Dai Xi
> **Role:** patron **Identity:** Wu Zhongzhun

2.2.2. Controlled Vocabularies vs. Controlled Format

While controlled vocabularies are organized sets of controlled terminology values (often with other information as well), the term *controlled format* refers to rules concerning the allowable data types and formatting of information. Fields may have controlled format in addition to being linked to controlled vocabulary, or the controlled format may exist in the absence of any finite controlled list of acceptable values.

Controlled format may govern the expression of Unicode or other characters in either a free-text field or in a field that is linked to a controlled vocabulary. Controlled format is also suitable for recording measurements, geographic coordinates, and other information in fields where numbers or codes are used. Restrictions may be placed on the field in order to regulate the number of digits allowed, the expression of decimals and negative numbers, and so on, ideally in compliance with ISO, NISO, or another appropriate standard where possible.

The examples below juxtapose a set of materials fields that use display and controlled vocabulary fields with a set of measurements fields. Fields such as Role and Material Name contain controlled vocabulary. However, in the measurements fields, the numbers in Value are indexed with controlled format but not controlled vocabulary.

Materials/Techniques Description: egg-tempera paint with tooled gold-leaf halos on panel
Role: medium **Material Name:** egg tempera | gold leaf
Role: support **Material Name:** wood panel
Technique Name: painting | gold tooling

Dimensions Description: comprises 10 panels; overall: 280 × 215 × 17 cm (110¼ × 84⅝ × 6¾ inches)
Extent: components
Value: 10 **Type:** count
Value: 280 **Unit:** cm **Type:** height
Value: 215 **Unit:** cm **Type:** width
Value: 17 **Unit:** cm **Type:** depth

Controlled format is also typically used for dates, such as the date of discovery or date of creation of an artwork. For such dates, controlled fields may be used in combination with a Display Date field.

The issues involved in recording data about dates illustrate the necessity of displaying information in a way that accurately expresses nuance and ambiguity to the end user, while at the same time formatting the dates consistently to allow retrieval. A free-text field for a Display Date can be used to express complex concepts and nuance, as in the examples below.

Display Creation Date: probably 1711
Display Creation Date: ca. 1910–ca. 1915
Display Creation Date: designed in the 1470s, constructed 1584–1627

The Display Date field should be combined with controlled Earliest Date and Latest Date fields that contain beginning and ending limits to enable searches on spans of time. The cataloger may estimate Earliest and Latest dates to allow for the leeway required by expressions such as *ca., before,* or *probably.*

The controlled Earliest and Latest fields do not contain controlled vocabulary per se, but they require a controlled format in which only numbers are allowed. A minus sign can be used to express dates BCE (Before Current Era) as negative numbers; dates CE (Current Era) are positive numbers. A rule should be in place ensuring that the latest date is always greater than or equal to the earliest date.

Display Creation Date: ca. 1913
Earliest: 1908 **Latest:** 1918

Display Creation Date: constructed 286–199 BCE
Earliest:–286 **Latest:**–199

Display Creation Date: 12th century
Earliest: 1100 **Latest:** 1199

Display Creation Date: Middle Minoan Palace period, ca. 1600 BCE
Earliest:–1630 **Latest:**–1570

Display Creation Date: 1039 anno Hegirae (1630 CE)
Earliest: 1630 **Latest:** 1630

Date fields should typically be controlled through locally defined rules rather than with default rules contained in the system. Although most systems promote the use of a special data type called *date* with predefined rules, this standard date data type does not generally work because art information requires the expression of dates up to many thousands of years BCE, and standard date data types are intended only for more modern dates (e.g., allowing 8-byte integers that represent dates ranging from 1 January of the year 0001 through 31 December of the year 9999).

2.3. Types of Controlled Vocabularies

Most controlled vocabularies discussed in this book are structured vocabularies. A structured vocabulary emphasizes relationships between and among the concepts represented by the terms or names in a vocabulary.

2.3.1. Relationships in General

In the context of this book, the term *relationship* means a state of connectedness or an association between two things in a database—in this case, fields or tables in a database for a controlled vocabulary.

One important type of relationship is between equivalents; for example, *Harlem Renaissance* and *New Negro Renaissance* refer to the same cultural movement that flourished in New York City in the 1920s.

Other relationships in a structured vocabulary include links that organize terms and provide context; for example, when discussing architectural drawings, an *orthographic projection* is a type of (child of) *parallel projection* and a sibling of *axonometric projection,* all of which are organized under *processes and techniques.*

The most common types of controlled vocabularies used for art and architecture include subject heading lists, simple controlled lists, synonym ring lists, taxonomies, and thesauri. Many of the definitions

Fig. 2. Display fields, as illustrated in the tombstone for this painting, are often indexed. The Display Materials field is indexed with controlled vocabulary. The Display Measurements field is indexed with controlled format for the numbers and a controlled list for the unit (centimeters, millimeters, inches, feet, square feet, among others) and type (height, width, depth, weight, area, circumference, among others).

Bartolomeo Vivarini (Italian, active from ca. 1440, died after 1500); *Polyptych with Saint James Major, Madonna and Child, and Saints;* 1490; tempera and gold leaf on panel; comprises 10 panels; overall: 280 × 215 cm (110¼ × 84⅝ inches); J. Paul Getty Museum (Los Angeles, California); 71.PB.30.

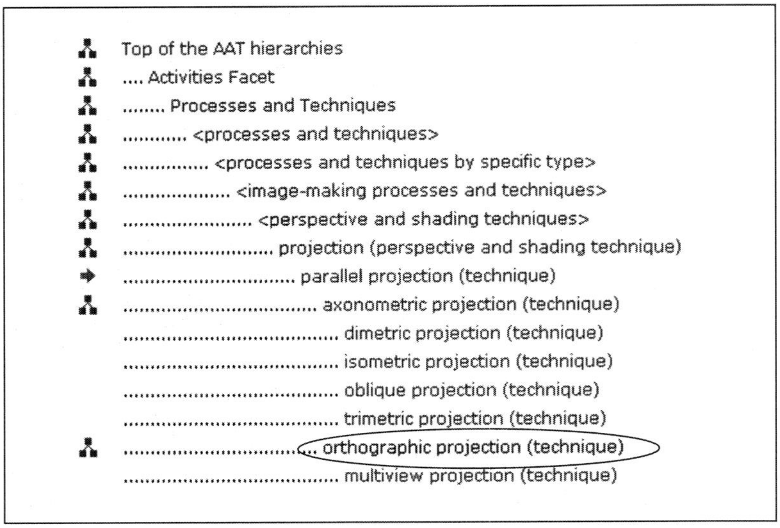

Fig. 3. A hierarchical display in the *AAT* illustrating *orthographic projection* with siblings and parents.

below are based on the discussions in *ANSI/NISO Z39.19-2005: Guidelines for the Construction, Format, and Management of Monolingual Controlled Vocabularies* and the related international standard, *ISO 2788:1986: Documentation—Guidelines for the Establishment and Development of Monolingual Thesauri.* Note that the types of vocabularies described below are not always mutually exclusive; for example, a single vocabulary can be both a thesaurus and an authority.

2.3.2. Subject Heading Lists

Subject headings, or simply *headings,* are uniform words or phrases intended to be assigned to books, articles, or other documents in order to describe the subject or topic of the texts and to group them with texts having similar subjects. The most commonly used subject headings in libraries in the United States are the *Library of Congress Subject Headings* (*LCSH*), which form a comprehensive list of preferred terms or strings, often with cross-references. Another well-known set of subject headings is the *Medical Subject Headings* (*MeSH*), which is used for indexing journal articles and books on medical science. *MeSH* incorporates a thesaurus structure with subject headings.

Subject heading lists are typically arranged in alphabetical order, with cross-references between the preferred, nonpreferred, and other related headings. This emphasis on a preferred entry and links to synonyms may be found in other types of authorities. However, subject headings differ from the other vocabularies discussed here in the following fundamental way: precoordination of terminology is a characteristic of subject headings in that they combine several unique concepts together in a string. For example, the heading *Medieval bronze vessels* combines a period, a material, and a work type in one heading.

Subject heading lists typically include separate listings of standardized subheadings (e.g., geographic locations) that may be combined with designated headings according to prescribed rules. Various styles of subject heading displays are included in the examples below. *LCSH* displays two dashes and parentheses or periods as required, while other styles may omit punctuation or use colons or em dashes for compound phrases. In *LCSH, MeSH,* and other authorities, the parts of a compound heading may be stored in separate MARC format subfields to allow variations in displays as desired.

Bicycle racing--United States
Cat family (Mammals)--Literary collections
South Africa. Arts and Culture Task Group
Architecture—Ancient Egypt
Film history: Movements and styles
Embryonic and Fetal Development
Medieval bronze vessels
Great Britain Description and travel 1801–1900

2.3.2.1. Other Headings

Other types of headings or labels may be used to uniquely identify or disambiguate one vocabulary entry from another. That is, the vocabulary record itself represents a single unique person, place, or thing, but its name is displayed with information in addition to the name. For example, the name of a creator may be listed with a short biographical string (e.g., *Flemish painter, 1423–1549*) to form a heading or label for display in a work record. This type of heading or label is discussed in **Chapter 7: Constructing a Vocabulary or Authority.**

2.3.3. Controlled Lists

A controlled list is a simple list of terms used to control terminology. In a well-constructed controlled list, the following is true: each term is unique; terms are not overlapping in meaning; terms are all members of the same class (i.e., having the same level of rank in a classification system); terms are equal in granularity or specificity; and terms are arranged alphabetically or in another logical order. These lists are also called *flat term lists* or *pick lists,* referring to the typical method of their implementation in an information system. Where appropriate, controlled lists should be derived from larger published standard vocabularies.

Controlled lists are usually designed for a very specific database or situation and may not have utility outside that context. They are best employed in certain fields of a database where a short list of values is appropriate and where terms are unlikely to have synonyms or ancillary information. However, as with any vocabulary for cataloging, it is preferable that definitions of the terms be made available to ensure consistency among catalogers. Below is an example of a controlled list for the Classification field in a work record.

architecture	manuscripts
armor	miscellaneous
books	paintings
coins	photographs
decorative arts	sculpture
drawings	site installation
implements	texts
jewelry	vessels

The advantage of such lists is that the cataloger or indexer has only a short list of terms from which to choose, thus ensuring more consistency and reducing the likelihood of error. In addition to the Classification field, examples of other art information fields that may benefit from a simple controlled list are Title Type (e.g., *artist's, descriptive, inscribed,* etc.), Title Language (e.g., *English, French, German, Italian, Spanish,* etc.), or Title Preference (e.g., *preferred, alternate*). Dozens of areas of a work record may be better suited for a short controlled list rather than a more complex controlled vocabulary. From the end-user perspective, such short lists may be easier to navigate than more complex lists, particularly for nonspecialist users.

2.3.4. Synonym Ring Lists

A synonym ring is a simple set of terms that are considered equivalent for the purpose of retrieval. Equivalence relationships in most controlled vocabularies should be made only between terms and names that have genuine synonymy or identical meanings. However, synonym rings are different. Even though they are classified as controlled vocabularies, they are almost always used in retrieval rather than indexing. They are used specifically to broaden retrieval (this is often referred to as query expansion): thus, synonym rings may in fact contain near-synonyms that have similar or related meanings, rather than restricting themselves to only terms with true synonymy.

Typically, synonym rings occur as sets of flat lists and are used behind the scenes of an electronic information system. They are most useful for providing access to content that is represented in texts and other instances of natural, uncontrolled language.

Even though catalogers do not use synonym rings for indexing, subject experts should be involved in the creation of synonym rings for retrieval. The most successful synonym rings are constructed manually by subject matter experts who are also familiar with the specific content of the information system, user expectations, and likely searches.

In the example below, synonym rings (each represented in an individual row) represent true synonyms as well as more generic terms and other terms that are related within the specific context of a given text. The example could represent a partial synonym ring list for a text about art depicting certain migrating birds. If a user enters *crows,* the search mechanism returns any text containing *birds* or any of the other terms in the same synonym ring as *crows.* Even though these terms are not synonyms, the implementer has judged that these links make sense for broad retrieval in this particular text. Other automated retrieval strategies may be in place as well; for example, the search algorithm may automatically truncate the *s* to allow matches in English on both singular and plural forms.

> birds, avian, storks, crows, ravens, herons, Ciconiidae, Corvus, Ardeidae
> migration, nonmigratory, migratory, travel, flying, altitude
> clouds, cumulus, nimbus, storm clouds, cloudy
> wind, windy, windstorm, wind damage, air flow, jet stream

2.3.5. Authority Files

An authority file is a set of established names or headings and cross-references to the preferred form from variant or alternate forms. Illustrated on the following page is the *LCNAF*—the *Library of Congress/NACO (Name Authority Cooperative Program) Authority File*—an authority widely used in libraries in North America.

Common types of authority files are name authority files and subject heading authority files. However, any listing of terms, names, or headings that distinguishes between a preferred term, name, or heading and alternate or variant names may be used as an authority. In other words, almost any type of controlled vocabulary—with the exception of a synonym ring list—may be used as an authority.

LC Control Number: n 79003969

HEADING: Moses, Grandma, 1860-1961

000 00578cz a2200193n 450

001 1418836

005 19910703055707.6

008 790117n| acannaab |a aaa

010 __ |a n 79003969

035 __ |a (DLC)n 79003969

040 __ |a DLC |c DLC |d DLC-R

100 10 |a Moses, |c Grandma, |d 1860-1961

400 00 |a Grandma Moses, |d 1860-1961

400 10 |w nna |a Moses, Anna Mary Robertson, |d 1860-1961

400 10 |a Mōzesu, |c Guranma, |d 1860-1961

670 __ |a Her Grandma Moses ... 1946.

670 __ |a Her Guranma Mōzesu ten, 1990: |b t.p. (Grandma Moses)

952 __ |a RETRO

953 __ |a xx00 |b zz00

Fig. 4. The *LCNAF* record for *Grandma Moses*, illustrating the established heading and cross-references for this artist.

Authority control refers as much to the methodology as to a particular controlled vocabulary. If a controlled vocabulary is accepted by a given community as authoritative, and if it is used in order to provide consistency in data, it is being used as an authority. A local authority file is often compiled from terminology from one or more published standard controlled vocabularies. The establishment of local authorities is discussed in **Chapter 6: Local Authorities.**

2.3.6. Taxonomies

A taxonomy is an orderly classification for a defined domain. It may also be known as a *faceted vocabulary.* It comprises controlled vocabulary terms (generally only preferred terms) organized into a hierarchical structure. Each term in a taxonomy is in one or more parent/child (broader/narrower) relationships to other terms in the taxonomy. There can be different types of parent/child relationships, such as whole/part, genus/species, or instance relationships. However, in good practice, all children of a given parent share the same type of relationship.

A taxonomy may differ from a thesaurus in that it generally has shallower hierarchies and a less complicated structure. For example, it often has no equivalent (synonyms or variant terms) or related terms (associative relationships). The scientific classifications of animals and plants are well-known examples of taxonomies. A partial display of

- **Bacteria**
  - **Atypical Bacterial Forms**
    - **L Forms**
    - **Spheroplasts**
  - **Bacteria, Aerobic**
  - **Bacteria, Anaerobic**
  - **Bacteroidetes**
    - **Bacteroidaceae**
      - **Bacteroides**
        - **Bacteroides fragilis**
      - **Porphyromonas**
        - **Porphyromonas endodontalis**
        - **Porphyromonas gingivalis**
      - **Prevotella**
        - **Prevotella intermedia**
        - **Prevotella melaninogenica**
        - **Prevotella nigrescens**
        - **Prevotella ruminicola**
    - **Flavobacteriaceae**
      - **Capnocytophaga**
      - **Chryseobacterium**
      - **Flavobacterium**
      - **Ornithobacterium**

Fig. 5. A display of data from the U.S. National Center for Biotechnology Information illustrating the taxonomic placement of *Flavobacteriaceae* with siblings and broader and narrower contexts.

Flavobacteria in the taxonomy of the U.S. National Center for Biotechnology Information is above.

In common usage, the term *taxonomy* may also refer to any classification or placement of terms or headings into categories, particularly a controlled vocabulary used as a navigation structure for a Web site.

2.3.7. Alphanumeric Classification Schemes

Alphanumeric classification schemes are controlled codes (letters or numbers, or both letters and numbers) that represent concepts or headings. They generally have an implied taxonomy that can be surmised from the codes. The Dewey Decimal Classification (DDC) system is an example of a numeric classification scheme with which many people are familiar, given that it is one of the two major systems used in libraries in the United States (the other is the Library of Congress Classification [LCC] system). In the Dewey system, the universe of knowledge is divided into sets of three-digit numbers. The arts are represented in the 700-number series; sculpture is represented by numbers between 730 and 739. For example, the number 735 has been established to indicate sculpture after the year 1400 CE. To that number may be added additional decimal indicators to further specify the topic by geographic or other categories. For example, 735.942 refers to sculpture dating after 1400 in England, because the extension 9 indicates geographic area, 4 indicates Europe, and 2 indicates England.

An alphanumeric classification scheme used for the iconography of art is *Iconclass,* discussed in **Chapter 4: Vocabularies for Cultural Objects.**

2.3.8. Thesauri

A thesaurus combines the characteristics of synonym ring lists and taxonomies, together with additional features. A thesaurus is a semantic network of unique concepts, including relationships between synonyms, broader and narrower (parent/child) contexts, and other related concepts. Thesauri may be monolingual or multilingual. Thesauri may contain three types of relationships: equivalence (synonym), hierarchical (whole/part, genus/species, or instance), and associative.

Thesauri may also include additional peripheral or explanatory information about a concept, including a definition (or scope note), bibliographic citations, and so on. A thesaurus is more complex than a simple list, synonym ring list, or simple taxonomy. Thesauri employ the versatile and powerful vocabulary control generally recommended for use as authorities in databases relating to art and cultural heritage.

The primary type of vocabulary discussed in this book is a thesaurus. Thesauri that contain art terminology include the Getty vocabularies, Chenhall's *Nomenclature,* and the *TGM,* which are discussed in **Chapter 4: Vocabularies for Cultural Objects.**

The term *thesaurus* may also be used for any controlled vocabulary arranged in a known order, displayed with standardized relationship indicators, and generally used for browsing in postcoordinated information storage and retrieval systems.

2.3.9. Ontologies

Whereas the vocabularies discussed above are the ones most commonly used for art information, discussions of controlled vocabularies may also include ontologies.

In common usage in computer science, an ontology is a formal, machine-readable specification of a conceptual model in which concepts, properties, relationships, functions, constraints, and axioms are all explicitly defined. Such an ontology is not a controlled vocabulary, but it uses one or more controlled vocabularies for a defined domain and expresses the vocabulary in a representative language that has a grammar

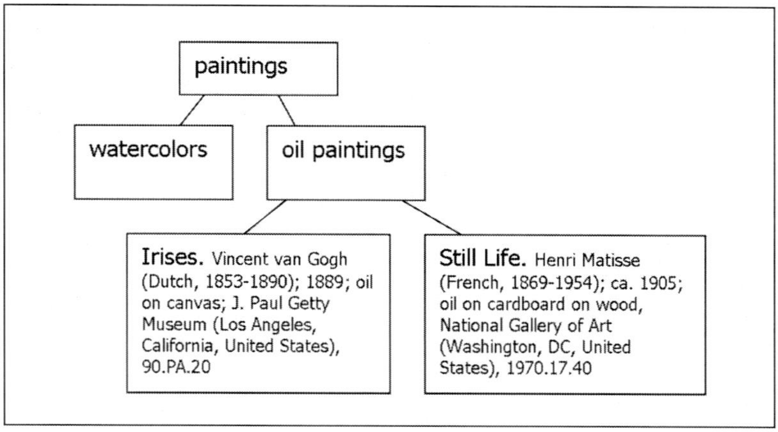

Fig. 6. A detail of a sample ontology for Vincent van Gogh's *Irises* and Henri Matisse's *Still Life*, illustrating how the works are part of a subset of *oil paintings* under the category *paintings*.

for using vocabulary terms to express something meaningful. Ontologies generally divide the realm of knowledge that they represent into the following areas: individuals, classes, attributes, relations, and events. The grammar of the ontology links these areas together by formal constraints that determine how the vocabulary terms or phrases may be used together. There are several grammars or languages for ontologies, both proprietary and standards-based. An ontology is used to make queries and assertions.

Ontologies have some characteristics in common with faceted taxonomies and thesauri, but ontologies use strict semantic relationships among terms and attributes with the goal of knowledge representation in machine-readable form, whereas thesauri provide tools for cataloging and retrieval.

Ontologies are used in the Semantic Web, artificial intelligence, software engineering, and information architecture as a form of knowledge representation in electronic form about a particular domain of knowledge.

In the example above, each item in the ontology belongs to the subclass above it. Items can also belong to various other classes, although the relationships may be different. For example, a watercolor is a painting, but it may also be classified as a drawing because it is a work on paper. Van Gogh's *Irises* could be classified with oil paintings (with the relationship type *medium is*) but also with Post-Impressionist art (with relationship type *style/period is*). Relationships in ontologies are defined according to strict rules, which are different than the equivalence, hierarchical, and associative relationships used for thesauri and other vocabularies discussed in this book.

2.3.10. Folksonomies

Folksonomy is a neologism referring to an assemblage of concepts represented by terms and names (called *tags*) that are compiled through social tagging. *Social tagging* is the decentralized practice and method by which individuals and groups create, manage, and share tags (terms, names, etc.) to annotate and categorize digital resources in an online social environment. This method is also referred to as *social classification, social indexing, mob indexing,* and *folk categorization.* Social tagging is not necessarily collaborative, because the effort is typically not organized; individuals are not actually working together or in concert, and standardization and common vocabulary are not employed.

Folksonomies do not typically have hierarchical structure or preferred terms for concepts, and they may not even cluster synonyms. They are not considered authoritative because they are typically not compiled by experts. Furthermore, they are by definition not applied to documents by professional indexers. Given that it is impossible for the large and varied community of creators and users of Web content to independently add metadata in a consistent manner, folksonomies are generally characterized by nonstandard, idiosyncratic terminology. Although they do not support organized searching and other types of browsing as well as tags from controlled vocabularies applied by professionals, folksonomies can be useful in situations where controlled tagging is not possible: they can also provide additional access points not included in more formal vocabularies. There may be great potential for enhanced retrieval by linking terms and names from folksonomies to more rigorously structured controlled vocabularies.

3. Relationships in Controlled Vocabularies

The three primary relationships relevant to the vocabularies discussed in this book are equivalence, hierarchical, and associative relationships. Relationships in a controlled vocabulary should be reciprocal. Reciprocal relationships are known as asymmetric when the relationship is different in one direction than it is in the reverse direction—for example, broader term/narrower term (BT/NT). If the relationship is the same in both directions, it is symmetric—for example, related term/related term (RT/RT).

3.1. Equivalence Relationships

Equivalence relationships are the relationships between synonymous terms or names for the same concept. A good controlled vocabulary should include terms representing different forms of speech and various languages where appropriate. Below are examples of terms in several languages that all refer to the same object type.

ceramics
ceramic ware
ware, ceramic
cerámica
Keramik

Ideally, all terms that share an equivalence relationship are either true synonyms or lexical variants of the preferred term or name or another term in the record.

3.1.1. Synonyms

Synonyms may include names or terms of different linguistic origin, dialectical variants, names in different languages, and scientific and common terms for the same concept. Synonyms are names or terms for which meanings and usage are identical or nearly identical in a wide range of contexts. True synonyms are relatively rare in natural language. In many cases, different terms or names may be interchangeable in some circumstances, but they should not necessarily be combined as synonyms in a single vocabulary record. Likewise, names for persons, places, events, and so on, may be used interchangeably in certain contexts, but their meanings may actually differ. Various factors must be considered when designating synonyms, including how nuance of meaning may differ and how usage may vary due to professional versus amateur contexts, historical versus current meanings, and neutral versus pejorative connotations. The creator of the vocabulary must determine whether or not the names or terms should be included in the same record or in separate records that are linked via associative relationships because they represent related concepts but are not identical in meaning and usage. In the examples below, each set of equivalent terms represents a single object type, style or culture, or person.

elevators
lifts

Ancestral Puebloan
Ancestral Pueblo
Anasazi
Basketmaker-Pueblo
Moqui

Le Corbusier
Jeanneret, Charles Édouard
Jeanneret-Gris, Charles Édouard

Fig. 7. Differences in language may account for differences in terminology in a vocabulary record, such as *hard paste porcelain* in English and *pâte dure* in French.

Unknown Chinese; *Lidded Vase;* Kangxi reign (ca. 1662/1722); hard paste porcelain, underglaze blue decoration; height: 59.7 cm (23½ inches); J. Paul Getty Museum (Los Angeles, California); 86.DE.629.

3.1.1.1. Lexical Variants

Although they are grouped with synonyms for practical purposes, lexical variants technically differ from synonyms in that synonyms are different terms for the same concept, while lexical variants are different word forms for the same expression. Lexical variants may result from spelling differences, grammatical variation, and abbreviations. Terms in inverted and natural order, plurals and singulars, and the use of punctuation may create lexical variants. In a controlled vocabulary, such terms should be linked via an equivalence relationship.

mice
mouse

watercolor
water color
watercolour
water-colour
color, water

Romania
ROM

In the example below, the past participle *embroidered* is included in the record for the process *embroidering* (needleworking (process), <needleworking and needleworking techniques>, . . . Processes and Techniques).

embroidering
embroidered
embroidery

Certain lexical variants could be flagged as *alternate descriptors* (AD), meaning that the AD and the *descriptor* (D) are equally preferred for indexing. For example, for objects, animals, and other concepts expressed as singular and plural nouns, the plural may be the descriptor, while the singular would be the alternate descriptor. In other cases, the past participle or an adjectival form may be an alternate descriptor.

baluster columns *(D)*
baluster column *(AD)*

laminating *(D)*
laminated *(AD)*

mathematics *(D)*
mathematical *(AD)*

3.1.1.2. Historical Name Changes

Political and social changes can cause a proliferation of terms or names that refer to the same concept. For example, the term used to refer to the ethnic group of mixed Bushman-Hamite descent with some Bantu admixture, now found principally in South Africa and Namibia, was previously *Hottentot.* That term now has derogatory overtones, so the term *KhoiKhoi* is preferred. However, a vocabulary such as the *AAT* would still link both terms as equivalents so that retrieval is thorough.

Names of people and places also change through history: People change their names, as when a title is bestowed or a woman marries. Place names change for a variety of reasons, as when *North Tarrytown, New York,* changed its name to *Sleepy Hollow* in 1996, or when the nation formerly known as the *Union of Burma* changed its name to the *Union of Myanmar* in 1989.

The issues that surround such historical changes are many. Determining when names are equivalents and when they instead refer to different entities is not always clear. For example, *Persia* is a historical name for the modern nation of Iran prior to 1935, yet ancient Persia was not entirely coextensive with modern Iran. Likewise, modern Egypt is not the same nation as ancient Egypt—neither in terms of borders nor of administration—therefore the names may be homographs, but not necessarily equivalents.

3.1.1.3. Differences in Language

Vocabularies may be monolingual or multilingual. Regional and linguistic differences in terminology are among the most common factors influencing variation among terms that refer to the same concept in monolingual vocabularies. Regional differences in terminology occur due to vernacular variations; for example, *English barn, Connecticut barn, New England barn,* and *Yankee barn* are all terms that refer to the same type of structure: a rectangular, gable-roofed barn that is divided on the interior into three roughly equal bays.

Multilingual vocabularies require the resolution of other issues in addition to those surrounding monolingual vocabularies. Cultural heritage communities around the world wish to share information, and users in many nations try to gain access to the same material on the Web. They need to retrieve the correct information on an object regardless of whether it has been indexed under *pottery, keramik,* or *céramique.* This is not always a simple prospect; forming equivalents is not just a matter of providing literal translations. For example, a nonexpert translator or a

AAT

copper (metal) (**preferred**,C,D,U,LC,English-P)
Cu (C,UF,U,A,English)
cuivre (metal) (C,D,U,French-P)
cuprum (C,D,U,Latin-P)
koper (C,D,U,Dutch-P)
Kupfer (C,D,U,German-P)
rame (C,D,U,Italian-P)
cobre (C,D,U,Portuguese-P,Spanish-P)
koppar (C,D,U,Swedish-P)

TGN

Beijing (**preferred**,C,V,N,Chinese (transliterated Pinyin)-P)	
Peking (C,V,N,Chinese (transliterated Wade-Giles)-P)	
Pékin (C,V,N)	
Pei-Ching (C,V,N)	
Pei-ching (C,V,N)	
Pei-p'ing (C,V,N)	
Peiching (C,O,N)	
Pekin (C,O,N)	
Pechino (C,O,N)	
Peiping (H,V,N)	 1928-1949
Peip'ing (H,V,N)	
Ch'i (H,V,N)	.... under the Chou Dynasty (1122-255 BCE)
Khanbalik (H,O,N)	
Cambaluc (H,O,N)	.... city with this name built 1260-1290

ULAN

Giambologna (**preferred**,V,display,LC, Italian-P)
Giovanni da Bologna (V, Italian)
Bologna, Giovanni da (V, Italian)
Giovanni Bologna (V, Italian)
Bologna, Giovanni (V, Italian)
Gian Bologna (V, Italian)
Bologne, Jean de (V, French-P)
Jean de Bologne (V, French)
Boulogne, Jean de (V)
Bologne, Jean (V, French)
Boulogne, Jean (V, French)
Jean Bologne (V, French)
Jean Boulogne (V, French)
Boullongne, Jean (V)
Boulongne, Jean (V)
Bolongne, Jean (V)

Fig. 8. Examples of terms flagged by language in the *AAT*, *TGN*, and *ULAN*.

computer program might translate the English term *toasting glasses* from the *AAT* vessels hierarchy into Spanish as *vasos para tostar,* which would seem to have something to do with a toaster oven rather than honoring someone with a toast (toasting glasses are tall, thin wineglasses with a small conical bowl, a stemmed foot, and a very thin stem that can easily be snapped between the fingers).

The names of people and places may also vary in different languages. As illustrated in the example on the previous page, this sixteenth-century Italian sculptor, who was born in Flanders (now Belgium) but worked in Italy, is known by many variations on his name, including the French *Jean de Bologne* and the Italian names *Giambologna* and *Giovanni da Bologna.* The name of *Mato Wanartaka,* the Native American artist who painted the Battle of the Little Big Horn, is translated into *Kicking Bear* in English. All these name variations must be linked together within a single vocabulary record as equivalents. Additional variations occur when names are transliterated by different methods into the Roman alphabet; for example, the names *Beijing, Peking,* and *Pei-Ching* all refer to the same city in China.

Further issues surrounding multilingual vocabularies and the mapping of terms between languages are discussed in **Chapter 5: Using Multiple Vocabularies.**

Names and terms that are similar or identical except for the use of diacritics should typically be included as variant names. Expressing names and terms in the original character sets or alphabets other than the Roman alphabet introduces additional issues, as discussed in **Chapter 9: Retrieval Using Controlled Vocabularies.**

3.1.2. Near Synonyms

Near synonyms are discussed under **2.3.4. Synonym Ring Lists**; they may be found in other vocabularies as well. Although it is generally advisable to link only true synonyms and lexical variants as equivalents, in some vocabularies the equivalence relationship may also include near synonyms and generic postings in order to broaden retrieval or cut down on the labor involved in building a vocabulary, among other reasons.

Near synonyms, also known as *quasi-synonyms,* are terms with meanings that are regarded as different, but the terms are treated as equivalents in the controlled vocabulary to broaden retrieval. Near synonyms are words that have similar but not identical meaning, such as *ice cream* and *gelato.* Both are frozen desserts made from dairy products, but ice cream is usually made with cream, and gelato is usually made with milk and has less air incorporated than ice cream. In other cases, antonyms—for example, *smoothness* and *roughness*—may be linked via the equivalence relationship in a vocabulary.

The phrase *generic posting* refers to the practice of putting terms with broader and narrower contexts together in the same record. For example, if *egg-oil tempera* were linked as an equivalent to *tempera,* this would be a generic posting because *egg-oil tempera* is a type of *tempera.*

In a vocabulary striving for more precise relationships, these terms should be linked with appropriate hierarchical relationships or associative relationships rather than as equivalents.

3.1.3. Preferred Terms

When multiple terms refer to the same concept, one term is generally flagged as a preferred term and the others are variant terms. In thesaurus jargon, the preferred term is always called a *descriptor,* and other terms may be called *alternate descriptors,* or *used for* terms.

For each concept or record, builders of a controlled vocabulary should choose one term or name among the synonyms as the preferred term. Preferred terms should be selected to serve the needs of the majority of users, relying upon established and documented criteria. For the sake of predictability, these criteria should be applied consistently throughout the controlled vocabulary. If, for example, American spelling is preferred over British spelling in a particular controlled vocabulary, the preferred terms or names should always be in American English. If the vocabulary is intended for a general audience, the preferred term should be the name or term most often found in contemporary published sources in the language of the users. The criteria for establishing preferred terms should be documented and explained to end users.

In the examples on the following page, *Georgia O'Keeffe* and *Mrs. Alfred Stieglitz* are names that refer to the same artist; the former name is preferred because this is the name by which she is most commonly known. In another example, the terms *still lifes* and *nature morte* refer to the same concept; the former term is preferred in English. In a third example, *Wien, Vienna,* and *Vindobona* refer to the same city; *Vienna* is the preferred current name in English, while *Wien* is the current German name, and *Vindobona* is a historical name.

The vocabulary may flag terms or names that are preferred in various languages. Terms preferred in other languages are also descriptors; that is, one record may have multiple descriptors. Each language represented may have a descriptor. However, only one of the descriptors should be flagged as preferred for the entire record.

3.1.4. Homographs

A homograph is a term that is spelled identically to another term but has a different meaning. For example, *drums* can have at least three

AAT

still lifes (preferred,C,D,U,English-P)
still life (C,AD,U,English)
still lives (C,UF,U,English)
still-lifes (C,UF,U,English)
still-life (C,UF,U,English)
stilleven (C,D,U,Dutch-P) .... in use from ca. 1650
nature morte (C,D,U,French-P,Italian) .... used from the mid-18th century

Stilleben (C,D,U,German-P)
natura morta (C,D,U,Italian-P)
naturaleza muerta (C,D,U,Spanish-P) .... in use from the early 19th century

TGN

Wien (**preferred,**C,V,N,German-P) .... name used by 1st century BCE
Vienna (C,O,N,English-P)
Vienne (C,O,N,French-P)
Beç (C,O,N,Magyar (Hungarian)-P) .... Hungarian name
Viden (C,O,N,Czech-P) .... Czech name
Wienis (H,V,N) .... name recorded in 1030
Wenia (H,V,N) .... name recorded in 881
Vindobona (H,V,N,Celtic language) .... Celtic for "white field"
Vindobna (H,V,N,Celtic language)
Vindomana (H,V,N)

ULAN

O'Keeffe, Georgia (preferred,V,index,LC)
Georgia O'Keeffe (V,display)
Stieglitz, Georgia O'Keeffe (V)
O'Keeffe, Georgia Totto (V)
Stieglitz, Mrs. Alfred (V)
Stieglitz, Alfred, Mrs. (V) .... in use 1924-1946
O'Keefe, Georgia (V) .... common misspelling

Fig. 9. Examples of preferred and variant names from the *AAT, TGN,* and *ULAN.* Preferred names are flagged *preferred* and are located at the top of each list. Names preferred in various languages are indicated with a *P* following the language.

meanings: components of columns, musical instruments classified as membranophones, or walls that support a dome. Words can be homographs whether or not they are pronounced alike. For example, *bows,* the forward-most ends of watercraft or airships, and *bows,* stringed projectile weapons designed to propel arrows, are spelled alike but pronounced differently. *Homophones* are terms that are pronounced the same but spelled differently, for example *bows* and *boughs;* controlled vocabularies generally need not concern themselves with labeling homophones.

Note that a controlled vocabulary is constructed differently from a dictionary. In a dictionary, homographs are listed under a single heading, with several definitions. For example, in a dictionary, *drum* would be listed as a noun, with several definitions under a single entry. In a controlled vocabulary, each homographic term is in a separate record.

3.1.4.1. Qualifiers

Controlled vocabularies must distinguish between homographs. One way to do this is to add a qualifier. A qualifier consists of one or more words used with the terms to make the specific meaning of each unambiguous, as seen in the examples below.

drums (column components)
drums (membranophones)
drums (walls)

Qualifiers should be distinguished from the term itself in displays. Traditionally, parentheses are used to identify the qualifier. In order to make construction of and use of the vocabulary more versatile, it is useful to place the qualifier in a separate field in the database rather than in the same field as the term itself.

If a term is a homograph to another term in the vocabulary, at least one qualifier is necessary. However, it is best to add a qualifier for both terms for clarity. Homographs and their qualifiers may occur not only with descriptors but also with alternate descriptors and *used for* terms. In addition, if a term is a homograph for another common term in standard language, even if the second term is not in the vocabulary, it is useful to add a qualifier for clarity.

A qualifier is sometimes also called a *gloss;* however, in linguistic jargon a gloss actually has the more general meaning of any term or phrase providing meaning or explanation for difficult words or passages. In contrast, a qualifier is used only to disambiguate homographs, not to define the term or provide context (although it may do so coincidentally because these characteristics may be what distinguish a term from its homograph).

Qualifiers should be used only to disambiguate homographs, not to represent a compound concept, define a term, or establish a term's hierarchical context. Some controlled vocabularies create qualifiers for these other purposes, but this is considered bad practice. Other situations should be handled in the following ways: To make a bound compound concept, construct a descriptor rather than using a qualifier (e.g., *phonograph record,* not *record (phonograph)*). Alternatively, if it is an unbound concept, rather than creating a qualified term in the thesaurus, end users should be allowed to construct a multiple-word search phrase in retrieval. For example, neither *cathedral (Baroque)* nor the descriptor *Baroque cathedral* (because that is an unbound concept) should be created in the thesaurus; instead, *Baroque AND cathedral* should be used in retrieval. The term should be defined in the scope note, not by using a qualifier. To establish context for the term in displays outside of homographic disambiguation, a heading or label for the term should be created rather than trying to do so with a qualifier (see **7.5.3.6.1. Headings or Labels**).

3.1.4.1.1. How to Choose a Qualifier for a Term

The builders of controlled vocabularies should establish detailed rules for how to compose qualifiers. Qualifiers should be as brief as possible, ideally consisting of one or two words.

In most cases, a word or words from a broader context of the term should be used as the qualifier (e.g., *stained glass (material),* where *stained glass* is a hierarchical descendant of *materials*). Qualifiers for all homographs should clearly disambiguate the terms in displays. For example, *stained glass (material)* and *stained glass (visual works)* distinguish the material from the artworks made from the material.

If words taken from the broader context do not sufficiently disambiguate between homographs, use words that describe another significant distinguishing characteristic.

Qualifiers should be standardized as much as possible within a controlled vocabulary. For example, *films* and *motion pictures* should not both be used as qualifiers because *films* is a *used for* term for *motion pictures.* When possible, the qualifier should have the same grammatical form as the term, as with the nouns and gerunds in the examples below.

Term: trailers **Qualifier:** motion pictures
Term: trailers **Qualifier:** vehicles

Term: forging **Qualifier:** copying
Term: forging **Qualifier:** metal forming

3.1.4.2 Other Ways to Disambiguate Names

Qualifiers are used frequently in controlled vocabularies containing terminology for object types, generic concepts, and so on, as illustrated above. For other vocabularies, such as personal name and geographic name vocabularies, data from various fields may be concatenated with the name or term to disambiguate entries. For example, the name of a person could be displayed with biographical information to create a heading—e.g., *Johnson, John (English architect, 1754–1814)*—or the name of a place could be displayed with place type and broader contexts taken directly from the hierarchy—e.g., *Springfield (inhabited place) (Tuolumne county, California, United States).* Headings and labels may be used not only

Johnson, John (British draftsman and engraver, died ca. 1797) [500007991]
Johnson, John (English architect, 1754-1814) [500008543]
Johnson, John (American photographer, died 1871) [500099783]
Johnson, John (British printer, 1882-1956) [500101358]

Fig. 10. A *ULAN* display containing homographs with additional distinguishing information for *John Johnson*, including a short biographical string and the unique numeric identification of the record in the *ULAN*.

to disambiguate homographs but also to provide context for terms and names when displayed in any horizontal string (see **7.5.3.6.1. Headings or Labels**).

3.2. Hierarchical Relationships

Hierarchical relationships are the broader and narrower (parent/child) relationships between logical records (where each record represents a concept). The hierarchical relationship is the primary feature that distinguishes a thesaurus or taxonomy from simple controlled lists and lists of synonym rings.

Hierarchical relationships are referred to by genealogical terms such as *child, children, siblings, parent, grandparent, ancestors, descendants,* etc. In the example on the following page, the *Upper Egypt* region is the parent of *Qinā* governorate; *Karnak* and *Luxor* are children of *Qinā* governorate and siblings of each other; and *Africa* is an ancestor of all these places. The display of hierarchical relationships is discussed in **Chapter 7: Constructing a Vocabulary or Authority.**

There are several types of hierarchical relationships, including whole/part, genus/species, and instance relationships.

3.2.1. Whole/Part Relationships

Hierarchical relationships are generally either whole/part, also called a *partitive relationship* (e.g., *Karnak* is a part of *Qinā* governorate), or genus/species, also called a *generic relationship* (e.g., *bronze* is a type of *metal*).

Whole/part relationships are typically applied to geographic locations, parts of corporate bodies, parts of the body, and other types of

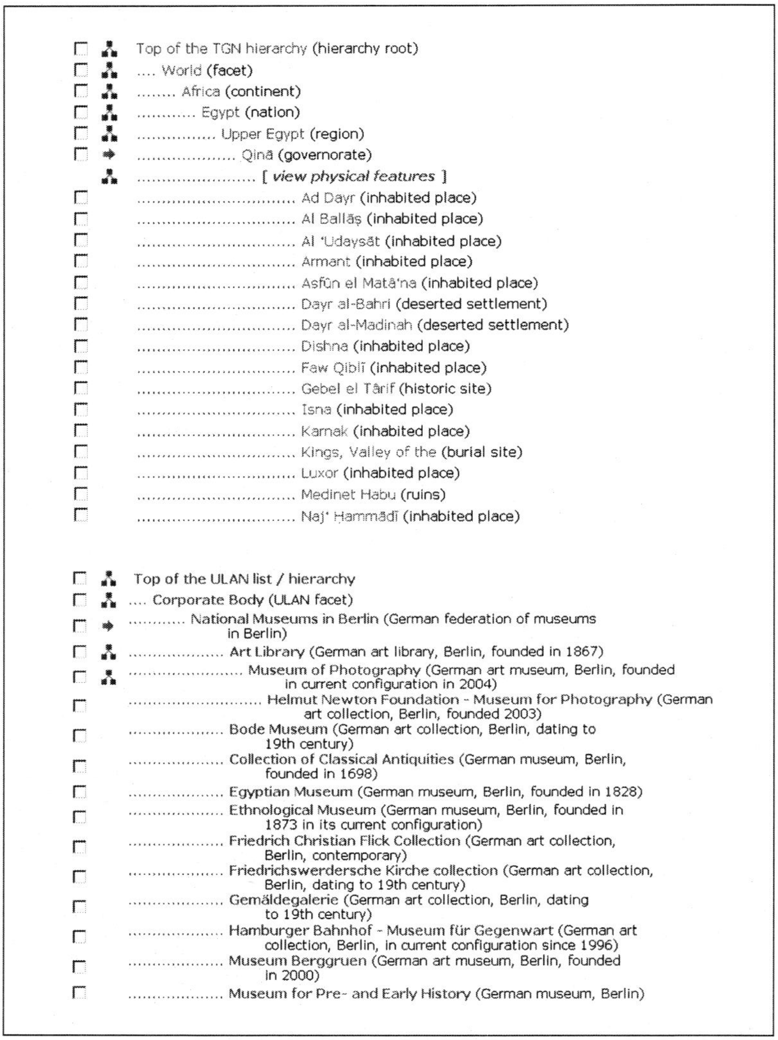

Fig. 11. Examples of hierarchical displays from the *TGN* and *ULAN*. Note that in these displays, the parenthetical words accompanying the names are place types (for the *TGN*) and biographical strings (for the *ULAN*); they are not generated from the qualifier field.

concepts that are not readily placed into genus/species relationships. Each child should be a part of the parent and all the other ancestors above it.

3.2.2. Genus/Species Relationships

The genus/species, or generic relationship, is the most common relationship in thesauri and taxonomies because it is applicable to a wide range of topics. All children in a genus/species relationship should be a *kind of*, *type of*, or *manifestation of* the parent (compare instance relationships

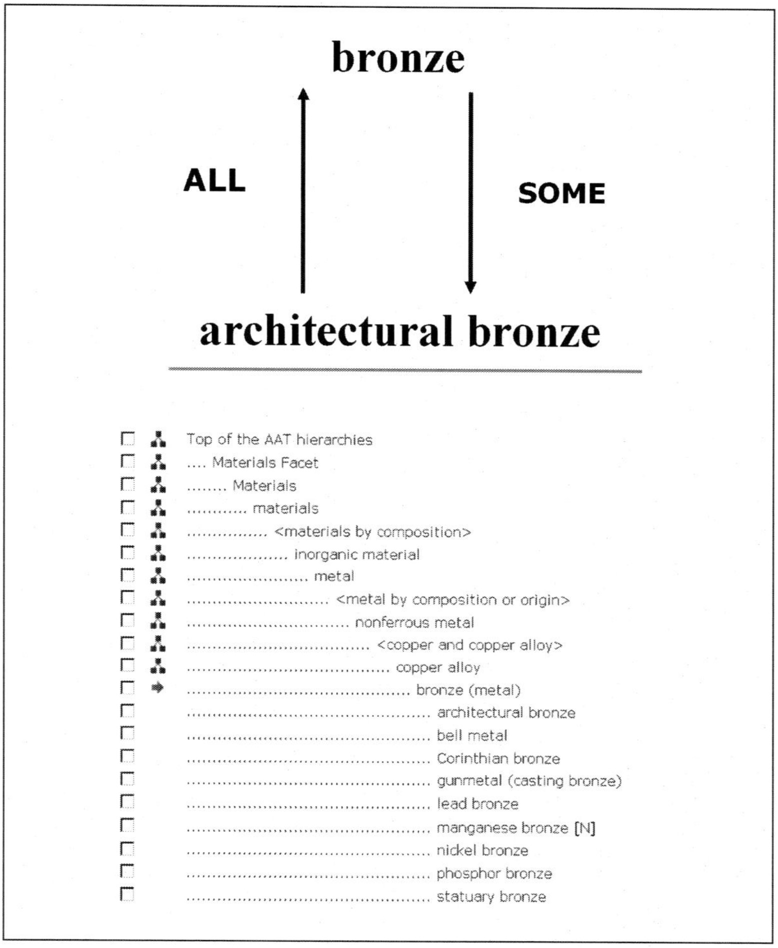

Fig. 12. Illustration of the all/some test for *architectural bronze* and the *AAT* hierarchical display for *architectural bronze* in a genus/species relationship as a child of *bronze*.

below). The placement of a child may be tested by the all/some argument. In the example of *bronze* above, *all* architectural bronze is bronze, but only *some* bronze is architectural bronze.

3.2.3. Instance Relationships

In addition to the whole/part and genus/species relationships, some vocabularies may utilize a third type of hierarchical relationship, the *instance relationship*. This is most commonly seen in vocabularies where proper names are organized by general categories of things or events, for example, if the proper names of mountains and rivers were organized under the general categories *mountains* and *rivers*.

mountains
- Alps
- Apennines
- Rocky Mountains
- Himalayas

rivers
- Amazon River
- Colorado River
- Mississippi River
- Nile River
- Ohio River
- Thames
- Yellow River

3.2.4. Facets and Guide Terms

Facets provide the primary subdivisions of a hierarchy, typically located directly under the *root* or top of the hierarchy. Subfacets, also called *hierarchies,* may subdivide the facets. Guide terms (types of *node labels*) are additional levels that collocate similar sets or classes of records (illustrated in the example below with angled brackets). They should logically illustrate the principles of division among a set of sibling terms, as discussed in **Chapter 7: Constructing a Vocabulary or Authority.**

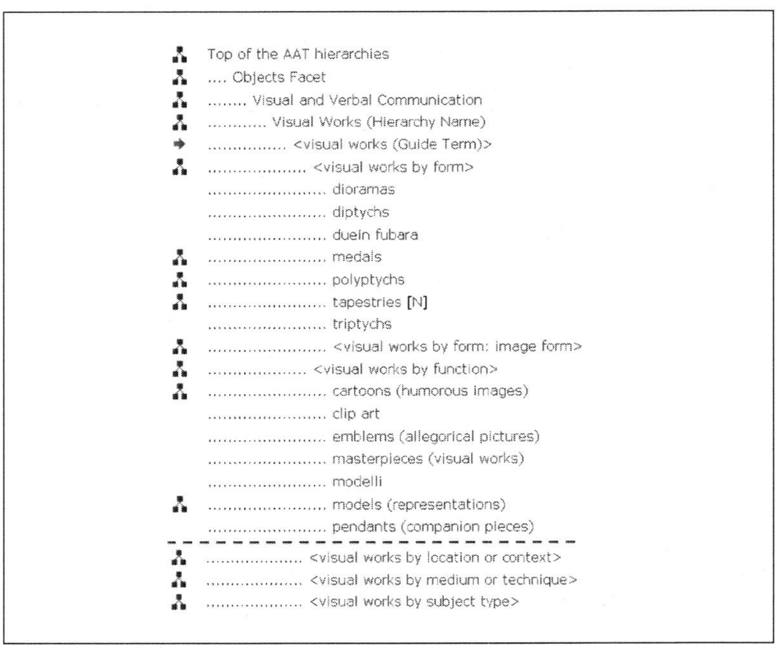

Top of the AAT hierarchies
.... Objects Facet
.... Visual and Verbal Communication
.... Visual Works (Hierarchy Name)
.... <visual works (Guide Term)>
.... <visual works by form>
.... dioramas
.... diptychs
.... duein fubara
.... medals
.... polyptychs
.... tapestries [N]
.... triptychs
.... <visual works by form: image form>
.... <visual works by function>
.... cartoons (humorous images)
.... clip art
.... emblems (allegorical pictures)
.... masterpieces (visual works)
.... modelli
.... models (representations)
.... pendants (companion pieces)
.... <visual works by location or context>
.... <visual works by medium or technique>
.... <visual works by subject type>

Fig. 13. A partial hierarchical display for *Visual Works* in the *AAT,* illustrating the logical classification of the terms under the top of the hierarchy, a facet, subfacet (hierarchy), and guide terms in angled brackets, which organize the terms by form, function, and other logical divisions.

3.2.5. Polyhierarchies

Some concepts logically belong to more than one broader context. To accommodate this situation, the data structure of a properly constructed thesaurus should allow *polyhierarchical relationships,* meaning that each record exists only once in the vocabulary but may be linked to multiple parents and can thus appear in multiple hierarchical views. Polyhierarchical relationships may exist in whole/part, genus/species, and instance relationship models. In the example below, *Siena* is part of the modern nation of *Italy,* but it was also part of the ancient confederation of *Etruria.*

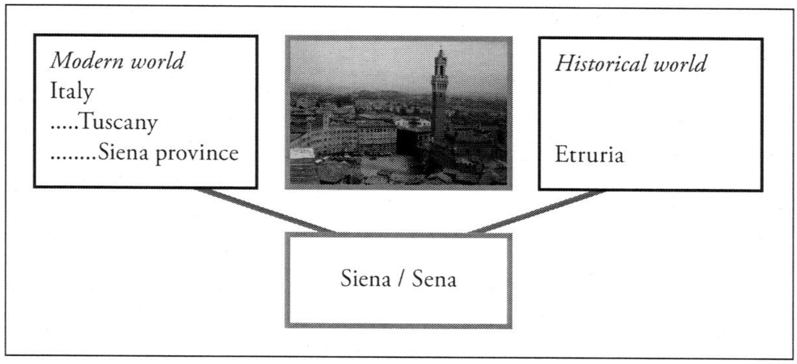

Fig. 14. Diagram of polyhierarchical relationships for *Siena,* linked to both *modern Italy* and *historic Etruria.*

The criteria for creating polyhierarchical relationships should be explicitly established. In the example below, the polyhierarchy is used to link a place to both its current and historical parents; the nonpreferred parent relationship is indicated with an *N* in brackets.

Fig. 15. A *TGN* hierarchical display showing *Siena* and other Italian towns linked to *Etruria,* where *N* indicates that this historical relationship is a nonpreferred hierarchical relationship.

Top of the TGN hierarchy (hierarchy root)
.... World (facet)
.... Europe (continent)
.... Italian Peninsula (peninsula)
.... Etruria (former group of nations/states/cities)
.... Arezzo (inhabited place) [N]
.... Bologna (inhabited place) [N]
.... Cerveteri (inhabited place) [N]
.... Chianciano Terme (inhabited place) [N]
.... Chiusi (inhabited place) [N]
.... Cortona (inhabited place) [N]
.... Fiesole (inhabited place) [N]
.... La Foce (inhabited place) [N]
.... Marzabotto (inhabited place) [N]
.... Orte (inhabited place) [N]
.... Orvieto (inhabited place) [N]
.... Perugia (inhabited place) [N]
.... Pisa (inhabited place) [N]
.... Populonia (inhabited place) [N]
.... Rusellae (deserted settlement) [N]
.... Siena (inhabited place) [N]
.... Tarquinia (deserted settlement) [N]
.... Veio (deserted settlement) [N]

The established classification scheme of the hierarchy should be considered, and terms should be placed under multiple parents when they logically belong to those parents. For example, in the *AAT*, a *backing hammer* should be located under the guide term *<bookbinding equipment>*, but it also belongs under *hammers (tools)*.

3.3. Associative Relationships

Associative relationships exist between records that are conceptually close, but where the relationship is neither equivalent nor hierarchical. The most basic type of associative relationship is simply *related to*. In some vocabularies, more specific types of associative relationships may be designated.

AAT

Final Neolithic (<transitional periods Stone Age to Bronze Age>, <three-age system>, ... Styles and Periods)

Note: Refers to the last stage of a Neolithic culture, which often partially overlaps with the Early Bronze Age. It is generally held to have occurred from around 4,000 BCE to around 3,000 BCE in Europe, lasting until around 2,000 BCE in parts of the British Isles.

Terms:
Final Neolithic (preferred,C,D,U,English-P)
Neolithic, Final (C,UF,U,English)

Related concepts:
meaning/usage overlaps with .... Early Bronze Age
.... (Bronze Age, <three-age system>, ... Styles and Periods) [300019276]

ULAN

Master of Moulins (painter, probably Netherlandish, active ca. 1480-1504 in France)

Note: Painter of South Netherlandish origin active in France. The Master of Moulins is possibly identified as Jean Hey. He is named after the triptych of the Virgin and Child Adored by Angels with Saints and Donors in Moulins Cathedral. Many of the works attributed to the Master of Moulins can be associated with members of the Bourbon court at Moulins, and he may have been their court painter. Given the poor survival rate of French 15th-century panels, a surprising number of works can be attributed to him and his workshop. His works combine the daring color and compositional ideas of van der Goes with the looser technique and Italianate motifs fashionable in France at the time.

Names:
Master of Moulins (preferred,V,display)
Maître de Moulins (V)
Master of the Bourbons (V)

Related People or Corporate Bodies:
patron was .... Cardinal Charles of Bourbon
.... (French cardinal and patron, 1426-1488) [500122258]
patron was .... Jean II, Duke of Bourbon
.... (French patron and collector, 1426-1488) [500122320]
possibly identified with .... Hey, Jean
.... (Netherlandish painter, active ca.1480-ca.1504, active in France) [500012005]
possibly identified with .... Prévost, Jean
.... (French glass painter and glazier, died 1503 or 1504) [500122083]

Fig. 16. Examples of associative relationships in the *AAT* and *ULAN*. In the *AAT*, concepts that may have overlapping meaning are linked—for example, *Final Neolithic* and *Early Bronze Age*. In the *ULAN*, patrons and a possible identification with a named artist are linked to the anonymous *Master of Moulins*.

3.3.1. Types of Associative Relationships

Associative relationships may be made between records in the same hierarchy or in different hierarchies. There may be relationships between overlapping siblings or other terms where the meanings are similar and the terms are occasionally (but not generally) used as synonyms.

In general, terms that are mutually exclusive do not require associative relationships, particularly if they cannot be confused with one another, whether or not they share the same parent. For example, it is not necessary to link *baluster columns* and *spiral columns* below because there is no reason why a user would confuse the two.

Fig. 17. Examples of the sibling *AAT* terms *baluster columns* and *spiral columns*, which are not linked by associative relationships.

ID: 300001577 **Record Type:** concept

baluster columns (<columns by form>, columns (architectural elements), ... Components (Hierarchy Name))

Note: Columns resembling balusters, composed of a base, a potlike element, a bulbous shaft, and a capital.

Terms:
baluster columns (preferred,C,D,U,English-P)
baluster column (C,AD,U,English)
columns, baluster (C,UF,U,English)
baluster shafts (C,UF,U,English)

ID: 300001626 **Record Type:** concept

spiral columns (<columns by form>, columns (architectural elements), ... Components (Hierarchy Name))

Note: Columns so shaped as to present a twisted or spiral form.

Terms:
spiral columns (preferred,C,D,U,English-P)
spiral column (C,AD,U,English)
columns, spiral (C,UF,U,English)
salomónicas (C,UF,U,English)
Solomonic columns (C,UF,U,English)
twisted columns (C,UF,U,English)
wreathed columns (C,UF,U,English)

However, there should be associative relationships between terms that are intended to be used as separate concepts but may be confused by users. In the first example on the following page, Lorraine, the current administrative region, and Lorraine, the historical entity, share the same name and some of the same territory; thus an associative relationship helps distinguish between the two and at the same time links them for possible retrieval. In the second example, the term *military bases* is distinguished from *military camps,* with which it is sometimes confused. If it is necessary to mention the second concept in the scope note in order to distinguish the two, the records should be linked through associative relationships.

TGN

ID: 7024272 **Record Type:** administrative

Lorraine (historical region)

Coordinates:
Lat: 49 00 00 N *degrees minutes* Lat: 49.0000 *decimal degrees*
Long: 006 00 00 E *degrees minutes* Long: 6.0000 *decimal degrees*

Note: Area of northwestern Europe contained in modern Belgium, the Netherlands, Luxembourg, Alsace-Lorraine (France), and northwestern Germany. The kingdom was established when the Carolingian empire split; it was divided into two duchies in 959. It was ruled by a ducal family from the 11th century. It was held permanently by France from 1766, except when it went to Germany (with Alsace) for a time after the Franco-Prussian War in 1871. See also the modern region of Lorraine, France.

Names:
Lorraine
(preferred,C,V,N,English-P,French-P)
Lothringen (H,V,N,Germanic language) .... named for grandson of Charlemagne, Lothair I
Lotharingia (H,V,N) .... name really applies to medieval kingdom of Lorraine, later divided
Lotharii Regnum (H,V,N,Latin-P) .... Latin for "kingdom of Lothair," named by Lothair II (died 869)

Hierarchical Position:
World (facet)
.... Europe (continent)
.... Lorraine (historical region) (H)

Place Types:
historical region (preferred, C)
kingdom (H) .... established 843

Related geographic places:
distinguished from .... Lorraine .... (region)
.... (World, Europe, France) [7002888]

AAT

ID: 300000476 **Record Type:** concept

military camps (military installations, <complexes by function>, ... Built Environment (Hierarchy Name))

Note: In contemporary military contexts this refers to groups of huts, tents, or other shelters set up temporarily for troops. In historical contexts the term connotes permanent or semipermanent places of encampment. Use "military bases" for contemporary permanent installations.

Terms:
military camps (preferred,C,D,U,English-P)
military camp (C,AD,U,English)
camps (military) (C,UF,U,LC,English)
camps, military (C,UF,U,English)
military encampments (C,UF,U,English)
military posts (camps) (C,UF,U,English)

Facet/Hierarchy Code: V.RG

Hierarchical Position:
Objects Facet
.... Built Environment (Hierarchy Name)
.... Built Complexes and Districts
.... complexes
.... <complexes by function>
.... military installations
.... military camps

Related concepts:
distinguished from .... military bases
.... (military installations, <complexes by function>, ... Built Environment (Hierarchy Name)) [300000455]

Fig. 18. Examples of associative relationships from the *TGN* and *AAT* linking records that are mentioned in the notes and linked as *distinguished from* one another.

Fig. 19. Partial lists of relationship types from the *ULAN*, *TGN*, and *AAT*, with each list reflecting the characteristic requirements of the vocabulary. Relationships are identified by numeric codes and text values. Where the reciprocal relationship differs from the target relationship, the reciprocal relationship is listed immediately following the target relationship (e.g., *1101/teacher of—1102/student of*).

ULAN

1000/related to
1003/associated with
1005/possibly identified with
1007/distinguished from
1100/<person to person – teaching/learning>
1101/teacher of – 1102/student of
1102/student of – 1101/teacher of
1105/apprentice of – 1106/apprentice was
1106/apprentice was – 1105/apprentice of

TGN

3000/related to
3001/formerly related to
3005/possibly identified as
3101/adjacent to
3102/coextensive with
3201/capital of – 3202/captial is
3202/capital is – 3201/capital of
3301/ally of
3401/moved from – 3402/moved to
3402/moved to – 3401/moved from

AAT

2000/related to
2001/formerly related to
2100/distinguished from
2110/meaning/usage overlaps with
2204/<thing caused by/causes an action> (e.g., carvings are caused by carving)
2205/resulting thing(s) are – 2206/causative action is
2206/causative action is – 2205/resulting thing(s) are
2207/<thing exists in location setting> (e.g., computers are located in computer rooms)
2208/locational context/setting is – 2208/thing(s) involved are

In addition to the relationships described above, antonyms may be treated as associative relationships. In fact, a vocabulary may require a substantial number of very specific additional associative relationships. These types of relationships vary from vocabulary to vocabulary, depending upon the nature of the terms and how they are intended for use in retrieval. For example, relationships between generic terms would differ from relationships between people, which could include familial and professional relationships. A vocabulary should list and define the types of associative relationships used. Partial lists of associative relationships for the Getty vocabularies appear above.

3.3.2. When to Make Associative Relationships

Only clear and direct associative relationships should be recorded. These direct relationships are typically current but occasionally may be historical. Given that associative relationships are more challenging to define than hierarchical relationships, care must be taken to consistently apply rules when assigning associative relationships in a vocabulary in order to prevent an excessive number of such relationships, which can have a negative effect when the thesaurus is used for retrieval.

Since associative relationships are often used not only for the reference of a user but also for retrieval, it is important to avoid making unnecessary links between related concepts. Relationships should be made only between records that are directly related, but where hierarchical and equivalent relationships are inappropriate. If a thesaurus is bound together by too many associative relationships between entities that are only loosely or indirectly related, the value of the relationships in retrieval is lost. Consider this question: if the end user is interested in retrieving Concept X, might he or she possibly also want to retrieve Concept Y? If not, there probably should not be an associative relationship between the two records.

Associative relationships may be displayed and described explicitly as in the example below or by using the generic notation *RT,* for *related term,* or the phrase *see also.*

collections
RT collecting

collections
see also *collecting*

Associative relationships are always reciprocal. For some relationships, the relationship type is the same on both sides of the link (e.g., *related to*); however, for others it is different depending upon

Fig. 20. Example of an associative relationship for *collections*, to which the activity *collecting* is related.

collections (object groupings) (<object groupings by general context>, <object groupings>, Object Groupings and Systems)

Note: Refers to groups of objects that have been brought together by an individual or organization.

Terms:
collections (object groupings) (preferred,C,D,U,English-P)
collection (object grouping) (C,AD,U,English)

Facet/Hierarchy Code: V.PC

Hierarchical Position:
Objects Facet
.... Object Groupings and Systems
.... <object groupings>
.... <object groupings by general context>
.... collections (object groupings)

Related concepts:
causative action is .... collecting
.... (collections management, <information handling functions>, ... Functions) [300077121]

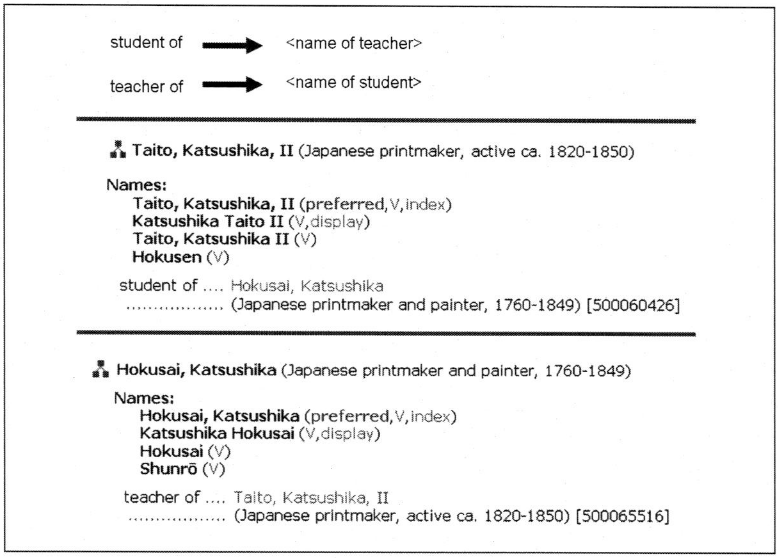

Fig. 21. Illustrations of associative relationships for *Katsushika Taito II* and *Katsushika Hokusai.* The relationships are reciprocal, meaning the link displays in the records for both artists, one as *student of* and the other as *teacher of.*

which record is the focus. Vocabulary editors must be very careful to choose the correct relationship for the focus record (i.e., the record being edited when the relationship is made). It is important to consider what will make sense when displayed to a user. For example, in an associative relationship between artists, *Katsushika Hokusai* was the *teacher of Katsushika Taito II;* their relationship is *teacher/student.* In the record of a student, the relationship type linking to the teacher is *student of,* because the artist in the focus record is the student of the artist in the linked record. In the record for the linked artist, the reciprocal relationship type is *teacher of.*

If a vocabulary has relationships that are homographs, or if values may change over time, it is best to identify the relationships with unique numeric codes rather than simply by text values.

When relationship types are homographs, the vocabulary editor must be careful to link to the correct code. As illustrated in the *ULAN* example on the following page, in linking an uncle to his niece, the vocabulary editor must be sure to link to *uncle of #1533,* which has the code for *niece of #1534* as its reciprocal code. The editor should not link to the homograph *uncle of #1532,* because its reciprocal code is for *nephew of.*

Fig. 22. Examples of relationship types for *uncle* in the *ULAN*, which may be reciprocally linked to *niece of* or *nephew of.*

Code	Focus Entity	Related Code
1531	nephew of	1532
1532	uncle of	1531
1533	niece of	1534
1534	uncle of	1533
1535	nephew of	1536
1536	aunt of	1535
1537	niece of	1538
1538	aunt of	1537

Peale, Mary Jane (American painter, 1826-1902)
Names:
Peale, Mary Jane (preferred,V,index)
Mary Jane Peale (V,display)
Peale, Mary Jean (V)
Peale, Miss Mary Jean (V)
Peale, Jean (V)
niece of .... Peale, Raphaelle
.... (American painter, 1774-1825) [500004821]
niece of .... Peale, Rembrandt
.... (American painter, 1778-1860) [500019719]
niece of .... Peale, Titian Ramsay
.... (American painter and naturalist, 1799-1885) [500017044]

Francken, Hieronymus, III (Flemish painter, 1611-after 1661)
Names:
Francken, Hieronymus, III (preferred,V,index)
Hieronymus Francken III (V,display)
Francken, Hieronymus III (V)
Hieronymus III Francken (V)
nephew of .... Francken, Ambrosius, II
.... (Flemish painter, ca. 1590 - 1632) [500092972]
nephew of .... Francken, Hieronymus, II
.... (Flemish painter, 1578-1623) [500024695]
nephew of .... Francken, Thomas
.... (Flemish artist, 1574-ca. 1625) [500000020]

4. Vocabularies for Cultural Objects

A wide range of controlled vocabularies may be used to describe and enhance access to art and material culture resources. Many of these vocabularies are created and maintained by research institutions, national and international cultural organizations, and professional societies and associations. They can be used individually or together, depending on the type of material being described. Only a sampling of the most commonly used vocabularies is discussed in this chapter. A fuller list of pertinent vocabularies and sources of terminology may be found in the **Appendix.**

4.1. Types of Vocabulary Terms

The types of terms that are necessary for describing art and architecture include the names for people, corporate bodies, geographic locations, objects, iconographic subjects, and genre terms.

Personal names are used for creators, publishers, donors, patrons, clients, and any other individual associated with the design, production, subject, or other aspect of cultural works.

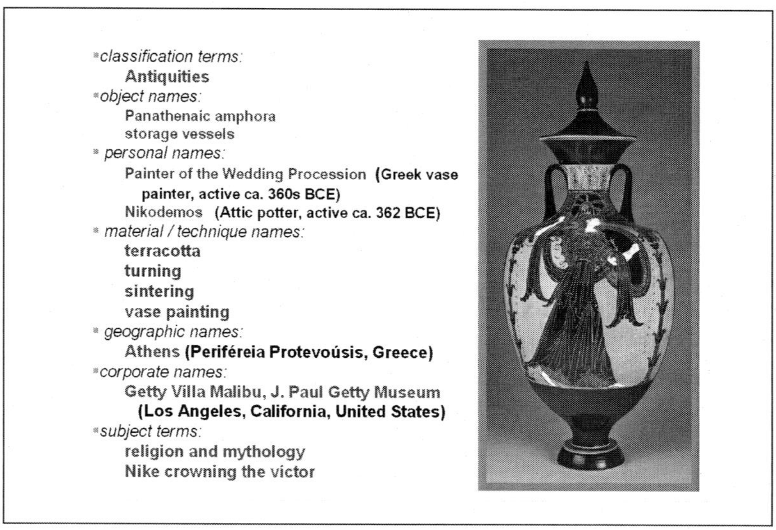

Fig. 23. Illustration highlighting the types of controlled terminology typically required for cataloging art and cultural heritage information.

Attributed to Painter of the Wedding Procession (Greek, active ca. 362 BCE); potter: signed by Nikodemos (Greek, active ca. 362 BCE); *Prize Vessel from the Athenian Games;* 363/362 BCE; terracotta; height with lid, 89.5 cm (35¼ inches), circumference at shoulder, 115 cm (44⅞ inches); J. Paul Getty Museum (Los Angeles, California); 93.AE.55.

Georgia O'Keeffe (American painter, 1887–1986)

Painter of the Wedding Procession (Greek vase painter, active ca. 360s BCE)

Corporate names are used for repositories, architectural and photographic firms, workshops, families of artists, and any other group of people working together as an entity who are associated with the work. The group need not be legally incorporated. Corporate names are often included in the same vocabulary as personal names.

Metropolitan Museum of Art (New York, New York, United States) (American art museum, formed in 1870)

Adler and Sullivan (American architectural firm, 1883–1924)

Geographic names are used for the current location, creation location, discovery location, various other former locations, places of conservation, subject (when the work depicts a named place), and any other geographic place associated with the work and its history.

Athens (Periféreia Protevoúsis, Greece) (inhabited place)

Taihezhen (Yunnan, China) (deserted settlement)

Pampa del Tamarugal (Chile) (plain)

Geographic names are also linked to the authority records for the artists, museums, and other people and corporate bodies listed in the work record. For example, if the *Metropolitan Museum of Art* is linked as the repository in a work record, the geographic location of the museum, *New York,* would by default also be associated with the work.

Generic terms—which are terms that may each refer generically to many things—are used for object types, materials, techniques, styles, and many other areas of the records for art and architecture. By definition, generic terms exclude proper names and are usually written in lowercase in English. However, the term may begin with a capital letter if a proper name is incorporated in a term (e.g., *Panathenaic amphorae*).

casein paint (tempera, water-base paint, Materials)

Panathenaic amphorae (neck amphorae, storage vessels, Furnishings and Equipment)

Iconographic subjects and themes, religious and mythological characters, events, and other such terminology also require controlled vocabulary.

Buddha (Buddhist iconography)

Nike Crowning the Victor (Story of Nike, Greek Iconography)

Battle of the Little Big Horn (American Indian Wars)

A discussion of several of the most prominent vocabularies used for art and architecture information is included below. In addition to the ones listed here, there are dozens of local and regional databases of vocabularies—such as *Artists in Canada,* compiled and maintained by the National Gallery of Canada Library, and Elizabeth Glass's *A Subject Index for the Visual Arts* (1969), developed to enhance access to the prints and drawings of the Victoria and Albert Museum—as well as published encyclopedias and other sources that are discussed in **Chapter 6: Local Authorities** and the **Appendix.**

4.2. The Getty Vocabularies

Three Getty vocabularies are thesauri that provide terminology, relationships, and other information about the objects, artists, concepts, and places important to various disciplines that specialize in art, architecture, and material culture: the *Art & Architecture Thesaurus* (*AAT*), the *Getty Thesaurus of Geographic Names* (*TGN*), and the *Union List of Artist Names* (*ULAN*). A fourth Getty vocabulary, the *Cultural Objects Name Authority* (*CONA*), is currently under development (as of this writing).

The Getty vocabularies can be used in three ways: as sources of terminology at the data entry stage by catalogers or indexers who are describing works of art, architecture, material culture, archival materials, visual surrogates, or bibliographic materials; as knowledge bases, providing information for researchers; and as search assistants to enhance end-user access to online resources.

Beginning in the 1980s, the Getty vocabularies were developed as sources of terminology for—and to supply scholarly information about—concepts needed to catalog and retrieve information about the visual arts and cultural heritage. The Getty vocabularies are thesauri containing names and other information about people, places, and things in the realm of art and cultural heritage, linked together to show relevant relationships. The focus of each record is the concept, to which terms are linked. The concepts are generally displayed in three ways: in hierarchies with indentation; in full records with all pertinent associated terms and names, other data, and relationships; and in abbreviated strings in results lists.

The Getty vocabularies are compilations of terms gathered from various cataloging and documentation projects. They are edited, managed, and distributed by the Getty Vocabulary Program. The vocabularies are not comprehensive; they are living thesauri that grow and evolve through work with internal and external contributors. Some of the current contributors to the Getty vocabularies include museums, libraries, archives, and bibliographic and documentation projects, including projects at the Getty

Research Institute such as the Getty Provenance Index, the Photo Study Collection, and the Research Library catalog. Former Getty projects were contributors in the past, including the *Avery Index to Architectural Periodicals,* the *Bibliography of the History of Art* (*BHA*), and the *Foundation for Documents of Architecture* (*FDA*). Various projects in the Getty Conservation Institute and the J. Paul Getty Museum also contribute data. External contributors include the Canadian Centre for Architecture; the Frick Art Reference Library; the Smithsonian National Museum of African Art; the Courtauld Institute of Art; the National Art Library in London; the Victoria and Albert Museum (V&A); the Mystic Seaport museum; the Harry Ransom Humanities Research Center at the University of Texas at Austin; the Bunting Visual Resources Library at the University of New Mexico; the Centro de Documentación de Bienes Patrimoniales, Chile; the Istituto Centrale per il Catalogo e la Documentazione, Rome; and the Canadian Heritage Information Network. Up-to-date information about contributors and how to make contributions is available on the Getty Vocabulary Program Web pages.

The Getty vocabularies are compliant with ISO and NISO standards for thesaurus construction. The terms and associated information in the *AAT, TGN,* and *ULAN* are valued as authoritative because they are derived from published sources and represent current research and usage in the art history and cultural heritage communities. The rules for content of the Getty vocabularies are available in comprehensive *Editorial Guidelines* that comply with *CDWA, CCO,* and other standards.

The Getty vocabularies are published in licensed files and in an online application that is free of charge to all Web users. They are integrated into various collections management systems. The primary users of the Getty vocabularies include museums, art libraries, archives, visual resources collection catalogers, bibliographic projects concerned with art, researchers in art and art history, and the information specialists who address the needs of these users. In addition, a significant number of users of the Getty vocabularies are students and members of the general public.

4.2.1. *Art & Architecture Thesaurus* (*AAT*)

The *AAT* is a structured vocabulary containing, as of this writing, approximately 131,000 terms and other information relating to objects, materials, techniques, activities, and other concepts. Terms in the *AAT* may be used to describe art, architecture, decorative arts, material culture, and archival materials.

The focus of each *AAT* record is called a *concept.* Currently there are approximately 34,000 concepts in the *AAT.* In the database, each concept's record (also called a *subject*) is identified by a unique numeric identifier. Linked to each concept record are terms, related concepts, a *parent* (that is, an immediate broader context), sources for the data, and notes. Each record has one preferred term in American English and may have other terms preferred in other languages. Additional synonymous terms may be included as well.

The *AAT* is a hierarchical database; its trees branch from a root called *Top of the AAT hierarchies* (*Subject_ID: 300000000*). The structure of the *AAT* allows for multiple broader contexts, making the *AAT* polyhierarchical; for example, *jade* has two broader contexts: *metamorphic rock* and *gemstone*. In addition to the hierarchical relationships, the *AAT* has equivalence and associative relationships.

4.2.1.1. Scope

The *AAT* includes terms describing concepts related to art and architecture, excluding proper names and iconographic subjects; thus, it contains information about generic concepts (as opposed to proper nouns or names). That is, each concept is a case of many (a generic thing), not a case of one (a specific thing). For example, the generic term *cathedral* is in the *AAT*, but the specific proper name *Chartres Cathedral* is out of scope for the *AAT* (*Chartres Cathedral* is in scope for *CONA*).

The temporal coverage of the *AAT* ranges from Antiquity to the present, and the scope is global. To be within scope, terms must be applicable to the creation, use, discovery, maintenance, description, appreciation, or conservation of art, architecture, decorative arts, archaeology, material culture, archival materials, or related concepts.

The *AAT* includes terminology to describe the type of artwork (e.g., *sculpture*), its material (e.g., *bronze*), activities associated with the work (e.g., *casting*), its style (e.g., *Art Nouveau*), the role of the creator or other persons (e.g., *sculptor, doctor*), and other attributes or various abstract concepts (e.g., *symmetry*). It may include the generic names of plants and animals (e.g., *domestic cat* or *Felis domesticus*), but not specific names. For example, *Fanchette,* as a literary character (the cat in the *Claudine* novels by Sidonie-Gabrielle Colette), would go in a Subject Authority. The *AAT* does not include proper names of persons, organizations, geographic places, named subjects, or named events.

The scope of the *AAT* is multicultural and international. Terms for any concept may include the plural form of the term, singular form, natural order, inverted order, spelling variants, various forms of speech, terms in different languages, and synonyms that have various etymological roots.

Fig. 24. *Composite order* is the descriptor, and *Roman order* and *italic order* are synonyms in the *AAT* for the architectural order illustrated in this print.

Draftsman: Antoine Babuty Desgodets (French, 1653–1728); engraver: George Marshall (Scottish, died ca. 1732); *The Temple of Vesta at Tivoli: Profile of the Capital of the Column;* plate: ca. 1682, published 1795; engraving; in *The Ancient Buildings of Rome;* published: London: I. and J. Taylor, 1795; Research Library; The Getty Research Institute (Los Angeles, California); 86-B5394-v.1-ch.5-p1.2.

4.2.1.1.1. Facets and Hierarchies in the AAT

New concepts must fit into the facets and hierarchies already established in the *AAT.* The facets are conceptually organized in a scheme that proceeds from abstract concepts to concrete, physical artifacts. A broader term provides an immediate class or genus to a concept and serves to clarify its meaning. The narrower term is always a type of, kind of, or generic manifestation of its broader context. For example, *orthographic projections* is the broader context for *plans (images)* because all plans are orthographic (i.e., the projectors are perpendicular to the picture plane).

The conceptual framework of facets and hierarchies in the *AAT* is designed to allow a general classification scheme for art and architecture. The framework is not subject-specific; for example, there is no defined portion of the *AAT* that is specific only for *Renaissance painting*. Terms to describe *Renaissance painting* are found in many locations in the *AAT* hierarchies. The following are the seven facets into which the *AAT* is divided:

> **Associated Concepts:** This facet contains abstract concepts and phenomena that relate to the study and execution of a wide range of human thought and activity, including architecture and art in all media as well as related disciplines. Also covered here are theoretical and critical concerns, ideologies, attitudes, and social or cultural movements. Examples are *beauty, balance, connoisseurship, metaphor, freedom,* and *socialism.*
>
> **Physical Attributes:** This facet concerns the perceptible or measurable characteristics of materials and artifacts as well as those features of materials and artifacts that are not separable as components. Included are characteristics such as size and shape, chemical properties of materials, qualities of texture and hardness, and features such as surface ornament and color. Examples are *strapwork, borders, round, waterlogged,* and *brittleness.*
>
> **Styles and Periods:** This facet provides terms for stylistic groupings and distinct chronological periods that are relevant to art, architecture, and the decorative arts. Examples are *French, Louis XIV, Xia, Black-figure,* and *Abstract Expressionist.*
>
> **Agents:** This facet contains terms for designations of people, groups of people, and organizations identified by occupation or activity, physical or mental characteristics, or social role or condition. Examples are *printmakers, landscape architects, corporations,* and *religious orders.*
>
> **Activities:** This facet encompasses areas of endeavor, physical and mental actions, discrete occurrences, systematic sequences of actions, methods employed toward a certain end, and processes occurring in materials or objects. Activities may range from branches of learning and professional fields to specific life

events, from mentally executed tasks to processes performed on or with materials and objects, from single physical actions to complex games. Examples are *archaeology, engineering, analyzing, contests, exhibitions, running, drawing (image-making),* and *corrosion.*

Materials: This facet deals with physical substances, whether naturally or synthetically derived. These range from specific materials to types of materials designed by their function, such as colorants, and from raw materials to those that have been formed or processed into products that are used in fabricating structures or objects. Examples are *iron, clay, adhesive, emulsifier, artificial ivory,* and *millwork.*

Objects: This facet is the largest of all the *AAT* facets. It encompasses discrete tangible or visible things that are inanimate and produced by human endeavor; that is, objects that are either fabricated or given form by human activity. In physical form, they range from built works to images and written documents. In purpose, they range from utilitarian to aesthetic. Also included are landscape features that provide the context for the built environment. Examples are *paintings, amphorae, façades, cathedrals, Brewster chairs,* and *gardens.*

4.2.1.2. What Constitutes a Term in the *AAT*?

Terms in all of the Getty vocabularies require literary warrant, meaning that they are found in an authoritative published source. The preferred term in the *AAT* is the term most often used in authoritative sources in American English. Descriptors in other languages may also be included.

4.2.1.2.1. Warrant for a Term

Whereas in the *TGN* and *ULAN* it is generally clear what word or combination of words is considered a place name or a person's name in a published source, the *AAT* presents a unique challenge: how to determine if a word or words truly represent a definable, unique concept in common and scholarly usage, or if it is simply a string of words (in which case it would not be included in the *AAT*). A *concept* is defined as a single word or multiple words that are used consistently to refer to the identical generic concept, type of work material, activity, style, role, or other attribute.

In order to determine whether or not the term is truly established by common usage in the community, that it consistently represents a definable concept, and that the preferred term (descriptor) is the one most often used to refer to this concept, the *AAT* generally requires three pieces of literary warrant (although exceptions are described in the guidelines for contributions).

4.2.1.2.2. Discrete Concepts

A *concept* in the context of the *AAT* is a discrete thing or idea. The *AAT* maintains *discrete concepts,* as opposed to *headings* or *compound terms,* in order to make the thesaurus more versatile in cataloging and more powerful in retrieval. However, a term for a discrete concept is not necessarily composed of only one word; examples of multiple-word terms describing discrete concepts include the following: *rose windows, flying buttresses, book of hours, High Renaissance,* and *lantern slides.* These terms are bound compound terms, meaning the words must remain joined in order to retain meaning.

In contrast to a discrete concept, a *subject heading* typically concatenates multiple terms or concepts together in a string. For example, *Pre-Columbian sculptures* is a heading composed of terms representing two discrete concepts: *Pre-Columbian* (a style and period) and *sculpture* (a type of work). *Pre-Columbian* as a style and period term can be combined with many other terms and retain its meaning, as may *sculpture.*

4.2.1.3. What Is Excluded from the *AAT*?

All terms in the *AAT* must refer to a case of many (generic things), not a case of one (unique things). In general, if a term is a proper name, it is excluded from the *AAT.* Therefore, individual people and named buildings, corporate bodies, and historical events are out of scope for the *AAT.*

Also excluded are concepts that are not directly related to the visual arts and architecture. Terms that are peripherally related to the visual arts may be included if the general user community deems them necessary for cataloging works of art and architecture and if the terms fit into the facets already established in the *AAT.* Brand names are generally excluded from the *AAT,* except in the rare case where the brand name has come to mean the generic item (e.g., *Bakelite*); unbound compound concepts and terms that have not been accepted in general language or by the scholarly community are also excluded.

4.2.1.4. Fields in the *AAT*

On the following page is a sample record from the published *AAT,* showing many of the fields in the record. In addition to these fields displayed to the public, there are additional fields hidden from public view but used for retrieval or administrative purposes in the production system. For a brief discussion of the *AAT* fields, see *About the AAT* on

ID: 300015613 **Record Type:** concept

graffiti (<visual works by location or context>, <visual works (Guide Term)>, ... Visual and Verbal Communication)

Note: In archaeology and art history, refers to casual scribbles or pictographs on walls, stones, or other surfaces. In the context of ancient Greek vase painting, graffiti refers to marks incised or cut into the ceramic, usually on the underside of the foot of the vase; they were generally trademarks. In recent times the term is applied to humorous, satiric, obscene, or gang-related writings or drawings executed anonymously in public places. Graffiti is distinct from "sgraffito," in that sgraffito is not casual, but is instead a formal decorative mark-making technique used on pottery, glass, or other surfaces.

Terms:
graffiti (**preferred**,C,D,U,LC,English-P,Italian-P)
graffito (writing) (C,AD,U,English,Italian)
grafitos (C,D,U,Spanish-P)
grafito (C,AD,U,Spanish)
graffites (C,D,U,French-P)
graffite (C,AD,U,French)

Facet/Hierarchy Code: V.VC

Hierarchical Position:
Objects Facet
.... Visual and Verbal Communication
.... Visual Works (Hierarchy Name)
.... <visual works (Guide Term)>
.... <visual works by location or context>
.... graffiti

Additional Parents:
Objects Facet
.... Visual and Verbal Communication
.... Information Forms (Hierarchy Name)
.... <information forms (Guide Term)>
.... <document genres>
.... <document genres by form>
.... inscriptions
.... graffiti

Related concepts:
creator(s) are .... graffiti artists
.... (muralists (painters), <painters by location or context>, ... People) [300312066]
distinguished from .... sgraffito (technique)
.... (<image-making processes and techniques>, <processes and techniques by specific type>, ... Processes and Techniques) [300266416]

Sources and Contributors:
graffite............ [VP]
.... Cassell's French Dictionary (1981)
graffites............ [VP]
.... Cassell's French Dictionary (1981) **220**
graffiti............ [VP Preferred]
.... Avery Index (1963-) **(source AAT)**
.... CDMARC Subjects: LCSH (1988-)
.... Clark, Elston and Hart, Understanding Greek Vases (2002) **96**
.... Mayer, Dictionary of Art Terms and Techniques (1969)
.... RIBA, Architectural Keywords (1982)
.... RILA, Subject Headings (1975-1990)
graffito (writing)............ [VP]
.... Cassell's Italian Dictionary (1983)
.... Clark, Elston and Hart, Understanding Greek Vases (2002) **96**
.... Oxford English Dictionary Online (2002-) **accessed 28 January 2004**
grafito............ [VP]
.... Cassell's Spanish Dictionary (1990)
grafitos............ **[VP, DIBAM preferred]**
.... Cassell's Spanish Dictionary (1990) **795**
.... Fatás Cabeza and Borrás Gualis, Diccionario (1980)
.... **Sturgis y Hollis, Entender la pintura (2002) 202**
.... **Tesauro de Arte & Arqu itectura (2000-)**

Subject: ..... [VP]
.... RIBA, Architectural Keywords (1982) **Vandalism**

Note: .... [VP]
.... Clark, Elston and Hart, Understanding Greek Vases (2002) **96**
.... Mayer, Dictionary of Art Terms and Techniques (1969)

Fig. 25. Example of a full record display for the concept *graffiti* in the *AAT.*

the *AAT* Web site. For a full description of the *AAT* fields and the methodology for compiling and editing the data, see the Getty Vocabulary Program *Editorial Guidelines* online.

4.2.2. *Getty Thesaurus of Geographic Names* (*TGN*)

The *TGN* is a structured vocabulary containing, at the time of this writing, approximately 1,115,000 names, as well as other information about places. It is a thesaurus containing hierarchical, equivalence, and associative relationships. The *TGN* is not a geographic information system (GIS). While many records in the *TGN* include coordinates, these coordinates are approximate and intended for reference only.

The focus of each *TGN* record is a place. There are approximately 895,000 places represented in the TGN. In the database, each place record (also called a *subject*) is identified by a unique numeric identifier. Linked to the place records are names, the place's parent (i.e., immediate broader context) in the hierarchy, other relationships, geographic coordinates, notes, sources for the data, and *place types,* which are terms describing the role of the place (e.g., *inhabited place* and *state capital*). Each record has at least one preferred name and may have additional names that are preferred in other languages. Names for a place may include names in the vernacular language, English, other languages, historical names, and names in natural order and inverted order. The *preferred name* is flagged in order to serve as a default in displays (although any name in the record may be preferred by users in different situations).

The *TGN* is a hierarchical database; its trees branch from a root called *Top of the TGN hierarchies* (*Subject_ID: 1000000*). Currently, most of the *TGN* data is located under the facet World. Under World, the places are generally arranged in hierarchies representing the current political and physical world, although some historical nations and empires are also included. There may be multiple broader contexts for a given place, making the *TGN* polyhierarchical; for example, the town of *Siena* is placed under modern *Italy,* but also under the historical confederation of *Etruria,* of which it was a part. The *TGN* also includes a facet called *Extraterrestrial Places.*

4.2.2.1. Scope

The temporal coverage of the *TGN* ranges from prehistory to the present, and the scope is global. The *TGN* includes administrative entities and physical features that have proper names, are of the types typically found in atlases and gazetteers, and are required for cataloging art and architecture.

4.2.2.1.1. Nations, Cities, Archaeological Sites

The *TGN* focuses on political and administrative bodies defined by administrative boundaries and conditions, including inhabited places, nations, empires, states, districts, townships, and some neighborhoods. These administrative entities include places defined by boundaries established by standard, independent sovereign states as well as entities with government and boundaries defined by ecclesiastical or tribal authorities. Archaeological sites and general regions without defined boundaries are also included.

4.2.2.1.2. Physical Features

Physical features are characteristics of the earth's surface that have been shaped by natural forces—including continents, mountains, forests, rivers, oceans, submerged islands, and former continents. The *TGN* generally excludes man-made features that may resemble physical features, such as roads, reservoirs, and canals. A small number of extraterrestrial places are included in the *TGN*.

4.2.2.1.3. Places That No Longer Exist

The *TGN* may include places that are no longer extant, such as deserted settlements, historical states, and lost physical features, such as submerged islands.

4.2.2.2. What Is Excluded from the *TGN*?

Smaller features typically found within the boundaries of a city—buildings, landmarks, and streets—are generally not included in the *TGN*. Also excluded are mythical and legendary places, such as the *Garden of Eden*. Lost sites may be included if they are generally believed to have existed, even if their precise historical location is not currently known.

4.2.2.2.1. Built Works

In general, architectural works are outside the scope of the *TGN* (but should be recorded in *CONA*). Building names are occasionally included in the *TGN*, but these are limited to names of structures or complexes that are located in the countryside (e.g., abbeys, villas, and shopping centers), where the name serves as a place name in the absence of a larger populated place. Certain other large, major man-made features, such as the *Great Wall of China* and the *Appian Way*, are also included in the *TGN*.

4.2.2.2.2. Cultural and Political Groups

Cultural and political groups are outside the scope of the *TGN*. However, the political state of a cultural or political group and the territory within its

ID: 7030330 **Record Type:** administrative

Epirus (province)

Note: Refers to the ancient region and province in northwestern Greece and southern Albania; Illyrium lay to the north and Macedonia to the east. The greatest Molossian king Pyrrhus (319-272) led a coalition of Epirote tribes and brought prosperity to the region; after the Third Macedonian War (171-168), Epirus was transferred to Roman rule, under which it prospered. The famous Battle of Actium (31 BCE) took place off the coast of Epirus. When the Roman Empire split in 395 CE, Epirus was the westernmost province of the Eastern Empire. When the Byzantine Empire became fragmented, an independent principality was maintained in Epirus from 1204 CE. See also the modern region of the same name, referring to area only within Greece; see also the general region of Epirus, consisting of coastal areas of northwestern Greece and southern Albania.

Names:
Epirus (preferred,C,V,N,English-P)
Epiros (C,V,N,English)
Ípiros (C,V,N,Greek)

Hierarchical Position:
World (facet)
.... Roman Empire (former nation/state/empire) (H)
.... Epirus (province) (H) ca. 167 BCE-395 CE

Additional Parents:
World (facet)
.... Byzantine Empire (former nation/state/empire) (H)
.... Epirus (province) (H) 395 CE-1337

Place Types:
province (preferred, H) .... of the Roman and Byzantine empire, from ca. 167 BCE
principality (H)
despotate (H) .... of the Byzantine Empire, 1204-1337
league (H) .... Epirote League, 232-170 BCE

Related geographic places:
distinguished from .... **Epirus** .... (general region)
.... (World, Europe) [7030329]
distinguished from .... **Epirus** .... (region)
.... (World, Europe, Greece) [7002705]

Sources and Contributors:
Epiros.......... [VP]
.... Encyclopaedia Britannica Online (2002-) accessed 1 July 2004
Epirus.......... [VP preferred, BHA preferred]
.... Encyclopaedia Britannica Online (2002-) accessed 1 July 2004
.... Times Atlas of World History (1993) 89
Ípiros.......... [VP]
.... Encyclopaedia Britannica Online (2002-) accessed 7 August 2006
Subject: ..... [VP]
.... Encyclopaedia Britannica Online (2002-) accessed 1 July 2004; accessed 7 August 2006
.... Times Atlas of World History (1993) 89
Note: .... [VP]
.... Encyclopaedia Britannica Online (2002-) accessed 1 July 2004

Fig. 26. Example of a full record display for the historical province *Epirus* in the *TGN*.

boundaries may be included in the *TGN*. For example, the *Ottoman Turks* are outside the scope of the *TGN*, but the *Ottoman Empire* is included.

4.2.2.3. Fields in the *TGN*

Above is a sample record from the published *TGN*, showing many of the fields in the record. In addition to the fields displayed to the public, there are additional fields hidden from public view but used for retrieval or administrative purposes in the production database. For a brief discussion of the *TGN* fields, see *About the TGN* on the *TGN* Web site. For a full description of the *TGN* fields and the methodology for compiling and editing the data, see the Getty Vocabulary Program *Editorial Guidelines* online.

4.2.3. *Union List of Artist Names* (*ULAN*)

The *ULAN* is a structured vocabulary containing, at the time of this writing, approximately 293,000 names and other information about artists and other creators of cultural works. Names in the *ULAN* may include given names and surnames, pseudonyms, variant spellings, names in multiple languages, and names that have changed over time (e.g., married names). Among these names, one is flagged as the *preferred name.*

Although it is usually displayed as a list, the *ULAN* is structured as a thesaurus, compliant with ISO and NISO standards for thesaurus construction; it contains hierarchical, equivalence, and associative relationships.

The focus of each *ULAN* record is an artist or other creator. As of this writing, there are approximately 120,000 individuals and corporate bodies represented in the *ULAN.* In the database, each person or corporate body record is identified by a unique numeric identifier. Linked to each record are names, related people and corporate bodies, sources for the data, and notes.

Even though the structure is relatively flat, the *ULAN* is constructed as a hierarchical database; its trees branch from a root called *Top of the ULAN hierarchies* (*Subject_ID: 500000001*); it currently has three published facets: Person, Corporate Body, and Unknown Artist. Entities in the Person Facet typically have no hierarchical children (if they have genetic children who are artists, they are linked as associative relationships). Entities in the Unknown Artist Facet may be arranged under guide terms. Entities in the Corporate Body Facet may branch into trees, for example with the departments or divisions of a museum or manufactory. There may be multiple broader contexts, making the *ULAN* structure polyhierarchical. In addition to the hierarchical relationships, the *ULAN* also has equivalence and associative relationships.

The *ULAN* includes records for individual people, whether or not their proper name is identified, such as *Katsushika Hokusai (Japanese printmaker and painter, 1760–1849)* and *Master of the Albrecht Altar (German painter, active 1430/1450).* It also includes records for corporate bodies, which are a legally incorporated entity or an organized, identifiable group of individuals working together in a particular place and within a defined period of time, such as the *Bisson Frères (French photography studio, 1841–1864).* The Unknown Artist Facet contains appellations used in cataloging to designate culture or nationality when the individual creator is unknown, such as *unknown Maya.*

4.2.3.1. Scope

The temporal coverage of the *ULAN* ranges from Antiquity to the present, and the scope is global. The *ULAN* includes records for individual artists, rulers and other patrons, architectural firms and other groups of artists working together, and repositories of artworks.

4.2.3.1.1. Artists

In the context of the *ULAN,* an *artist* or *artisan* is any person or group of people who create art or other items of high artistic merit. The definition hinges upon the sometimes nebulous, often controversial, constantly changing definition of art. For the *ULAN,* artists and artisans represent creators who have been involved in the design or production of the visual arts that are of the type collected by art museums. Included are the creators of fine art such as paintings, sculpture, drawings, photographs and other prints, as well as the craftsmen who make ceramics, furniture, jewelry, calligraphy, costume, and many other types of works. The objects themselves may be in an art museum; an ethnographic, anthropological, or other museum; or owned by a private collector.

4.2.3.1.2. Architects

In the context of the *ULAN,* a creator of architecture may be included if he or she was involved in the design or creation of structures or parts of structures that are the result of conscious construction, are of practical use, are relatively stable and permanent, and are of a size and scale appropriate for—but not limited to—habitable buildings. Architecture is often limited to the built environment that is typically classified as fine art, meaning that it is generally considered to have aesthetic value, was designed by an architect, and constructed with skilled labor.

4.2.3.1.3. Non-Artists

The *ULAN* may include people and corporate bodies closely related to artists, such as prominent patrons (e.g., *Hadrian* or *Louis XIV*). Museums and other repositories of art are included as well. Other examples of persons include teachers, patrons, famous spouses, or other family members. Examples of corporate bodies include associated firms, art academies, museums, and other repositories of art.

4.2.3.1.4. Workshops and Families

A workshop may be included if the workshop itself is a distinct, definable group of people collectively responsible for the creation of art (e.g., the thirteenth-century group of French illuminators known as the *Soissons atelier*). Generic attributions to studios or workshops are outside the scope of the *ULAN.* For example, when a painting is attributed to an unknown hand in the workshop of a known artist (e.g., as might be expressed in an object record as *workshop of Raphael*), this is outside the scope of the *ULAN.* Families of artists may be included as corporate bodies.

4.2.3.1.5. Anonymous and Unknown Artists

Anonymous artists are placed in the Person Facet if the hand of the anonymous artist has been identified. In such cases, it is common for scholars or a museum to have created an identity for him or her (e.g., *Monogrammist A. C.* or *Master of the Aeneid Legend*). The Unknown Artist Facet includes designations for cultures or nationalities that are used for cataloging when the work is not attributed to an identified artistic personality with an established oeuvre—for example, *unknown Ancient Egyptian.*

4.2.3.1.6. Amateur Artists

Amateur artists are individuals who create art as a pastime rather than as a profession, and who are typically not formally trained in creating art. Such artists may be included in the *ULAN* if their work is of the type and caliber typically collected by art museums and if their work has been documented by an authoritative source or reviewed in a published source. A criterion for inclusion is the availability of information for all required *ULAN* fields, including a published source (which may be an entry in a museum catalog).

4.2.3.2. What Is Excluded from the *ULAN*?

Excluded from the *ULAN* are those professionals who may play one of the roles described above—such as painters, sculptors, printmakers, photographers, ceramicists, architects, etc.—but whose products are not considered art. For example, a portrait painter is considered an artist, but a house painter is not. Photographers who create still photographs of landscapes, portraits, still lifes, events, or abstract compositions of the caliber of *art* are artists, but photographers producing forensic photographs are generally outside the scope of the *ULAN.* Likewise, an engineer involved in the artistic process of designing architecture is included in the *ULAN,* but engineers who design diesel engines and biomedical engineers are not.

Note that the nature of a designated role may be typically artistic in one period but not in another. A medieval mason was often involved in the creative design process, while a modern bricklayer generally is not. A cabinetmaker in the court of Louis XVI was probably producing high-quality furnishings considered art, while the work of a modern craftsman who remodels a kitchen is probably not considered art.

Creators outside the scope of the *ULAN* include those who create in media not typically collected by art museums. For example, still photographers are included, but cinematographers are generally outside the scope of the *ULAN,* as are authors, choreographers, directors of plays and movies, composers of music, dancers, musicians, singers, and actors. A creator may be included in the *ULAN* even if his or her primary or most famous life role was not that of an artist or architect. For example, Thomas Jefferson is best known as a founding father and president of the United States, but he was also an influential architect. Conversely, history remembers Leonardo da Vinci primarily as a painter and draftsman (i.e., artist), and for these roles he is included in the *ULAN*, but in his own time, his role as military engineer was one of his most important activities.

4.2.3.3. Fields in the *ULAN*

On the following page is a sample record from the published *ULAN*, showing many of the fields in the record. In addition to these fields displayed to the public, there are additional fields hidden from public view but used for retrieval or administrative purposes in the production database. For a brief discussion of the *ULAN* fields, see *About the ULAN* on the *ULAN* Web site. For a full description of the *ULAN* fields and the methodology for compiling and editing the data, see the Getty Vocabulary Program *Editorial Guidelines* online.

4.2.4. *Cultural Objects Name Authority* (*CONA*)

CONA is the fourth Getty vocabulary and is in the early stages of development, as of this writing. It will be released initially with a core set of data from Getty projects and will be enlarged over the years through contributions from the user community. *CONA* fills a need for brief authoritative records for works of art and architecture. The target users are the visual resources, academic, and museum communities. *CONA* is a hierarchical database containing names, titles, and other core information for works of art. It is structured as a thesaurus and is compliant with ISO and NISO standards, as are the other three Getty vocabularies. Although *CONA* is an authority—not a full-blown database of object information—it complies with the cataloging rules for adequate minimal records described in *CDWA* and *CCO*.

4.2.4.1. Scope

CONA includes authority records for cultural works, including architecture and movable works such as paintings, sculpture, prints, manuscripts, photographs, performance art, archaeological artifacts, and various functional objects that are from the realm of material culture and of the type collected by museums. The focus of *CONA* is works cataloged in scholarly literature, museum collections, visual resources collections, archives, libraries, and indexing projects with a primary emphasis on art, architecture, and archaeology. The coverage is global, from prehistory through the present. Names or titles for the works may be current, historical, and in various languages.

Fig. 27. Example of a full record display for the artist *Mark Rothko* in the *ULAN.*

ID: 500014869 **Record Type:** Person

Rothko, Mark (American painter, born in Russia, 1903-1970)

Note: Noted as one of the primary artists of Abstract Expressionism and color field painting. Rothko moved to Portland in 1913. He attended Yale University for two years before moving to New York in 1925, where he attended the Art Students League and studied under Max Weber. He was a founding member of a group of abstract painters called Ten. In 1936, Rothko worked with the WPA Federal Art Project in the easel painting division. In 1945, he had a solo show in Peggy Guggenheim's Art of This Century gallery in New York. He also taught at the California School of Fine Arts in San Francisco with Clyfford Still. Rothko finished his first commission in 1958, a monumental painting for the Four Seasons restaurant in New York. He also painted murals for Harvard University and a chapel in Houston, which was dedicated to him after his death. Rothko committed suicide on February 25, 1970, in New York.

Names:
Rothko, Mark (preferred,V,index, English-P)
Mark Rothko (V,display)
Rothkowitz, Marcus (V,BN, Russian-P) .... the name given to him at birth in Russia (today in Latvia)

Nationalities:
American (preferred)
Russian
Jewish

Roles:
artist (preferred)
painter
abstract artist

Gender: male

Birth and Death Places:
Born: Daugavpils (Daugavpils district, Latvia) (inhabited place)
Died: New York City (New York state, United States) (inhabited place)

Events:
immigration: in 1913 United States (North and Central America) (nation)

Related People or Corporate Bodies:
colleague of .... Still, Clyfford taught at the California School of Fine Arts, San Francisco
.... (American painter, 1904-1980) [500020155]
parent of .... Rothko, Kate
.... (American, born 1950) [500069309]
student of .... Weber, Max Art Students League
.... (American painter, printmaker, and sculptor, 1881-1961) [500029261]
teacher of .... Frey, Viola
.... (American sculptor and ceramicist, 1933-2004) [500061622]
teacher of .... Hultberg, John
.... (American painter, 1922-2005) [500030565]

List/Hierarchical Position:
.... Person
.... Rothko, Mark

Biographies:
(American painter, born in Russia, 1903-1970) ..... [VP Preferred]
(American artist, 1903-1970) ..... [WCI]
(American artist, 1903-1970) ..... [WCP]
(American painter, 1903-1970) ..... [GRLPSC]
(American painter, 1903-1970) ..... [BHA]
(American artist, 1903-1970) ..... [WL-Courtauld]

Sources and Contributors:
Mark Rothko .... [VP]
.... Getty Vocabulary Program rules
Rothko, Mark .... [BHA Preferred, GRLPSC Preferred, VP Preferred, WCI Preferred, WCP Preferred, WL-Courtauld Preferred]
.... Grove Dictionary of Art online (1999-2002) accessed 1 April 2003
.... Museum of Modern Art (MoMA) [online] (2003) accessed 1 April 2003
.... RILA/BHA (1975-2000)
.... Witt Library, Authority files
Rothkowitz, Marcus .... [VP, WCI]
.... Witt Computer Index database

Note: .... [VP, WL-Courtauld]
.... Bruce and Wells, Art and Context, the '50s and '60s (2006) 30
.... Museum of Modern Art (MoMA) [online] (2003) accessed 1 April 2003

Subject: .... [BHA, GRLPSC, VP, WCI, WCP, WL-Courtauld]
.... Bruce and Wells, Art and Context, the '50s and '60s (2006) 30
.... Bénézit, Dictionnaire des Peintres (1976)
.... Getty Vocabulary Program rules
.... Grove Dictionary of Art online (1999-2002) accessed 1 April 2003
.... Museum of Modern Art (MoMA) [online] (2003) accessed 1 April 2003
.... RILA/BHA (1975-2000)
.... Who Was Who in America (1943-)
.... Who Was Who in American Art (1985)
.... Witt Computer Index database
.... Witt Library, Authority files

With the exception of performance art, *CONA* records unique physical works. However, *CONA* may include works that were never built or that no longer exist—for example, designs for a building that was not constructed or a work that has been destroyed.

4.2.4.1.1. Built Works

Built works within the scope of *CONA* are architecture, which includes structures or parts of structures that are the result of conscious construction, are of practical use, are relatively stable and permanent, and are of a size and scale appropriate for—but not limited to—habitable buildings. Most built works in *CONA* are manifestations of the built environment typically classified as fine art, meaning it is generally considered to have aesthetic value, was designed by an architect (whether or not his or her name is known), and was constructed with skilled labor.

4.2.4.1.2. Movable Works

The term *movable works* is borrowed from legal jargon, referring to tangible objects capable of being moved or conveyed from one place to another, as opposed to real estate or other buildings. It is useful to

Fig. 28. *CONA* includes records for built works as well as for paintings, sculpture, and other movable works. Both *Hagia Sophia* and the photograph of *Hagia Sophia* would be within scope.

James Robertson (English, 1813–1888); *Hagia Sofia, Constantinople, Turkey*; 1855; salt print; image: 25.7 × 30 cm (10⅛ × 11¹³⁄₁₆ inches), mount: 44.5 × 61.3 cm (17½ × 24⅛ inches); from *Photographs of the Crimea and Constantinople* (album); J. Paul Getty Museum (Los Angeles, California); 84.X0.1375.54.

separate the two types of works into different facets in *CONA* because movable works are typically located in a repository, have a repository identification number, have a provenance of former locations, and have other characteristics that generally differ from built works.

Movable works within the scope of *CONA* include the visual arts that are of the type collected by art museums, although the objects themselves may actually be held by an ethnographic, anthropological, or other type of museum, or owned by a private collector. Performance art is included in *CONA* under this facet as well.

4.2.4.2. What Is Excluded from *CONA*?

In general, *CONA* does not include records for objects in natural history or scientific collections, although there are exceptions for works of particularly fine craftsmanship that are of the type collected by art museums. *CONA* does not include names of musical or dramatic art, titles of documentary or feature films, or titles of literature. Exceptions that are included in *CONA* are illuminated manuscripts or illustrated books, artists' books, and artists' films. *CONA* does not include records for corporate bodies, although the building that houses the corporate body would be included, even if it has the same name as the corporate body. For example, the buildings of the *National Gallery of Art* in Washington, D.C., are included in *CONA;* however, the corporate body that inhabits those buildings, also called the *National Gallery of Art,* is outside the scope of *CONA* (but within the scope for the *ULAN*).

4.2.4.3. Fields in *CONA*

On the opposite page are draft sample records of a built work and a movable work appropriate for *CONA.*

4.2.5. *Conservation Thesaurus* (*CT*)

At the time of this writing, the Getty Conservation Institute, working with the Getty Vocabulary Program, is embarking on the development of the *Conservation Thesaurus* (*CT*), which is intended to improve consistency in indexing and to allow more efficient vocabulary-assisted retrieval of professional literature and other records related to the discipline of conservation. The *CT* will be developed in collaboration with the professional conservation community. It will be designed to be integrated with the *AAT,* with which there will be some overlap.

Fig. 29. Drafts of full record display in *CONA* for the architectural work *Hagia Sophia* and for the print *Great Wave at Kanagawa*, by Katsushika Hokusai.

ID: 1000001 **Record Type:** built work

Hagia Sophia (Istanbul, Turkey; 532-537 CE; museum)

Note: Nothing remains of the earlier two basilicas on this site: a 4th-century church and a 5th-century one built by Constantius, the son of Constantine the Great, which burned during the Nika riots of 532. The current church was rebuilt under the personal supervision of emperor Justinian I .

Names/Titles:

Hagia Sophia (preferred)
Church of the Holy Wisdom
Ayasofya (Turkish)
Agia Sofia
Agia Sophia
Sancta Sophia (Latin)

Current Location: Istanbul (Marmara region, Turkey) **Location type:** geographic
Repository ID:

Display Creator: architects: Anthemios of Tralles (Byzantine architect and mathematician in Asia Minor, ca. 474-ca. 534) and Isidoros of Meletus, the Elder (Byzantine architect and engineer in Asia Minor, active mid-6th century)

Related People/Corporate Bodies:

Anthemios of Tralles **Role:** architect
Isidoros of Miletus **Role:** architect

Display Creation Date:

original structure dated from 4th century CE; present structure built 532-537 CE; rebuilt in 12th century
[start: 532 end:9999]

Work Type:

church *Display Date:* from 4th century
[start: 300 end: 1500]
mosque *Display Date:* under Ottomans
[start: 1400 end:1934]
museum *Display Date:* since 1934
[start: 1934 end: 9999]

Technique/Medium display: system bearing masonry, centralized plan ; interior surfaces are sheathed with polychrome marble, porphyry, and mosaics

indexing Tech/Med: •masonry •load-bearing walls •centralized plan

Measurements display: central dome: diameter 31 meters (102 feet); height 56 meters (184 feet)

indexing measurements: *value:31 unit:m type: diameter: extent:* dome *value:*56 *unit:*m *type:*height

Style: **Culture:**

Subject: •architecture •religion/mythology • Holy Wisdom (Christian iconography) • worship

Related Works:

List/Hierarchical Position:

.... Built works
.... Hagia Sophia

Sources and Contributors:

Hagia Sophia ...... [BHA Preferred, VP Preferred, Avery Preferred]
Fletcher, History of Architecture (1987) 286 ff.
.... Grove Art Online (2002-) "Istanbul: Hagia Sophia," accessed 17 March 2010
Church of the Holv Wisdom .... [VP]
.... Grove Art Online (2002-) "Istanbul: Hagia Sophia," accessed 17 March 2010
Ayasofya · [BHA]
.... Kaliopi, Architecture of Hagia Sophia (1988) 12
Agia Sofia ...... [BHA]
.... Kaliopi, Architecture of Hagia Sophia (1988) 12
Agia Sophia .... [Avery]
.... Avery database
Sancta Sophia [VP]
.... Britannica online (2002-) accessed 17 March 2010

Note: .... [VP]
.... Fletcher, History of Architecture (1987) 286 ff.
.... Grove Art Online (2002-) "Istanbul: Hagia Sophia," accessed 17 March 2010

Subject: .... [BHA, Avery, VP]
.... Kaliopi, Architecture of Hagia Sophia (1988) 12
.... Fletcher, History of Architecture (1987) 286 ff.
.... Grove Art Online (2002-) "Istanbul: Hagia Sophia," accessed 17 March 2010
.... Britannica online (2002-) accessed 17 March 2010

Fig. 29. (continued)

ID: 1000002 **Record Type:** movable work

Great Wave at Kanagawa (Katsushika Hokusai; ca. 1831-1833; color woodcut; Metropolitan Museum of Art, New York)

Note: The large wave dominates the scene, with the small mountain in the background. It is said to have inspired said to have inspired both Debussy's "La Mer" and Rilke's "Der Berg."

Names/Titles:

Great Wave at Kanagawa (preferred, English-P)
In the Hollow of a Wave off the Coast at Kanagawa (alternate)
La Vague (French-P)
Die große Welle (German-P)

Current Location: **Metropolitan Museum of Art, New York, New York, USA)**
Location type: corporate body
Repository ID: **JP1847**

Display Creator: **Katsushika Hokusai (Japanese, 1760-1849); published by Nishimura Eijudo (Japanese, 19th century)**

Related People/Corporate Bodies:

Hokusai, Katsushika Role: **printmaker**
Nishimura Eijudo Role: **publisher**

Display Creation Date: ca. 1831/1833
[Start: 1828 • End: 1836]

Work Type:

color woodcut Display Date: [Start: • End:]

Technique/Medium display: woodcut, polychrome ink and color on paper
Indexing Material [links]: • polychrome ink •paper • color (pigment) Technique [links]: • woodcut

Measurements display: 25.7 x 37.9 cm (10 1/8 x 14 15/16 inches)
•Value: 25.7 Unit: cm Type: height | •Value: 37.9 Unit: cm Type: width

Style: Edo Culture:

Subject: •seascape •wave •fishermen •boat •Mount Fuji (Chubu, Japan) •Kanagawa (Kanto, Japan)

Related Works:

Relationship Type:
Link to related work:

List/Hierarchical Position:

... **Movable works**
...... **Thirty-six Views of Mount Fuji: First Series: Katsushika Hokusai ; 1827-1837**
.... **Great Wave at Kanagawa: Katsushika Hokusai; ca. 1831-1833**

Sources and Contributors

Great Wave at Kanagawa ...... [BHA Preferred, VP Preferred]
Janson, History of Art), 3rd Edition (1986) index.
.... Metropolitan Museum of Art online (2000-) accessed 17 March 2010

In the Hollow of a Wave off the Coast of Kanagawa .. [VP]
.. Grove Art Online (2002-) accessed 17 March 2010

La Vague .... [BHA]
.... BHA database (2000-)

Die große Welle .... [VP]
.... Kollontai, Wege der Liebe (1925)

Note: .... [VP]
.... Metropolitan Museum of Art online (2000-) accessed 17 March 2010
.... Grove Art Online (2002-) accessed 17 March 2010

Subject: .... [BHA, VP]
.... Janson, History of Art, 3rd Edition (1986)

4.3. Chenhall's *Nomenclature for Museum Cataloging*

The *Revised Nomenclature for Museum Cataloging* is a revised and expanded version of Robert Chenhall's system for classifying man-made objects. *Nomenclature* was first published in 1978 as a cataloging tool for historical organizations. It was developed at the Strong Museum in Rochester, New York, under the guidance of museum director Robert Chenhall and in consultation with a group of museum professionals. The goal was to provide names of object types for indexing materials in the Strong Museum, other history museums, and other types of museums. It was to be based on taxonomic approaches already being used by the scientific community. The book was revised and expanded in 1988 by a committee of expert users and museum professionals. *Nomenclature* underwent another significant revision by a committee of experts and was published under the title *Nomenclature 3.0 for Museum Cataloging.*

4.3.1. Organization and Scope of *Nomenclature for Museum Cataloging*

Nomenclature is organized alphabetically and also by hierarchy, based on artifact categories and classifications. It was designed as an open-ended system into which new terms could be added over time. In organizing his system of classification, Chenhall tried to avoid overlapping and inconsistent categories, which he saw as a problem with previous classification schemes. He decided that the unifying principle of his classification would be original functional context of each object.

The revised *Nomenclature* contains six levels of hierarchy, arranged in ten categories: (1) Structures, (2) Furnishings, (3) Personal Artifacts, (4) Tools and Equipment for Materials, (5) Tools and Equipment for Science and Technology, (6) Tools and Equipment for Communication, (7) Distribution and Transportation Artifacts, (8) Communication Artifacts, (9) Recreational Artifacts, and (10) Unclassifiable Artifacts.

Subclassifications have been created as necessary, designating more specific functional groupings—for example, Storage and Display Furniture. The terms actually used for indexing are positioned alphabetically under these subdivisions. In the third edition, the earlier alphabetical listing has been replaced by a three-level object-term hierarchy, with primary object terms at the broadest level; under these primary terms there may be narrower secondary and tertiary terms.

4.3.2. Terms in *Nomenclature for Museum Cataloging*

Nomenclature makes a distinction between what it calls *object names* and *object terms.* In the context of *Nomenclature,* an *object name* is the common word or phrase used to designate an object, while an *object term* is the preferred designation for that object in *Nomenclature.* For example, in local usage, a particular type of chair may be called a *rocker;* this is its local object name. However, when that object is indexed using *Nomenclature,* the cataloger is advised to use the preferred *Nomenclature* term *chair, rocking.* In this case, the object name *rocker* is not included in *Nomenclature* as an alternate term for *chair, rocking;* however, local catalogers are advised to include the object name *rocker* in the local catalog record for retrieval by their users. In this example, the object name is a true synonym for the object term; in other cases, the object term may be a broader context for an object name that is not included in *Nomenclature.*

The use of the words *names* and *terms* is different in *Nomenclature* than in the *AAT,* although the same principle of distinguishing preferred terms from common terms and other variants exists in both. In the *AAT,* terms representing the same concept (including objects) are gathered into records. The terms are flagged as *preferred, alternate preferred, used for* (UF), as well as designations such as *common term, scientific term,* and *neologism,* among others. In the case of *rocking chairs,* the term *rockers* is included in the *AAT* as a *used for* term.

4.3.3. *Nomenclature for Museum Cataloging* vs. the *AAT*

Users of vocabularies often ask how Chenhall's *Nomenclature* differs from the *AAT.* There is some overlap, but the two vocabularies differ in several ways; thus, catalogers often need to use both.

- *Nomenclature* is more generalist, with shallow coverage of more disparate types of cultural artifacts, and it has headings in addition to terms. For art and architecture, the *AAT* has broader and deeper coverage.
- The only overlap between *Nomenclature* and the *AAT* is in the *AAT* Objects Facet.
- The *AAT* has incorporated all of *Nomenclature* that is within scope for the *AAT.*
- Much of *Nomenclature* is out of scope for the *AAT* (e.g., medical and surgical equipment) because the *AAT* focuses on art and cultural heritage.
- The *AAT* is a polyhierarchical thesaurus, compliant with national and international standards for thesaurus construction. The first two editions of *Nomenclature* were categorized authority lists. The third edition more closely approaches the model of a monohierarchical thesaurus. Accepted usage practice of the third edition of *Nomenclature* allows for objects

to be cataloged with more than one term for cross-indexing purposes. By contrast, in the first two editions, standard practice was to assign only one term to an object, which discouraged and complicated cross-indexing of objects with multiple functional contexts.

- *Nomenclature* has fewer *used for* terms than the *AAT.* In *Nomenclature,* nonpreferred terms do not appear in the hierarchical list of terms but in the alphabetical list of terms in the back of the book, with the preferred term noted.
- *Nomenclature* has no qualifiers, while the *AAT* has qualifiers.
- *Nomenclature* is in English. The base language of the *AAT* is English; however, terms may exist in multiple languages.
- *Nomenclature* includes some compound terms (headings) that *AAT* users would construct for themselves.
- The third edition of *Nomenclature* will have definitions for broad terms at the category, classification, and subclassification level. Object terms will not have definitions, although some terms will be accompanied by helpful hints about usage. The *AAT* has scope notes for most terms at all levels.
- At the time of this writing, the draft revision of *Nomenclature* prefers capitalized and inverted terms, while the *AAT* prefers terms in lowercase and expressed in natural order.
- *Nomenclature* does not include the published warrant for each term. The *AAT* cites published sources and institutional contributors for most terms.

4.4. *Library of Congress Authorities*

The *Library of Congress Authorities* include subject, name, and title authority records created by or for the Library of Congress. These authorities comprise a tool used by librarians to establish forms of names for persons, places, meetings, and organizations as well as titles and subjects (i.e., topics) indexed in bibliographic records. Although the authorities were designed to provide uniform access and cross-references to materials in library catalogs, catalogers of art and art information who work outside the museum community also use the *Library of Congress/NACO Authority File* (*LCNAF*) and *Library of Congress Subject Headings* (*LCSH*). The Library of Congress Authorities and Vocabularies Service uses the *MARC 21 Format for Authority Data,* which provides a carrier for information concerning the authorized forms of names and subjects to be used as access points in MARC records.

4.4.1. *Library of Congress/NACO Authority File* (*LCNAF*)

At the time of this writing, the *LCNAF* includes over seven million personal names, corporate names, geographic names, and meeting names. Personal names include authors and other creators, such as editors, performers, photographers, and artists. The *LCNAF* also includes group authors and creators, such as corporate entities, government bodies, conferences, and jurisdictions.

LCNAF entries are established by the cooperating partners, which are primarily libraries in the United States, the British Library, the National Library of New Zealand, the National Library of South Africa, and the National Library of Australia. The Library of Congress also participates in the Program for Cooperative Cataloging (PCC), an international cooperative effort to provide cataloging that meets mutually accepted standards of libraries around the world. Rules for establishing name forms are found in the *Anglo-American Cataloguing Rules* (*AACR2*) manuals (currently under revision, with the working title *Resource Description and Access* [*RDA*]).

LCNAF exemplifies a controlled vocabulary that contains equivalence relationships between terms (or headings) and other relationships between related entities. For example, in the *LCNAF* MARC record, the 100 field may contain the preferred name for a person, and the 400 fields may contain variant names that refer to the same person;

Fig. 30. Example of the *LCNAF* record for *Diego Rivera,* including the control number, heading, additional names, and citations.

LC Control Number: n 79056051
HEADING: Rivera, Diego, 1886-1957
000 01088cz a2200229n 450
001 1889574
005 20081004072447.0
008 790702n| acannaabn |b aaa
010 __ |**a** n 79056051
035 __ |**a** (OCoLC)oca00289158
040 __ |**a** DLC |**b** eng |**c** DLC |**d** DLC |**d** OCoLC
100 1_ |**a** Rivera, Diego, |**d** 1886-1957
400 1_ |**a** Rivera Barrientos, Diego María, |**d** 1886-1957
400 1_ |**a** Barrientos, Diego María Rivera, |**d** 1886-1957
400 1_ |**a** ריוערא, דיעגא, |**d** 18861957-
667 __ |**a** Machine-derived non-Latin script reference project.
667 __ |**a** Non-Latin script reference not evaluated.
670 __ |**a** Worcester Art Museum, Worcester, Mass. Exhibition of sketches ...
670 __ |**a** Rivera Barrientos, M. del P. Mi hermano Diego, 1986: |**b** p. 11 (Diego María Rivera Barrientos) p. 24 (b. 12/8/1886) p. 219 (Diego Rivera; b. Guanajuato) p. 221 (d. 11/24/57; muralista)
670 __ |**a** His Diego Rivera, una retrospectiva, 1986: |**b** p. 9 (José Diego María de la Concepción Juan Nepomuceno Estanislao de la Rivera Barrientos Acosta y Rodríguez)
952 __ |**a** RETRO
953 __ |**a** xx00 |**b** bv16

in other words, they are synonyms for the concept. Preferred names for authors are generally the inverted form of the name found on the title page of books and other published works. The 500 fields may contain references to related entities, such as between a group and the members of the group. The *LCNAF* record may include information in addition to the names/terms, such as biographical information including the birth and death dates. The LC Control Number provides a stable, unique numeric identification for the record.

4.4.2. *Library of Congress Subject Headings* (*LCSH*)

The *LCSH* system was originally designed as a controlled vocabulary for indexing the subject and form of the books and serials in the Library of Congress collection. Most libraries in the United States have now adopted the *LCSH* system. The *LCSH* was originally developed for print material, but it is also used for moving images, art objects, and architecture, primarily by art libraries or librarians. The Library of Congress participates in the Subject Authority Cooperative Program (SACO), a component of the PCC.

The *LCSH* authority contains approximately four hundred thousand Subject Authority records that are maintained by the Library of Congress. These subject headings are applied to every item within a library's collection and are designed to allow access to items that have similar subject matter; the cross-references may represent near-synonymous relationships rather than true synonyms. In the example on the following page, the heading in the 150 field, *Motion pictures,* is the preferred term for the concepts in the 450 fields—*Films, Feature Films, Movies,* and *Cinema*—which have similar, but not identical, meanings.

The *LCSH* system is often used as a subject retrieval tool in an automated environment that is very different from that for which it was developed. Displays may sometimes label entries with thesaurus codes for broader and narrower concepts, scope notes, etc.; however, it was not designed as a thesaurus, and the links do not always comply with standards for thesaurus construction.

A subject heading representing a single concept or object may appear as one word or as a multiple-word phrase that usually includes a noun and an adjectival or prepositional phrase (e.g., *Human settlements*). A heading may also comprise a precoordinated multiple-concept heading, which is made of two or more otherwise individual or independent concepts coordinated or related through one or more linking devices. Precoordination results in phrase headings or main-heading/subdivision combinations (e.g., *Maya—Kings and rulers*).

LC Control Number: sh 85088084
HEADING: Motion pictures
000 01888cz a2200349n 450
001 4738393
005 20080909002741.0
008 860227i| anannbabn |a ana
035 __ |**a** (DLC)sh 85088084
035 __ |**a** (DLC)85078
035 __ |**a** (DLC)5715683
035 __ |**a** (DLC)sp 85088084
035 __ |**a** (DLC)287562
035 __ |**a** (DLC)7606751
035 __ |**a** (DLC)406855
906 __ |**t** 0834 |**u** te04 |**v** 0
010 __ |**a** sh 85088084 |**z** sj 96005965
040 __ |**a** DLC |**c** DLC |**d** DLC
053 _0 |**a** PN1993 |**b** PN1999
150 __ |**a** Motion pictures
360 __ |**i** subdivision |**a** In motion pictures |**i** under names of countries, cities, etc., and under names of individual persons, families, and corporate bodies, and headings of the type [topic] in motion pictures, e.g. |**a** Children in motion pictures; Death in motion pictures; |**i** and titles of individual motion pictures

450 __ |**a** Cinema
450 __ |**a** Feature films |**x** History and criticism
450 __ |**a** Films
450 __ |**a** Movies
450 __ |**w** nne |**a** Moving-pictures
550 __ |**w** g |**a** Audio-visual materials
550 __ |**w** g |**a** Mass media
550 __ |**w** g |**a** Performing arts
680 __ |**i** This heading is used as a topical heading for general works about motion pictures themselves, including motion pictures as an art form, copyrighting, distribution, editing, plots, production, etc. Works about the technical aspects of making motion pictures and their projection onto a screen are entered under |**a** Cinematography. |**i** Works about the technical aspects of making video recordings, i.e., creating and storing moving images in an electronic form and displaying them on an electronic display are entered under |**a** Video recording. |**i** Works about the artistic aspects of making video recordings are entered under |**a** Video recordings--Production and direction.
681 __ |**i** Notes under |**a** Cinematography; Video recording; Video recordings--Production and direction
953 __ |**a** xx00 |**b** lg14

Fig. 31. *LCSH* record for *Motion pictures*, including a control number, the heading, and cross-references.

4.5. *Thesaurus for Graphic Materials* (*TGM*)

The *Thesaurus for Graphic Materials* (*TGM*) was developed from a list of terms for visual images used by the Library of Congress Prints and Photographs Division, including subject terms and descriptive terms. The Library of Congress developed the *TGM* in recognition of the differences in terms for visual rather than textual materials. Since its original appearance in 1980, the *TGM* has evolved into two separate lists, the *TGM I: Subject Terms* and the *TGM II: Genre and Physical Characteristic Terms.*

Civil rights

--[country or state]--[city]

Public Note	Search also under the subdivision --CIVIL RIGHTS used with names of ethnic, racial, and regional groups and classes of persons (Appendix A).
Catalogers Note	Used in a note under CIVIL LIBERTIES and CIVIL RIGHTS DEMONSTRATIONS.
Used For	Civil rights movements
	Freedom from discrimination
	Rights, Civil
Broader Term	Civil liberties
Narrower Term	Children's rights
	Employee rights
	Gay rights
	Veterans' rights
	Women's rights
Related Term	Abolition movement
	Civil rights demonstrations
	Civil rights leaders
	Discrimination
	Integration
	Legal aid

Fig. 32. Example of the *TGM* record for *Civil rights*, including a heading, usage note, cross-references (*used for* headings), broader and narrower terms, and related terms.

4.5.1. Scope of the *TGM*

The principal source for terms in the *TGM* was the *LCSH.* Other sources include the *Legislative Indexing Vocabulary* (*LIV*) for political and social issues, the *AAT,* and published dictionaries and encyclopedias. Although the *TGM* is in large part based on the *LCSH,* the *TGM* differs fundamentally in that it has, from the outset, applied a consistent hierarchical structure to the terms.

The format of the *TGM* is as an alphabetical display. Hierarchical, equivalence, and associative relationships may be included. The example above is a screen shot from the *TGM I.*

4.5.2. The *TGM* vs. the *AAT*

How does the *TGM* differ from the *AAT*? The *TGM* aims for a broader application, dealing with topics not generally covered in the *AAT.* However, the *AAT* has deeper, more comprehensive coverage of art and architecture. The *TGM* entries are presented with initial capital letters rather than lowercase; uses the standard thesaural abbreviations UF (used for), BT (broader term), NT (narrower term), and RT (related term); uses PN (public note) and CN (cataloger's note), which are unique to the *TGM;* and often omits scope notes (SN). The *TGM* thesaurus is displayed as a single alphabetical list of terms rather than as indented hierarchies.

TGM

Altarpieces

--[country or state]--[city]

Used For Predellas
Reredoses
Retables
Retablos

Broader Term Religious architectural elements

Related Term Altars
Art
Churches

Control Number lctgm000273

Hierarchy
<<<(3)Architectural & site components(+)
<<(2)Architectural elements
<(1)Religious architectural elements
Altarpieces

AAT

ID: 300075940 **Record Type:** concept

altarpieces (<religious visual works>, <visual works by function>, ... Visual and Verbal Communication)

Note: Refers to painted or carved image-bearing objects in a Christian church. Altarpieces are characterized by usually being framed and either set on the rear part of the altar abutting the back of the altarblock or hung on the wall behind the altar. Altarpieces may be set on both the central high altar and side altars. The subject of the image is typically a religious figure or figures, often included in a narrative or didactic scene; it may also include a patron of the church.

Terms:
altarpieces (preferred,C,D,U,American English-P)
altarpiece (C,AD,U,American English)
altar-pieces (C,D,U,British English-P)
altar-piece (C,AD,U,British English)
tableaux d'autel (C,D,U,French-P)
tableau d'autel (C,AD,U,French)
tableaux d'autels (C,UF,U,French)
retable (altarpiece) (C,UF,U,French)
postautel (C,UF,U,French)
Altaraufsatze (C,D,U,German-P)
Altaraufsatz (C,AD,U,German)
Altäre (altarpieces) (C,UF,U,German)
Altare (altarpieces) (C,UF,U,German) .... Austrian spelling
Altar (altarpiece) (C,UF,U,German)
Altarbild (C,UF,U,German)
Altarretabel (C,UF,U,German)
pale d'altare (C,D,U,Italian-P)

Fig. 33. Examples comparing the *TGM* and *AAT* records for *altarpieces.*

pala d'altare (C,AD,U,Italian) .... from the Latin "pallium," meaning cloak and referring to the ancient practice of hanging drapery behind the altar

cuadros de altar (C,D,U,Spanish-P)
cuadro de altar (C,AD,U,Spanish)

Facet/Hierarchy Code: V.VC

Hierarchical Position:

Objects Facet
.... Visual and Verbal Communication
.... Visual Works (Hierarchy Name)
.... <visual works (Guide Term)>
.... <visual works by function>
.... <religious visual works>
.... altarpieces

Related concepts:

distinguished from .... **devotional images**
.... (<religious visual works>, <visual works by function>, ... Visual and Verbal Communication) [300178241]

distinguished from .... **dossals (curtains)**
.... (<altar and altar component coverings and hangings>, <coverings and hangings for religious building fixtures>, ... Furnishings and Equipment) [300204851]

distinguished from .... **superfrontals**
.... (<altar and altar component coverings and hangings>, <coverings and hangings for religious building fixtures>, ... Furnishings and Equipment) [300204866]

locational context/setting is .... **altars (religious building fixtures)**
.... (<altars and altar components>, <religious building fixtures>, ... Components (Hierarchy Name)) [300003725]

thing(s) involved are .... **predellas**
.... (<visual works components>, <components by specific context>, ... Components (Hierarchy Name)) [300003745]

Sources and Contributors:

Altar (altarpiece)............ [VP]
.... Grove Dictionary of Art online (1999-2002)
Altaraufsatz............ [VP]
.... Grove Dictionary of Art online (1999-2002)
Altaraufsatze............ [VP]
.... Cassell's German Dictionary (2002)
Altarbild............ [VP]
.... Grove Dictionary of Art online (1999-2002)
Altäre (altarpieces)............ [VP]
.... Cassell's German Dictionary (2002) 27
Altare (altarpieces)............ [VP]
.... Cassell's German Dictionary (2002) 27
altarpiece............ [VP]
.... Chenhall, Revised Nomenclature (1988)
altar-piece............ [VP]
.... Oxford English Dictionary Online (2002-)
altarpieces............ [DIBAM, VP Preferred]

Fig. 33. (continued)

The *TGM* users are encouraged to add nationality, geographic, chronological, and topical facet indicators when creating indexing entries, as is done in the *LCSH* (e.g., *Civil rights—Georgia—Atlanta*).

The *TGM* is intended to be a controlled vocabulary for describing a broad range of subjects, including activities, objects, and types of people, events, and places depicted in still pictures. While much of the *TGM* overlaps with the *AAT,* the *TGM* has subject terms that are typically out of scope for the *AAT,* such as *Hammer & sickle.* However, the *TGM* has fewer terms to describe the art objects themselves; for example, the *TGM* often includes narrower terms as UFs rather than as NTs (i.e., generic postings), making it more difficult to adopt the indexing principle of using the most specific term available.

Differences between the *TGM* and the *AAT* are illustrated in the example on the previous page. The hierarchical placement of the term differs in each vocabulary, based on the distinct logical structure inherent in each. The *TGM* includes generic postings, while the *AAT* does not: in the *TGM,* components of an altarpiece (*predellas*) and types of altarpieces (*retables* and *reredoses*) are UFs, while in the *AAT* they are all separate entries, though linked through associative relationships. In the *AAT,* the UFs and other variant terms are always true synonyms for the descriptor. This allows the *AAT* to be more precise, while the generic postings of the *TGM* allow it to be less complex (if less precise). In the example, there is no note defining the scope or usage of the term in the *TGM,* while most *AAT* terms have scope notes.

4.6. *Iconclass*

Iconclass was originally conceived by Henri van de Waal. It is now maintained by the Dutch art history institute Rijksbureau voor Kunsthistorische Documentatie (RKD) in The Hague.

4.6.1. Structure and Scope of *Iconclass*

Iconclass is an alphanumeric classification scheme designed for the iconography of art, focusing primarily on religious and mythological stories and themes in Western art. Each alphanumeric code in *Iconclass* has an associated natural language entry in English (called a *textual correlate*) that identifies the meaning of the code. The textual correlates have been translated into several other languages.

Iconclass alphanumeric codes are used as a controlled vocabulary to describe and classify subjects of artworks in a standardized manner. Unlike other vocabularies, *Iconclass* is not based on terms per se. The textual correlates are generally long and too unwieldy to use as controlled terms. *Iconclass* has been supplemented with an index of keywords that

9 Classical Mythology and Ancient History
......94 the Greek heroic legends (I)
.... 94L (story of) Hercules (Heracles)
....................94L1 early life, prime youth of Hercules
....................94L2 love-affairs of Hercules
....................94L3 most important deeds of Hercules: the Twelve Labours
...........................94L31 preliminaries to the Twelve Labours of Hercules
..........................94L32 the Twelve Labours: first series
.................................94L321 (1) Hercules chokes the Nemean lion with his arms
.................................94L322 (2) the Hydra of Lerna is killed by Hercules
.................................94L323 (3) the Ceryneian hind of Arcadia is captured by Hercules
.................................94L324 (4) the Erymanthian boar is captured by Hercules
.................................94L325 (5) Hercules cleanses the stables of Augeas by diverting the rivers...
.................................94L326 (6) the Stymphalian birds are shot by Hercules, or driven away with .
.................................94L327 (7) the Cretan bull is captured by Hercules
.................................94L328 (8) the four mares of King Diomedes are captured; when Diomedes is slai
.................................94L329 (9) Hippolyte, the Amazon, offers her girdle to Hercules
..........................94L33 the Twelve Labours of Hercules: second series
......................94L4 aggressive, unfriendly activities and relationships of Hercules
......................94L5 non-aggressive, friendly or neutral activities and relationships of Hercules
......................94L6 suffering, misfortune of Hercules
......................94L7 specific aspects, allegorical aspects of Hercules; Hercules as patron
......................94L8 attributes of Hercules

Fig. 34. Example illustrating how a section of *Iconclass* could be displayed as a hierarchy constructed from the alphanumeric classification codes. *Iconclass* is managed by the RKD (Rijksbureau voor Kunsthistorische Documentatie/Netherlands Institute for Art History). All rights reserved RKD, The Hague, The Netherlands.

help users locate the entries; however, these keywords are not unique and cannot be used as controlled vocabulary terms. Thus, the main indexing component of *Iconclass* remains the alphanumeric classification, which is explained to the user via textual correlates; the textual correlates are then indexed with keywords to provide additional access.

A standard entry in the *Iconclass* system consists of an alphanumeric notation and its textual correlate. The *Iconclass* system allows implementers to use additional features to increase the accuracy of meaning of a notation, including the addition of bracketed texts and designated *keys,* which are supplementary terms taken from an authorized list.

The main divisions of the *Iconclass* system are represented by the digits 0 to 9:

0 for Abstract, Nonrepresentational Art
1 for Religion and Magic
2 Nature
3 Human Being, Man in General
4 Society, Civilization, Culture
5 Abstract Ideas and Concepts
6 History
7 Bible
8 Literature
9 Classical Mythology and Ancient History

Within each division of *Iconclass,* entries are organized in increasing specific order. Each main division may be further divided by adding a second digit to the right of the first one. A third level of specificity may be attained by adding a letter in upper case. After that, subsequent levels of specificity are made by extending the notation to the right with more digits. Through this method of increasing specificity, the codes may be used to create a hierarchy, descending from broader to more specific.

In the example on the previous page, the *Iconclass* codes were used as the starting point to create the appearance of a hierarchy with indentation. The broader/narrower relationships represent a genus/species relationship.

5. Using Multiple Vocabularies

Catalogers of art information require multiple vocabularies because no single vocabulary provides the full set of terminology needed to catalog or index a given set of cultural heritage data; therefore, a combination of vocabularies is necessary for indexing. Furthermore, separate vocabularies may be required for retrieval; ideally, retrieval vocabularies are based on indexing vocabularies but may be optimized and applied differently for this purpose. Strategies for using vocabularies for indexing and for retrieval are further discussed in **Chapter 8: Indexing with Controlled Vocabularies** and **Chapter 9: Retrieval Using Controlled Vocabularies.**

In order to overcome the obstacles involved with using multiple vocabularies, systems developers should investigate the interoperability of vocabularies and the creation of local authorities.

5.1. Interoperability of Vocabularies

In the context of controlled vocabularies, *interoperability* refers to the ability of two or more vocabularies and their systems or components of their systems to map to each other's data, with the goals of exchanging information and enhancing discovery. Interoperability of controlled vocabularies is a complex topic that has been researched in the field of information science since the 1960s.

Interoperability deals with the two conflicting demands that underlie the development and use of controlled vocabularies. The first demand is that specialized vocabularies be developed for a certain community, such as the art and cultural heritage community; these vocabularies reflect the specific terms and concepts needed by catalogers to index and classify that material. However, no single vocabulary can be comprehensive, not even for its given scope. Interoperability may thus come into play as catalogers assign indexing terms to material, because cataloging art information requires a broad range of terminology that comes from different sources.

The second demand is made by end users who want to use a single search to find resources (e.g., texts, data, images, etc.) in federated settings across resources in different domains and created by different communities. Interoperability between resources and vocabularies is also a critical factor in meeting this demand.

Mappings between vocabularies may be used to facilitate faster indexing when two or more vocabularies are used by the indexer. When the indexer selects a term from the first vocabulary, the system can respond by offering corresponding terms from the second vocabulary. The indexer then confirms appropriate selections and rejects those that do not apply. In addition, creating interoperability between vocabularies for retrieval can expand retrieval options for a given collection without the cost of additional indexing by indexers having to select terms from the second vocabulary.

5.2. Maintenance of Mappings

The use of multiple controlled vocabularies across multiple databases and systems involves the mapping of terms and the design of methods to use those terms for indexing and retrieval. In addition, it requires plans for maintenance of the vocabularies and the mapping; terminologies tend to change significantly over time, thus rendering the mapping obsolete if a maintenance plan is not in place.

The issues surrounding interoperability are discussed in detail in *ANSI/NISO Z39.19-2005: Guidelines for the Construction, Format, and Management of Monolingual Controlled Vocabularies; BS 8723-4:2007: Structured Vocabularies for Information Retrieval: Interoperability between Vocabularies;* and *ISO/CD 25964-1: Thesauri and Interoperability with Other Vocabularies. Part 1: Thesauri for Information Retrieval* (in development at the time of this writing). A brief discussion of the issues appears below. Additional issues surrounding retrieval using vocabularies are addressed in **Chapter 9: Retrieval Using Controlled Vocabularies.**

5.3. Methods of Achieving Interoperability

Achieving interoperability requires adapting two or more vocabularies—which were probably developed to stand alone—to work in a new environment where search terms drawn from one link to terms found in the other. Often the search is conducted across two or more resources. The resources may have been indexed using one, all, or none of the vocabularies being used in retrieval.

Thus, interoperability may involve merging or adapting two or more controlled vocabularies to actually or virtually form a new controlled vocabulary that combines all the concepts and terms contained in the originals. It could also involve merging or adapting two or more resources that have been indexed using different controlled vocabularies. Various methodologies for direct mapping and switching may be used.

5.3.1. Direct Mapping

Direct mapping generally refers to the matching of terms one-to-one in each controlled vocabulary. The vocabularies need not be the same size (one may be smaller or larger) or cover exactly the same content, but there should be significant overlap in content. This technique assumes that where overlap exists, there is the same meaning and level of specificity between the two terms in each controlled vocabulary. In the broadest application, interoperability allows vocabularies developed for completely different domains to be combined in a comprehensive conceptual and terminological map. Successful mappings typically begin with a master vocabulary to which one or more subsidiary vocabularies are mapped, rather than mapping back and forth across both or all vocabularies.

Mapping may be done by computer algorithm or human mediation, but often both methods are employed together. The advantage of human mediation in creating mappings is that a subject expert can make a judgment about inexact equivalents. However, the use of automation or partial automation in a first pass at mapping may be beneficial.

Automated mapping may employ sets of terms found through comparisons and analysis. In one example, *co-occurrence mapping,* a set of terms may be created based on clusters of related terms gathered from the target resources. Related terms are determined by the frequency with which the terms appear together in the data. The result is a body of sets of presumably loosely related terms. The terms used for the co-occurrence mapping may be selected from individual metadata fields in the resources, from uncontrolled keywords assigned to the content or from the full text of the content in the resources. The loosely mapped term clusters discovered via this approach may be used in mapping between controlled vocabularies or used directly for indexing and retrieval.

In another automated strategy, links between vocabularies may be made through a temporary union list created dynamically in response to user queries. Such algorithms may map terms that are not necessarily conceptual equivalents but may be related in some way and may be used to map to existing controlled vocabularies. Capturing these clusters of presumably related terms is intended to enhance indexing and retrieval at the time a user enters a query, but no new controlled vocabulary is permanently generated.

5.3.2. Switching Vocabulary

Switching refers to the use of a third vocabulary, a switching vocabulary, that itself can link to terms in each of the two original controlled vocabularies. As with direct mapping, this type of mapping also assumes that the meaning of the terms can be reconciled—in this case, between all three terms: the original two controlled vocabulary terms and one switching term. The advantage of this method is that the scope and format of the switching term may be made broad enough to compensate for differences between the two original terms. Another application of switching occurs when the third vocabulary provides notations or a classification scheme under which terms from both original controlled vocabularies may be grouped. For example, *carriage cradles* in one vocabulary and *swinging cradles* in a second vocabulary could both be mapped as children of *cradles* in a switching vocabulary. This approach enables a single, unifying hierarchical display for terms that originated in multiple sources.

A further example of using a third vocabulary to map two or more original vocabularies involves a *lexical database*. This kind of database can be used to link terms from multiple controlled vocabularies into clusters of related concepts for which the types of relationships are defined, such as synonyms, antonyms, hierarchical relationships, and associative relationships.

5.3.3. Factors for Successful Interoperability of Vocabularies

The achievement of interoperability depends upon various factors, including the following:

Scope of mapping: The greater the number of elements included in the mapping, the more difficult the mapping becomes. At minimum, a mapping between vocabularies should match terms to terms. If a mapping intends to link not only terms but also scope notes, relationships, and other elements of the records from each vocabulary, more human intervention is required to harmonize the results.

Similarity of content: The more similarity there is in the content of each of the vocabularies and of the resources being searched, the more likely it is that successful interoperability will be achieved. For example, since there is little overlap in the content, trying to map an art vocabulary to a medical vocabulary for indexing and retrieval purposes has little advantage over using each vocabulary separately in indexing and retrieval. Even when both controlled vocabularies comply with standards such as those from ISO or NISO thesaurus standards, if the content is not similar, differences and variability in terminology, meaning, and syntax will hamper cross-domain interoperability.

Intended audience: If the purposes or intended audiences of the resources or vocabularies are very different, mappings of vocabularies are difficult or impossible and search results are uneven. If one database is indexed using terms for nonspecialists while the other is indexed for subject experts, users from both communities are likely to be disappointed with the combined retrieval results. For example, the resources and vocabularies required for an audience of K–12 students typically differ from those required for scholars and subject experts.

Format and hierarchical structure: The more there is similarity in the format and hierarchical structure of the vocabularies, the more likely interoperability between them is successful. If terms from the different vocabularies vary in format and hierarchical structures, indexing and retrieval results may be poor, even when the combined vocabularies are similar in content and used to search across similar domains. For example, mapping subject headings to thesaurus terms is typically only marginally successful, because subject headings are made of multiple terms and other information—such as dates—concatenated together, usually without hierarchical structure, while each term in a thesaurus is a single word or short phrase representing a discrete concept that is organized in a strictly defined hierarchical context. Interoperability between two or more such controlled vocabularies usually must reduce or eliminate structure while attempting to maintain meaning, which is difficult with a thesaurus because meaning is implied by the hierarchical context of the term.

Precoordination and postcoordination: Differences in the application of precoordinated and postcoordinated terminology in the vocabularies complicate mapping efforts if one vocabulary contains headings while the other contains unique terms. For example, a two-to-one match rather than a one-to-one match is required for the heading *Baroque cathedral* if the second vocabulary places the style *Baroque* in one hierarchy and the building type by function, *cathedral,* in a second hierarchy.

A related issue concerns the differences in precoordination and postcoordination expected in the search methodologies of the resources being searched; if one database is indexed for precoordinated terms and the second expects terms to be postcoordinated in retrieval, results are uneven. Libraries have agreed on a common search protocol—*Information Retrieval: Application Service Definition and Protocol Specification* (*ANSI/NISO Z39.50*)—to perform searches across multiple Online Public Access Catalogs (OPACs). More recently developed search protocols are *Search/Retrieve via URL* (*SRU*), *Search Retrieve Web Service* (*SRW*), and *Metasearch XML Gateway* (*MXG*). However, resources in other communities do not typically have a common protocol, causing challenges in the interpretation of search terms and search results.

Granularity and specificity: The differences in degree of specificity or granularity of the controlled vocabularies themselves, and of the indexers' applications of the vocabularies in the target resources, may result in uneven results in indexing and retrieval. For example, if one vocabulary contains very specific terms for a given domain while another contains only general terms, mapping between them will be difficult. If an exact equivalent is not available, mappings should attempt to link to broader terms, narrower terms, or to terms that have overlapping, if not synonymous, meaning.

Conversely, if indexers of both resources have used the same vocabulary for indexing, even if they use varying degrees of specificity and granularity in indexing terms, retrieval using that vocabulary across resources is still likely to be relatively successful because the broader and narrower terms are logically linked in the vocabulary and may be applied together in a search.

Synonymy and near synonymy: Differences in how synonyms and near synonyms are handled affects the ability to make a successful mapping between vocabularies. If one vocabulary links near synonyms as *used for* terms for a concept, while the other links only true synonyms, it is difficult to make a one-to-one match between concepts. For example, *levitation* and *flight* may be related in a very general way and could both be terms in a single thesaurus record, but they are not true synonyms because their meanings are different, thus they comprise two separate records in a thesaurus employing only true synonymy.

Authoritativeness: If vocabularies differ in the level of authoritativeness by which they are developed, mapping them is difficult. For example, if the literary, organizational, and user warrants allowed in developing the various vocabularies are quite different, there may be little commonality among the terms across the vocabularies or different meanings for the same term.

5.3.4. Semantic Mapping

A *semantic network* comprises relationships between terms and concepts based on their meanings or the nature of the relationships between them. The semantic relationships are sometimes derived from the vocabularies. In other cases, they are extrapolated from the target content databases.

A semantic network may be used to map terms from one or more controlled vocabularies according to a defined underlying organizational structure or conceptual scheme. The relationships may range from a simple hierarchical structure with generic broader/narrower relationships to a more complex set of carefully defined relationships, such as *contained in, agent for, process is,* etc. The relationships may be categorized to indicate the degree of closeness between linked terms, for example

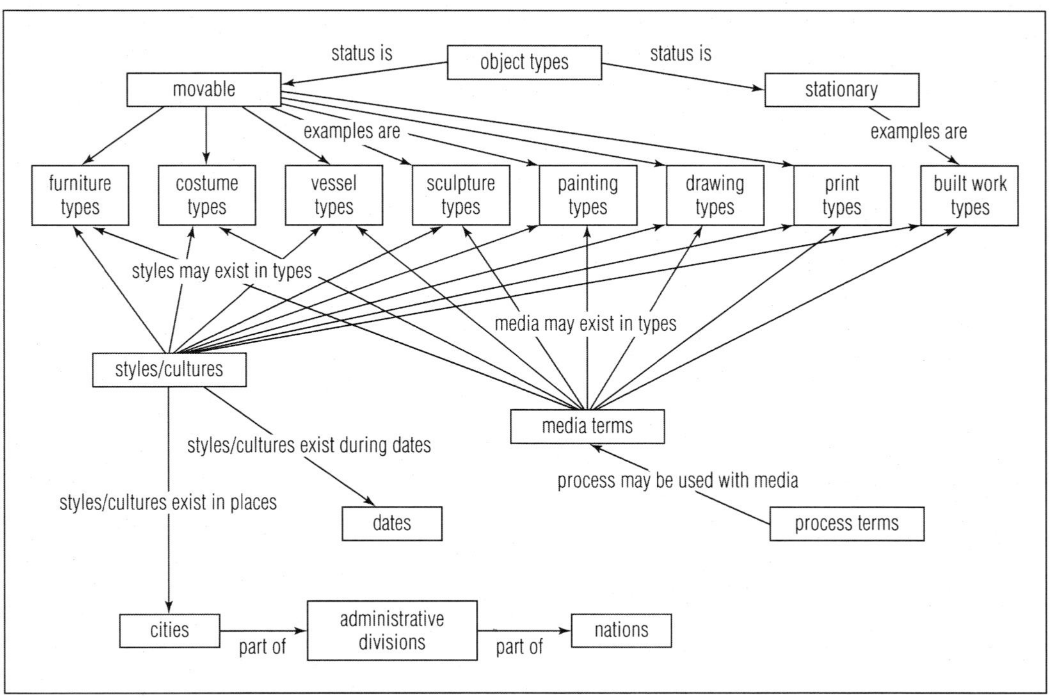

Fig. 35. Diagram of an example generic semantic mapping for artworks, where elements in rectangular boxes are linked to other elements using the relationships designated (e.g., *status is*).

exact synonyms, near synonyms, closely related terms, loosely related terms, and *antonyms.*

A semantic mapping based on categories and relationships is illustrated in the diagram on the previous page. See also the discussion of ontologies in **Chapter 2: What Are Controlled Vocabularies?**

5.4. Interoperability across Languages

Multilingual controlled vocabularies are sometimes treated as a special case of interoperability. If unique vocabularies have been developed independently using different languages, utilizing the two together as a multilingual controlled vocabulary is generally not effective without extensive human intervention in the mapping process. This is due to the problems and idiosyncrasies of translation and usage of terms in various languages, which are not resolved with the simple employment of an automated dictionary or data mining.

5.4.1. Issues of Multilingual Terminology

The issues surrounding the development or implementation of multilingual terminology are discussed in detail in *ISO 5964:1985: Documentation—Guidelines for the Establishment and Development of Multilingual Thesauri.* In brief, issues related to mapping problems are listed below, ranked according to the difficulty of the solutions, from simplest to most complex.

> **Exact equivalence:** The most desirable match involves terms in each language that are identical, or nearly identical, in meaning and scope of usage in each language. For example, the English *prayer nut* and the Italian *noce di preghiera* have the same meaning.
>
> **Inexact and partial equivalences:** In cases where a suitable preferred term with the exact meaning and usage of the original term is not available in the second language, terms are sometimes linked as equivalents when they have only inexact or partial matches in scope and meaning. For example, the English *science* and the German *Wissenschaft* have overlapping but not identical meanings.
>
> **Single-to-multiple term equivalence:** If there is no match in scope and meaning between terms, sometimes a concept in one vocabulary is matched to multiple descriptors in the second language. For example, the Spanish term *relojero* means both

watchmaker and *clockmaker* in English; however, in translation, the Spanish term could be repeated as a homograph and distinguished with the qualifiers *relojero (de pulsera)* and *relojero (de pared)* in order to map to the English terms.

Nonequivalence: Sometimes there is no exact match, no term in the second language has partial or inexact equivalence, and there is no combination of descriptors in the second language that would approximate a match. For example, the French term *trompe l'oeil* has no equivalent in English.

In the absence of an exact match between terms in different languages, inexact and partial equivalences may be used. Terms may be linked where both represent the same general concept, or where one term is broader and the second is narrower in meaning. When single-to-multiple term equivalences are made, a concept that is represented by a single preferred term in one language is represented by a combination of descriptors or a heading or phrase in the second language. In all of these cases, the definition or scope of the concept must be modified to cover the meanings of terms in all the languages.

None of the scenarios in the above paragraph is ideal. If the meanings of the terms differ significantly, it is better to fill a gap in one language with a loan term from the other language. A *loan* term is a foreign word or phrase that is routinely used instead of a translation of the term into the native language. For example, the term *lits à la romaine* refers to a particular type of bed peculiar to late-seventeenth-century French furniture; the best way to represent that term in an English language vocabulary is to use the French term as a loan term. Less desirable solutions include the adoption of a coined term in the second language. A *coined* term is a new term invented for the purpose of making a match between languages, generally by translating the term, but without authoritative literary warrant for the usage of the term. Terms without literary warrant should be avoided because they do not represent usage in the other language (and documenting usage is a critical criterion in creating terms); in addition, coined terms are often awkward at best and meaningless at worst. For example, if the French Gothic style term *Rayonnant* were translated into English as *Radiating,* it would be meaningless; the French term should be used in English.

If a new vocabulary is intentionally developed as a translation of an existing vocabulary, mapping between the two separate vocabularies is relatively easy. Mapping should occur from terms in an original language (called the *source* language) to terms in the second language (called the *target* language).

5.4.2. Dominant Languages

In a completely multilingual vocabulary, all languages are treated equally, with none serving as a so-called dominant language. However, in practical applications, it is often necessary to treat one language as the default dominant language, particularly when the vocabulary is rich and complex. An example is the *AAT,* in which each concept record includes over one hundred fields or data elements in addition to the term itself. With such vocabularies, it is impractical to maintain the data values of flags, notes, dates, hierarchies, and other subsidiary information in several languages. For the *AAT,* English is the dominant language, although terms and scope notes may be in multiple languages. In addition, if every term in the original source language has not been assigned equivalents in all other target languages, the status of the other languages is not equal to that of the source language, and they are known as *secondary* languages.

If a vocabulary such as the *AAT* is developed as a single unified vocabulary—but one in which the terms may exist in multiple languages—problems and issues with translations are resolved in the development process rather than in later mappings. Methods of development may entail the manual translation of the terms of the entire original vocabulary into another language or the addition of terms in several languages as each concept record is created. Creating such a vocabulary on the development side, rather than trying to map separate vocabularies later, makes the resulting set of multilingual terms very effective in searching across resources in different languages. In such a vocabulary, terms in different languages are exact equivalents, ideally linked only when meaning is synonymous and usage is identical or nearly identical. Issues of specificity and cultural context are taken into consideration in the selection of terms and the creation of relationships between concepts. Hierarchies and other relationships are likely to differ between comparable terminology in different languages, but such differences can be harmonized in development.

5.5. Satellite and Extension Vocabularies

Satellite and extension vocabularies may be considered *microcontrolled vocabularies* (also known as *microthesauri*), because they are specialized vocabularies that may fit into the structure of a larger, broader, or more generic controlled vocabulary.

A *satellite vocabulary* is characterized by having been constructed with the goal of being interoperable with an existing vocabulary. The satellite may be linked at multiple points to the original vocabulary. An example is a narrow specialty vocabulary that is intended to be integrated with the superstructure of a larger vocabulary.

An *extension vocabulary* is typically also constructed with the goal of being interoperable with an existing vocabulary, but is usually linked at one or a small number of nodes rather than being integrated at many points in the original vocabulary. *Node* or *leaf linking* is the method that links a specialized vocabulary to a node in the hierarchical structure of a broader controlled vocabulary so that the specialized vocabulary becomes a virtual new branch (or extension vocabulary) to the original vocabulary.

With either approach, the resulting family of controlled vocabularies should be consistent in structure, term format, and editorial oversight. By using satellite or extension vocabularies, specialized users may have access to the desired levels of specificity in the new controlled vocabulary without swamping the original controlled vocabulary with detail that may not be needed by most users. Furthermore, as noted in the discussion of local authorities in the following chapter, satellite and extension vocabularies can allow a particular set of users to access only the specialized vocabulary terms that apply to their indexing needs, thus excluding the full original vocabulary from these users, while ensuring that their specialized terms are still compatible with the full vocabulary in retrieval.

6. Local Authorities

Systems for cataloging art information should incorporate local authorities to control terminology. Local authorities should be populated with terms from published vocabularies; however, maintaining local authorities rather than relying exclusively upon external sources of terminology allows the multiple vocabularies necessary for cataloging to be combined or linked. Local authorities may also be streamlined or otherwise optimized for the particular requirements of local cataloging and retrieval applications in ways that using an external published authority would not facilitate.

A common way of creating local authorities is through *derivation* (also called *modeling*) based on a published vocabulary. In this approach, an appropriate controlled vocabulary is selected as a model for developing controlled terminology for local use, so that the local terms will be interoperable with the larger original vocabulary. This method encourages consistency in term selection, hierarchical structure, and format between the local authority and the published vocabulary. For example, many users of the *AAT* use only the portions of that thesaurus that apply to their own art or image collections. They often add their own local terminology to these core *AAT* terms. If the local terms are within scope for the *AAT,* they are submitted as contributions, so that the published *AAT* grows and reflects users' needs over time. See the additional discussion on interoperability in **Chapter 5: Using Multiple Vocabularies.**

Local authorities may provide terms not found in published authorities, including local terms that are out of scope for published vocabularies, nonexpert terms, and even so-called wrong terms that provide access to nonspecialist users. In the example on the opposite page, a collections management system includes the *AAT* as part of its thesaurus maintenance module. The *front* screen illustrates how local terminology for nonexpert end-user displays may be added to the system, in this case, dividing the collection into broad classifications based on function, such as *medical* or *decorative.* The local terms are flagged as such, and they may be submitted to the *AAT* for inclusion; however, in the model of broad generality underlying the *AAT,* these terms would likely not appear together in a specific area such as *decorative,* as they do in the local application.

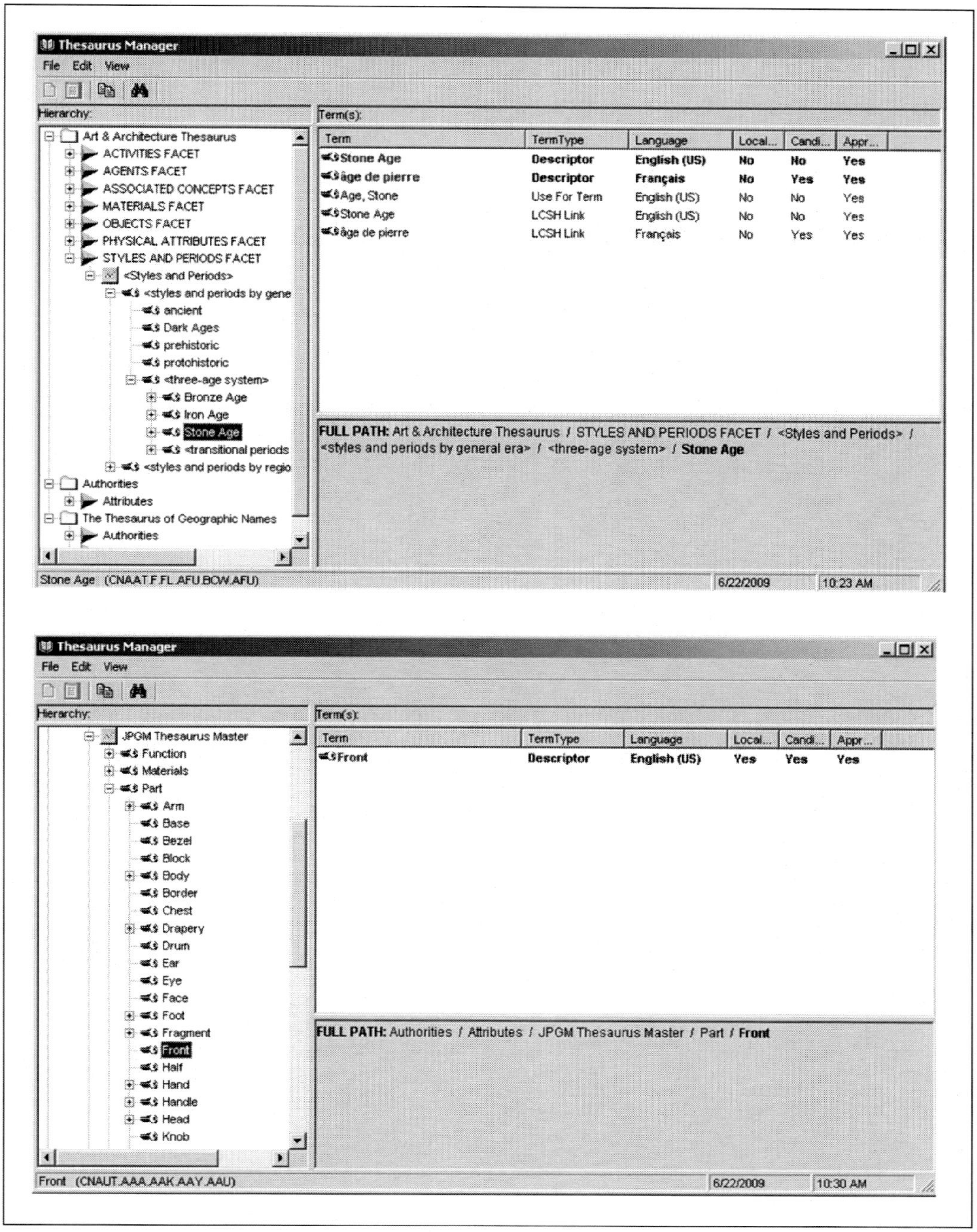

Fig. 36. Displays of published (*AAT*) and local (*JPGM Thesaurus Master*) thesauri in a museum's collection management system.

6.1. Which Fields Should Be Controlled?

Systems developers must understand that a system for cataloging art and cultural heritage objects requires certain fields that allow data to be formatted for display to end users. Display information may be free text or concatenated from controlled data, depending upon the requirements of a given field. For many other fields, it is necessary to use controlled vocabulary for indexing. A general guideline is that any information

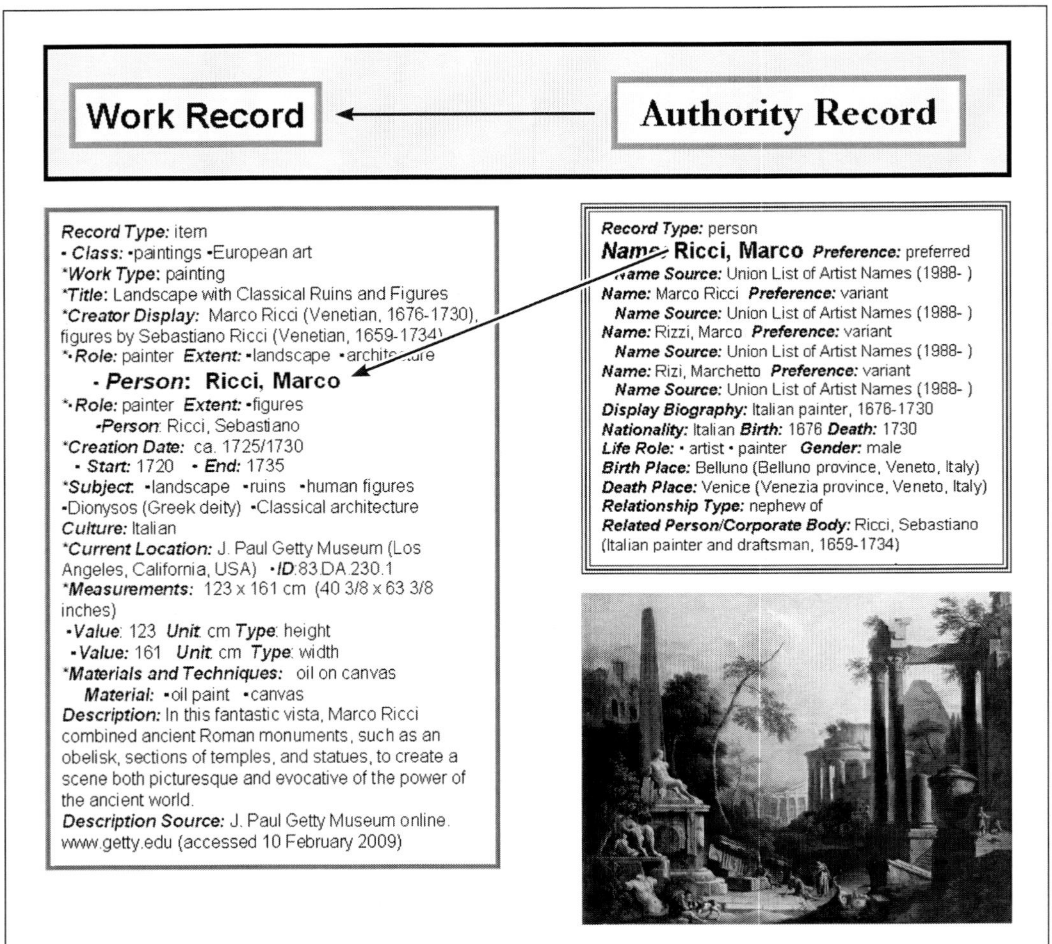

Fig. 37. Diagram of a work record linked to an authority record. Values in many fields are best controlled by an authority, including the indexing field for the creator. The authority in this example contains the variant names for Marco Ricci as well as biographical information. This information is entered or loaded once in the authority and can then be linked to all pertinent work records where Marco Ricci is the artist.

Marco Ricci (Italian, 1676–1730) and Sebastiano Ricci (Italian, 1659–1734); *Landscape with Classical Ruins and Figures;* 1720s; oil on canvas; 123 × 161 cm (48⅜ × 63⅜ inches); J. Paul Getty Museum (Los Angeles, California); 70.PA.33.

required as a variable in a retrieval query should be indexed in controlled fields to allow efficient retrieval. The distinction between display and indexed information is discussed in **Chapter 2: What Are Controlled Vocabularies?**

Systems developers must also understand that fields for indexing require various forms of control. In some cases, the format needs to be controlled, but no prescribed set of terminology is necessary, as in a field that contains numbers. For other fields, a simple, flat controlled list of terminology is sufficient, particularly where the list is relatively short and there is no need for synonyms or other relationships. However, for many fields, a linked local authority is the best way to control terminology and provide synonyms and thesaural relationships. Local authorities should be structured as thesauri whenever possible. Such local authorities should be populated with terminology from standard published controlled vocabularies and local terms and names as necessary.

One of the primary advantages of linking fields in work records to authority records is that when names or other information in the authority are updated, it need be done only once rather than repeatedly in every work record to which that authority information applies. In addition, the authority record can contain full information on the concept, making the power of the variant names and other information available to every linked work record, as represented in the example on the opposite page.

6.2. Structure of the Authority

If possible, local authorities should be compliant with ISO and NISO standards for thesauri; they should be structured as hierarchical, relational databases, as recommended and discussed in *CDWA* and *CCO*. These standards recommend the use of a relational database because of the complexity of cultural information and the importance of linking to authority records. A *relational database* provides a logical organization of interrelated information (e.g., data about works and images, authority files, and so on) that is managed and stored in a single information system. The data structure of an art information system should provide a means of relating works to each other, works to images, and works and images to authorities. When records of the same type are related, they have a reciprocal relationship. Hierarchical relationships between records of the same type should be possible.

6.3. Unique IDs in the Authority

Referencing unique numeric identifiers is a common way to express relationships in an information system.

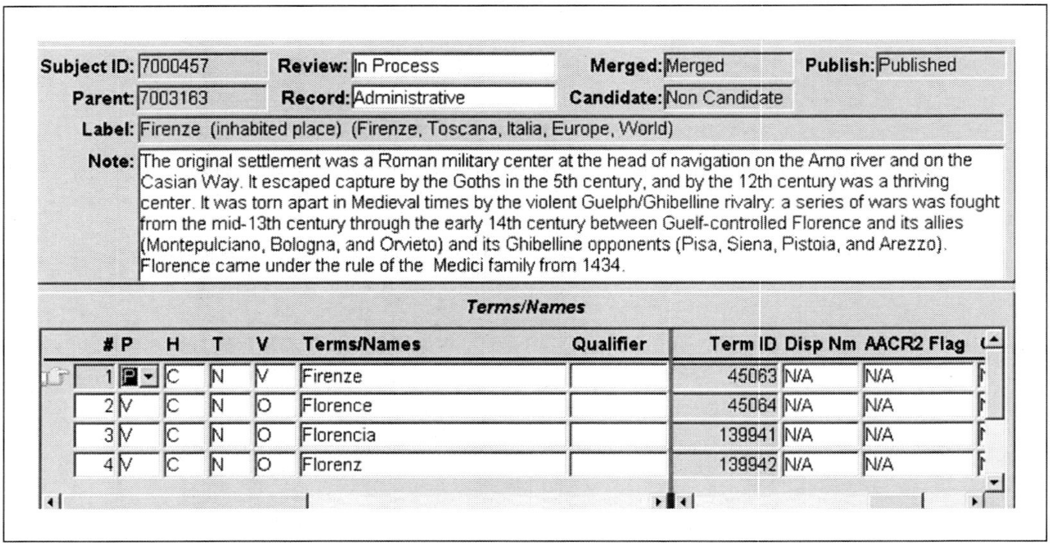

Subject ID: 7000457 Review: In Process Merged: Merged Publish: Published
Parent: 7003163 Record: Administrative Candidate: Non Candidate
Label: Firenze (inhabited place) (Firenze, Toscana, Italia, Europe, World)
Note: The original settlement was a Roman military center at the head of navigation on the Arno river and on the Casian Way. It escaped capture by the Goths in the 5th century, and by the 12th century was a thriving center. It was torn apart in Medieval times by the violent Guelph/Ghibelline rivalry: a series of wars was fought from the mid-13th century through the early 14th century between Guelf-controlled Florence and its allies (Montepulciano, Bologna, and Orvieto) and its Ghibelline opponents (Pisa, Siena, Pistoia, and Arezzo). Florence came under the rule of the Medici family from 1434.

Terms/Names

#	P	H	T	V	Terms/Names	Qualifier	Term ID	Disp Nm	AACR2 Flag
1	P	C	N	V	Firenze		45063	N/A	N/A
2	V	C	N	O	Florence		45064	N/A	N/A
3	V	C	N	O	Florencia		139941	N/A	N/A
4	V	C	N	O	Florenz		139942	N/A	N/A

Fig. 38. Display in the *TGN* editorial system illustrating unique numeric identifiers for the record (Subject ID), broader context (Parent ID), and terms (Term ID).

Note that qualifiers, parent strings, or other such methods of disambiguation are for the benefit of human users; they are not intended to uniquely identify terms in a database. Whether dealing with homographs or any other record in an authority, it is recommended to use a unique numeric or alphanumeric identification to uniquely distinguish each record and each term in the record. Reliance upon the name or term itself to identify the record in a database is not recommended, because names and terms may change over time. See also **Chapter 9: Retrieval Using Controlled Vocabularies.** In the example above, a *TGN* record illustrates several unique identification numbers: a Subject ID (meaning the ID for the focus record), a Parent ID (by which hierarchies are built), and a Term ID (for each name in the record).

The specifics of how records are linked and related is a local database design issue not explicitly prescribed in this book. However, a few basic requirements are illustrated in the simplified entity-relationship model illustrated on the opposite page, where several local authorities are linked to work records in an art information system. If images are cataloged, the authorities should also link to image records. Systems developers should allow for a given authority file to be used to control terminology in multiple elements (e.g., a Concept Authority to control Work Type, Materials, etc.). Furthermore, a given element may use controlled terms from multiple authorities (e.g., the Subject element of a Work may use terms from several authorities).

CDWA and *CCO* provide a full discussion of these issues, advice regarding which work and image fields require links to which vocabu-

Fig. 39. Entity-relationship diagram for work records and linked authorities.

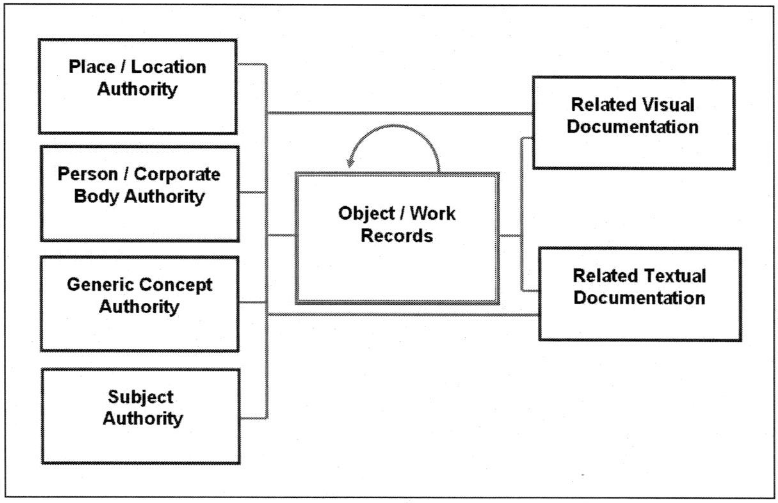

laries, and basic editorial rules for constructing various local authorities. A brief discussion of the issues surrounding some specific types of authorities is included below. Additional information regarding building a local authority or a vocabulary for broader distribution is found in **Chapter 7: Constructing a Vocabulary or Authority.**

6.4. Person/Corporate Body Authority

The Person/Corporate Body Authority should contain information about artists, architects, and other individuals and corporate bodies responsible for the design and production of works of art and architecture. This authority may also contain information about patrons, repositories, and other people or corporate bodies important to the record for the work or image.

People: This authority should contain information about individual people whose biographies are well known (e.g., *Vincent van Gogh (Dutch painter and draftsman, 1853–1890)*) as well as anonymous creators with identified oeuvres but whose names are unknown and whose biography is surmised (e.g., *Aberdeen Painter (Attic vase painter, active mid–5th century BCE)*). This authority is limited to real, historical people. Fictional people should be recorded in the subject authority.

Corporate bodies: This authority should contain information about corporate bodies, which are organized, identifiable groups of individuals working together in a particular place and within a defined period of time. Included are legally incorporated entities, such as a modern architectural firm (e.g., *Adler and Sullivan*) as well as studios, families (e.g., *della Robbia family*), or repositories. Certain events, such as conferences, are typically treated as corporate bodies and recorded in this authority; however, named historical events, such as the *U.S. Civil War,* would be recorded in the Subject Authority.

Anonymous creators: If the hand of a creator has been identified, but his or her name is unknown, it is common to create an identity for the creator by devising an appellation (e.g., *Master of St. Verdiana*) and recording his or her deduced locus of activity and approximate dates of activity. By establishing an identity, all works by this anonymous individual may be associated with that identity. For example, many paintings have been attributed to a particular person who worked in Florence, Italy, in the late fourteenth and early fifteenth centuries; he seems to have been influenced by the painter Orcagna. However, no one has yet been able to ascertain his name, so he is called the *Master of St. Verdiana* after a saint in an altarpiece by his hand, the *Santa Verdiana Triptych.*

Unknown creators: Unidentified artistic personalities may be recorded in this authority. Unknown creators are defined here as unidentified artistic personalities with unestablished oeuvres. If the identity of a hand is not established, a generic identification is often devised for the creator in the work record, such as *unknown Florentine* or *unknown Maya.* The generic identification differs from an anonymous creator in that it does *not* refer to one identified, if anonymous, individual; instead, the same heading refers to any of hundreds of unidentified artistic personalities. Including such designations in the authority is useful because the authority records may be used to control terminology and link all unattributed works by unknown artists that fit this description.

Hierarchical relationships: Although records for individual people do not typically have hierarchical depth (given that this authority is not used to build family trees), records for corporate bodies in this authority may have hierarchical administrative structures. For example, works may be created by *Feature Animation,* which is a part of *Disney Studios,* which in turn is part of *The Walt Disney Company.* The authority could follow the same model as the *ULAN,* where there are separate facets for individual people and corporate bodies.

Associative relationships: Persons or corporate bodies may have associative relationships, meaning they are related nonhierarchically to other people or corporate bodies. Corporate bodies may be related to single individuals, as a workshop or architectural firm should be related to its members. Corporate bodies may be related to other corporate bodies, such as when the architectural firm Adler and Sullivan succeeded Dankmar Adler and Company. Likewise, single individuals may be related to other single individuals, as a master is related to a student, or a father is related to a daughter. All such relationships should be accommodated in this authority.

6.4.1. Sources for Terminology

All information in the authority record should be derived from published sources, where possible. A short list of sources appears below; fuller lists of authoritative published sources are found in *CDWA, CCO,* and the *ULAN Editorial Guidelines.* Variant names from all sources consulted should be included, with preference given to the most authoritative, up-to-date sources available, which may include the following, arranged in a general descending order of preference:

Standard general reference sources

- *Union List of Artist Names* (*ULAN*)
- *Library of Congress Authorities*
- *Grove Art Online*
- *Thieme-Becker Allgemeines Lexikon der bildenden Künstler*
- Saur's *Allgemeines Künstlerlexikon*
- Emmanuel Bénézit's *Dictionnaire des peintres, sculpteurs, dessinateurs et graveurs*
- *Macmillan Encyclopedia of Architects*
- American Association of Museum's *Official Museum Directory* textbooks such as *Gardner's Art through the Ages* and *Janson's History of Art*
- general biographical dictionaries

Other authoritative sources

- repository publications, including catalogs and official Web sites
- general encyclopedias and dictionaries

- authoritative Web sites other than museum sites (e.g., university sites)

Other sources

- inscriptions on art objects, coins, or other artifacts
- journal and newspaper articles
- archives, historical documents, and other original sources
- authority records of the cataloging institution's databases

6.4.2. Suggested Fields

Below is a relatively extensive list of fields that may be used for a Person/ Corporate Body Authority, as discussed in *CDWA*. A subset of these fields is discussed in *CCO*. Suggested required fields are flagged *core*. Builders of local authorities may decide to use only the core fields, adding any others that may be useful for their specific needs. In any case, it is advised to record the sources of all vocabulary and to allow for periodic additions and updates from published vocabularies, such as the *ULAN*.

Record Type
Name Core
  Preference
  Language
  Historical Flag
  Name Source Core
    Page
  Name Type
  Name Date
    Earliest Date
    Latest Date
Display Biography Core
Birth Date Core
Death Date Core
Birth Place Place
Nationality/Culture/Race Core
  Preference
  Type
Gender
Life Roles
  Preference
  Role Date
    Earliest Date
    Latest Date
Event
  Event Date
    Earliest Date
    Latest Date
  Event Place
Related Person/Corporate Body
  Relationship Type
  Relationship Date
    Earliest Date
    Latest Date
Broader Context
  Broader Context Date
    Earliest DateDeath
    Latest Date
Label/Identification
Descriptive Note
  Note Source
    Page
Remarks
Citations
  Page

Below are examples of authority records from *CDWA,* illustrating fuller and less full records, records for individual people and for corporate bodies, and records for both anonymous and unknown people.

This is a brief authority record for a person:

> **Record Type:** person
> **Name:** Harpignies, Henri-Joseph
> **Preference:** preferred
> **Name Source:** Thieme-Becker, *Allgemeines Lexikon der Kunstler* (1980–1986)
> **Name Source:** *Union List of Artist Names* (1990–)
> **Name Source:** *Witt Checklist of Painters c. 1200–1976* (1978)
> **Name:** Henri-Joseph Harpignes
> **Preference:** variant
> **Name Source:** Thieme-Becker, *Allgemeines Lexikon der Kunstler* (1980–1986)
> **Display Biography:** French painter and printmaker, 1819–1916
> **Birth Date:** 1819 **Death Date:** 1916
> **Nationality/Culture/Race:** French
> **Life Role:** artist
> **Life Role:** painter
> **Life Role:** printmaker
> **Gender:** male
> **Relationship Type:** teacher of
> **Related Person/Corporate Body:** Bouchaud, Jean (French painter and draftsman, 1891–1977)

This is a fuller authority record for a person:

> **Record Type:** person
> **Name:** Riza
> **Preference:** preferred
> **Name Source:** *Union List of Artist Names* (1990–)
> **Name:** Reza
> **Preference:** variant
> **Name Source:** *Union List of Artist Names* (1990–)
> **Name:** Riza-yi ʻAbbasi
> **Preference:** variant
> **Name Source:** *Union List of Artist Names* (1990–)
> **Display Biography:** Persian painter, ca. 1565–1635
> **Nationality:** Persian
> **Birth Date:** 1560 **Death Date:** 1635
> **Life Role:** artist

Life Role: painter
Life Role: court artist
Gender: male
Role Date: under Abbas I (reigned 1588–1629)
Earliest Date: 1588 **Latest Date:** 1635
Birth Place: Kashan (Esfahan province, Iran)
Death Place: Esfahan (Esfahan province, Iran)
Event: active **Place:** Mashhad (Khorasan, Iran)
Relationship Type: parent of
Related Person/Corporate Body: Muhammad Shafi' (Persian painter, active ca. 1628–1674)
Relationship Type: teacher of
Related Person/Corporate Body: Muhammad Qasim Tabrizi (Persian illustrator, painter, and poet, died 1659)
Descriptive Note: Riza, son of 'Ali Asghar, was a leading artist under the Safavid shah Abbas I (reigned 1588–1629). He is noted primarily for portraits and genre scenes. The various names for this artist and the attributions of paintings in his oeuvre are somewhat uncertain, since his signatures and contemporary documentary references to him are ambiguous.
Note Source: *Grove Dictionary of Art* online (1999–2002)
Page: accessed 6 Aug 2003

This is an authority record for a firm:

Record Type: corporate body
Name: Eero Saarinen & Associates **Preference:** preferred
  Name Source: *Union List of Artist Names* (1990–)
Nationality: American
Birth Date: 1950 **Death Date:** 1961
Life Roles: architectural firm
Gender: not applicable
Event: location **Place:** Birmingham (Michigan, United States)
Event: location **Place:** Camden (Connecticut, United States)
Relationship Type: founder
Related Person/Corporate Body: Eero Saarinen (American architect, 1910–1961)

This is an authority record for a repository:

Record Type: corporate body
Name: Museo Nacional de Arte Moderno
  Preference: preferred **Language:** Spanish
  Name Source: *Union List of Artist Names* (1990–)

Name: National Museum of Modern Art
Name Source: *Union List of Artist Names* (1990–)
Preference: variant **Language:** English
Display Biography: Guatemalan museum
Nationality: Guatemalan
Birth Date: 1850 **Death Date:** 9999
Life Role: art museum
Gender: not applicable
Event: location **Place:** Guatemala City (Guatemala department, Guatemala)

This is an authority record for an anonymous person:

Record Type: person
Name: Painter of the Wedding Procession
Preference: preferred
Language: English
Name Source: *Union List of Artist Names* (1990–)
Name: Wedding Procession Painter
Preference: variant
Name Source: *Union List of Artist Names* (1990–)
Name: Der Maler des Hochzeitszugs
Preference: variant
Language: German
Name Source: *Union List of Artist Names* (1990–)
Name Source: Schefold, Karl. *Kertscher Vasen* (1930)
Nationality: Ancient Greek
Display Biography: Greek vase painter, active ca. 360s BCE
Birth Date:–0390 **Death Date:**–0330
Role: artist **Role:** vase painter
Event: active **Place:** Athens (Periféreia Protevoúsis, Greece)
Descriptive Note: Working in Athens in the 300s BCE, the Painter of the Wedding Procession decorated pottery primarily in the red-figure technique. As with most vase painters, his real name is unknown, and he is identified only by the style of his work. He decorated mostly large vases, such as hydriai and lebetes. He was also one of the many vase painters who received a commission for Panathenaic amphorai, which were always decorated in the old-fashioned black-figure technique. The Painter of the Wedding Procession was among the last vase painters working in Athens before the tradition of painted ceramics died out in Greece. He produced vases in the Kerch style, named for a city on the Black Sea in southern Russia where many vases in this style have been found.

Note Source: J. Paul Getty Museum, collections online (2000–)
Page: accessed 21 January 2009

Finally, this is a generic authority record for an unknown artist:

Record Type: person
Name: unknown Indian
Display Biography: Indian artist
Nationality: Indian
Birth Date: 1400 **Death Date:** 1800
Life Role: artist

6.5. Place/Location Authority

The Place/Location Authority should contain information about geographic places directly related to the work of art, architecture—such as locations or subjects—or creators of works. This authority includes administrative entities, such as nations or cities, and physical features, such as rivers or continents.

Physical geographic features: Geographic authorities for art and cultural information typically focus on the names of cities and towns. However, physical features may be included, as necessary. Physical features include entities that are part of the natural physical condition of the planet, such as continents, rivers, and mountains. Surface features as well as underground and submarine features may be included, as necessary. Former features, such as submerged islands and lost coastlines, may also be included, as necessary.

Administrative geographic entities: Most records in this authority probably represent nations and the administrative subdivisions and inhabited places belonging to them. Administrative geographic entities include man-made or cultural entities that are circumscribed by political and administrative boundaries: examples are empires, nations, states, districts, townships, and cities. In addition to such administrative entities set up by independent sovereign states, entities established by ecclesiastical or tribal governing bodies may also be included, as necessary. Both current and historical places (e.g., deserted settlements and former nations) may be included.

Recording streets within cities is generally not appropriate to this authority, because it adds an unnecessary level of complexity; however, the authority could accommodate the names of streets if this level of detail is considered important by the cataloging institution. Built works are outside the scope of the Place/Location Authority. They should be recorded as works or in the Subject Authority. Repositories, in the sense of administrative bodies that have control of art objects (not the building housing the artwork), should be recorded as corporate bodies in the Person and Corporate Name Authority.

The Place/Location Authority may contain names for archaeological sites (e.g., *trench 6A (Bundy-Voyles site, Morgan County, Indiana, United States)*) and street addresses. This authority may also include *general regions,* which are recognized, named areas with undefined, controversial, or ambiguous borders. An example is the *Middle East,* which refers to an area in southwestern Asia and northeastern Africa that has no defined borders and may be variously interpreted to mean different sets of nations.

Terminology for generic cultural and political groups (e.g., the Incas) is outside the scope of this geographic authority file; it should be recorded in the Concept Authority. However, the political state of a cultural or political group, and the territory within its boundaries (e.g., the Inca Empire), are within the scope of the Place/Location Authority.

Hierarchical relationships: If possible, this authority should be compliant with ISO and NISO standards for thesauri; it should be structured as a hierarchical, relational database. A geographic thesaurus such as a Place/Location Authority should be polyhierarchical, because geographic places often have multiple parents or broader contexts.

Associative relationships: Places may have associative relationships, meaning they are related nonhierarchically to other places, including relationships described as *distinguished from, ally of, predecessor of, possibly identified as, adjacent to,* etc.

6.5.1. Sources for Terminology

All information in the authority record should be derived from published sources, where possible. A short list of sources appears below; fuller lists of authoritative published sources are found in *CDWA, CCO,* and the *TGN Editorial Guidelines.* Variant names from all sources consulted should be included, with preference given to the most authoritative, up-to-date sources available, which may include the following, arranged in a general descending order of preference:

Standard general reference sources

- *Getty Thesaurus of Geographic Names* (*TGN*)
- National Geospatial-Intelligence Agency's *GEOnet Names Server* (*GNS*)
- U.S. Geological Survey (USGS)
- *Times Comprehensive Atlas of the World*
- *Oxford Atlas of the World*
- *National Geographic Atlas of the World*
- Rand McNally's *New International Atlas*
- *Merriam-Webster's Geographical Dictionary*
- *Columbia Gazetteer of the World*
- *Princeton Encyclopedia of Classical Sites*
- *Grove Art Online*
- other atlases, loose maps, and gazetteers
- other geographic dictionaries, general encyclopedias, and guidebooks
- government Web sites for other nations or regions

Other authoritative sources

- newsletters from the ISO and United Nations
- communications with embassies
- *Library of Congress Authorities*

Other material on topics of geography or current events

- books, journal articles, and newspaper articles
- archives and other original sources

Other sources

- books on the history of art and architecture
- inscriptions on art objects, and catalog records of repositories of art objects

6.5.2. Suggested Fields

Below is a relatively extensive list of fields that may be used for a Place/ Location Authority, as discussed in *CDWA*. A subset of these fields is discussed in *CCO*. Suggested required fields are flagged *core*. Builders of local authorities may decide to use only the core fields, adding any others that may be useful for their specific needs. In any case, it is advised to record the sources of all vocabulary and to allow for periodic additions and updates from published vocabularies, such as the *TGN*.

Record Type
Place Name Core
  Preference
  Language
  Historical Flag
  Name Source Core
    Page
  Name Type
  Name Date
    Earliest Date
    Latest Date
Coordinates
Place Types Core
  Preference
  Place Type Date
    Earliest Date
    Latest Date
Related Places
  Relationship Type
  Relationship Date
    Earliest Date
    Latest Date
Broader Context Core
  Broader Context Date
    Earliest Date
    Latest Date
Label/Identification
Descriptive Note
  Note Source
  Page
Remarks
Citations
  Page

Below are examples of authority records from *CDWA,* illustrating full records for an administrative place, a physical feature, and a historical place.

This is a full record for a historical region, administrative:

Record Type: administrative entity
Name: Burgundy
  Preference: preferred **Language:** English
  Name Source: *Getty Thesaurus of Geographic Names* (1997–)
Name: Bourgogne
  Preference: preferred vernacular
  Name Source: *Getty Thesaurus of Geographic Names* (1997–)
Name: Burgund
  Preference: variant
  Name Source: *Getty Thesaurus of Geographic Names* (1997–)
Name: Bourgogne, duché de
  Preference: variant
  Name Source: *Getty Thesaurus of Geographic Names* (1997–)
Name: Duchy of Burgundy
  Preference: variant
  Name Source: *Getty Thesaurus of Geographic Names* (1997–)
Broader Context: Europe
  Europe (continent)
    France (nation)
    Burgundy (historical region)

Place Types: historical region, kingdom, duchy
Coordinates:
  Lat: 47 00 00 N degrees minutes
  Long: 004 30 00 E degrees minutes
  (**Lat:** 47.0000 decimal degrees)
  (**Long:** 4.5000 decimal degrees)
Descriptive Note: Historic region that included a kingdom founded by Germanic people in the 5th century CE. It was conquered by the Merovingians and incorporated into the Frankish Empire in the 6th century. It was divided in the 9th century, and united as the Kingdom of Burgundy or Arles in 933. The area flourished culturally during the 14th–15th centuries.
  Note Source: *Webster's Geographical Dictionary* (1988)
  Page: 191
Citation: *Cambridge World Gazetteer* (1990) **Page:** 211

This is a full record for a geographic feature, physical:

Record Type: physical feature
Name: Ötztaler Alps **Preference:** preferred
  Name Source: *Getty Thesaurus of Geographic Names* (1997–)
Name: Ötztal Alps **Preference:** variant
  Name Source: *Getty Thesaurus of Geographic Names* (1997–)
Name: Oetztaler Alps **Preference:** variant
  Name Source: *Getty Thesaurus of Geographic Names* (1997–)
Name: Venoste, Alpi **Preference:** variant
  Name Source: *Getty Thesaurus of Geographic Names* (1997–)
Name: Ötztaler Alpen **Preference:** variant
  Name Source: *Getty Thesaurus of Geographic Names* (1997–)
Broader Context: Alps (Europe)
  Europe (continent)
    Alps (mountain system)
    Ötztaler Alps (mountain range)
Place Type: mountain range
Coordinates:
  Lat: 46 45 00 N degrees minutes
  Long: 010 55 00 E degrees minutes
  (**Lat:** 46.7500 decimal degrees)
  (**Long:** 10.9167 decimal degrees)
Descriptive Note: Located in the eastern Alps on the border of South Tirol, Austria, and Trentino-Alto Adige, Italy.

Citation: *Webster's Geographical Dictionary* (1988) **Page:** 906
Citation: NIMA, *GEOnet Names Server* (2000–) **Page:** accessed 23 November 2003

This is a full record for a city:

Record Type: administrative entity
Name: Alexandria
  Preference: preferred **Language:** English
  Name Source: *Getty Thesaurus of Geographic Names* (1997–)
  Name Date: used since 4th century BCE, named after Alexander the Great
  Earliest:–399 **Latest:** 9999
Name: Al-Iskandariyah
  Preference: preferred vernacular
  Name Source: *Getty Thesaurus of Geographic Names* (1997–)
  Name Date: Arabic name used since 640 CE
  Earliest: 0640 **Latest:** 9999
Name: Alexandrie
  Preference: variant **Language:** French
  Name Source: *Getty Thesaurus of Geographic Names* (1997–)
Name: Alejandría
  Preference: variant **Language:** Spanish
  Name Source: *Getty Thesaurus of Geographic Names* (1997–)
Name: Alessandria
  Preference: variant
  Name Source: *Getty Thesaurus of Geographic Names* (1997–)
Name: Alexandria Aegypti
  Preference: variant **Historical:** historical
  Name Source: *Getty Thesaurus of Geographic Names* (1997–)
  Name Date: Roman name
  Earliest:–100 **Latest:** 1500
Name: Rhakotis
  Preference: variant **Historical:** historical
  Name Source: *Getty Thesaurus of Geographic Names* (1997–)
  Name Date: name of original village on the site
  Earliest:–800
  Latest:–300
Broader Context: Urban region (Egypt)
  Africa (continent)
    Egypt (nation)
      Urban (region)
        Alexandria (inhabited place)

Fig. 40. Names and other information for places such as *Alexandria, Egypt,* would be collected in the Place/Location Authority.

Foto Zurich (Swiss firm, 19th–20th centuries); *Cemetery and Column of Pompey the Great in Alexandria, Egypt;* ca. 1906; from *Basse Egypte Janvier 1906* (album), in *Travel Albums from Paul Fleury's Trips to Switzerland, the Middle East, India, Asia, and South America* (collection); Research Library; The Getty Research Institute (Los Angeles, California); 91.R.5-v01.3-p.2r.

Place Types: inhabited place, city, regional capital, port
Coordinates:
  Lat: 31 12 00 N degrees minutes
  Long: 029 54 00 E degrees minutes
  (**Lat:** 31.2000 decimal degrees)
  (**Long:** 29.9000 decimal degrees)
Descriptive Note:
The city is located on a narrow strip of land between the Mediterranean Sea and Lake Mariut; it is now partially submerged. Alexandria was built by the Greek architect Dinocrates for Alexander the Great, and was the renowned capital of the Ptolemies when they ruled Egypt. It was noted for its library and a great lighthouse on the island of Pharos. It was captured by Julius Caesar in 48 BCE, taken by Arabs in 640 and by Turks in 1517. The city was famed for being the site of convergence of Greek, Arab, and Jewish ideas. Occupied by the French 1798–1801, by the British in 1892; evacuated by the British in 1946.

Note Source: *Princeton Encyclopedia* (1979) **Page:** 36
Citation: NIMA, *GEOnet Names Server* (2000–)
Page: accessed 18 April 2003

6.6. Generic Concept Authority

The Generic Concept Authority should contain information about generic concepts needed to catalog or describe works or images, including the type of object, materials, activities, its style, other attributes, or the role of a creator.

This authority includes terms used to describe generic concepts. It does not include proper names of persons, organizations, places, named events, or named subjects. This authority file may include terminology used to describe the type of work (e.g., *sculpture*); its material (e.g., *bronze*); activities associated with the work (e.g., *casting*); its style (e.g., *Art Nouveau*); the role of the creator, other people, or corporate bodies (e.g., *sculptor, architectural studio*); and other attributes or various abstract concepts (e.g., *symmetry*). It may include the generic names of plants and animals (e.g., *house mouse* or *Mus musculus,* but not *Mickey Mouse*).

Divisions of the authority: In the Generic Concept Authority, dividing terms into various logical categories (called *facets* in the jargon of thesaurus construction) makes the authority file more useful, easier to maintain, and more effective in retrieval. Terminology might fall into the following categories (which are derived from the facets of the *AAT*): objects (e.g., *cathedral*); materials (e.g., *oil paint*); activities (e.g., *exhibitions*); agents (e.g., *printmakers*); styles, periods, and cultures (e.g., *Renaissance*); physical attributes (e.g., *waterlogged*); and associated concepts (e.g., *beauty*).

Hierarchical relationships: If possible, this authority should be compliant with ISO and NISO standards for thesauri; it should be structured as a hierarchical, relational database. It should be polyhierarchical, because generic concepts often have multiple parents or broader contexts.

Associative relationships: Generic concepts may have associative relationships (related nonhierarchically to other generic concepts), including relationships described as *distinguished from, usage overlaps with, causative action is, activity performed is,* etc.

6.6.1. Sources for Terminology

All information in the authority record should be derived from published sources, where possible. A short list of sources appears below; fuller lists of authoritative published sources are found in *CDWA, CCO,* and the *AAT Editorial Guidelines.* Variant names from all sources consulted should be included, with preference given to the most authoritative, up-to-date sources available, which may include the following, arranged in a general descending order of preference:

Standard general reference sources

- *Art & Architecture Thesaurus* (*AAT*)
- Other authoritative thesauri and controlled vocabularies, such as Robert Chenhall's *Revised Nomenclature for Museum Cataloging*
- major encyclopedias, such as *Encyclopedia Britannica*
- major authoritative dictionaries of the English language, including *Merriam-Webster's, Random House, American Heritage,* and the *Oxford English Dictionary* (for the *OED,* be aware that words may be spelled differently in American English)
- dictionaries in languages other than English
- *Library of Congress Subject Headings* (*LCSH*)
- *Oxford Companion to Art*
- Ralph Mayer's *Artist's Handbook of Materials and Techniques*
- Library of Congress *Thesaurus for Graphic Materials II: Genre and Physical Characteristic Terms*
- Association of College and Research Libraries (ACRL)/ American Library Association (ALA) *Genre Terms* and *Paper Terms*

Other authoritative sources

- textbooks such as *Gardner's Art through the Ages* and *Janson's History of Art*

Other material on pertinent topics

- books, journal articles, and newspaper articles
- archives, historical documents, and other original sources (for historical terms only)

Other sources

- articles or databases on museum or university Web sites

6.6.2. Suggested Fields

Below is a relatively extensive list of fields that may be used for a Generic Concept Authority, as discussed in *CDWA*. A subset of these fields is discussed in *CCO*. Suggested required fields are flagged *core*. Builders of local authorities may decide to use only the core fields, adding any others that may be useful for their specific needs. In any case, it is advised to record the sources of all vocabulary and to allow for periodic additions and updates from published vocabularies, such as the *AAT*.

Record Type
Term **Core**
  Term Qualifier
  Preference
  Language
  Historical Flag
  Term Source **Core**
    Page
  Term Type
  Term Date
    Earliest Date
    Latest Date
Related Generic Concepts
  Relationship Type
  Relationship Date
    Earliest Date
    Latest Date
Broader Context **Core**
  Broader Context Date
    Earliest Date
    Latest Date
Label/Identification
Scope Note **Core**
  Note Source **Core**
    Page
Remarks
Citations
  Page

Below are examples of authority records from *CDWA,* illustrating full records for an object type, material, style, and animal species.

This is a full record for an object type:

Record Type: concept
Term: dinoi
  Preference: preferred **Term Type:** descriptor
  Term Source: *Art & Architecture Thesaurus* (1990–)
Term: dinos
  Preference: variant **Term Type:** alternate descriptor
  Term Source: *Art & Architecture Thesaurus* (1990–)
Broader Context: vessels (containers)
  Objects Facet
    Furnishings and Equipment
      containers
        <containers by form>
          vessels (containers)
            dinoi

Relationship Type: distinguished from
Related Generic Concept: lebetes
Scope Note: Used by modern scholars to refer to ancient Greek large, round-bottomed bowls that curve into a wide, open mouth, and that often stood on a stand. Metal vessels of this shape were probably used for cooking and those made of terracotta were used for mixing wine and date from the mid-seventh through the late fifth centuries BCE. They are distinguished from "lebetes" by their larger size. Ancient literary evidence suggests that the term was originally applied to drinking cups rather than bowls, and that such bowls were at that time called "lebetes."
  Note Source: Clark, Elston and Hart, *Understanding Greek Vases* (2002) **Page:** 87
Citations: *Grove Dictionary of Art* (1996) **Page:** 8:906
Citations: Boardman, *Athenian Black Figure Vases* (1988) **Page:** 30

This is a full record for a material:

Record Type: concept
Term: travertine
  Preference: preferred
  Term Type: descriptor **Language:** American English
  Term Source: *Art & Architecture Thesaurus* (1990–)
Term: travertine
  Preference: variant
  Term Type: descriptor **Language:** Italian
  Term Source: *Art & Architecture Thesaurus* (1990–)
Term: lapis tiburtinus
  Preference: variant
  Term Type: used for term **Language:** Latin
  Term Source: *Art & Architecture Thesaurus* (1990–)
Term: travertine marble
  Preference: variant
  Term Type: used for term
  Term Source: *Art & Architecture Thesaurus* (1990–)
Term: roachstone
  Preference: variant
  Term Type: used for term
  Term Source: *Art & Architecture Thesaurus* (1990–)
Broader Context: sinter, limestone
  Materials

rock
sedimentary rock
limestone
sinter
travertine

Scope Note: A dense, crystalline or microcrystalline limestone that was formed by the evaporation of river or spring waters. It is named after Tivoli, Italy ("Tibur" in Latin), where large deposits occur, and it is characterized by a light color and the ability to take a good polish. It is typically banded, due to the presence of iron compounds or other organic impurities. It is often used for walls and interior decorations in public buildings. It is distinguished from "tufa" by being harder and stronger.
Note Source: *Art & Architecture Thesaurus* (1990–)
Relationship Type: distinguished from
Related Generic Concept: tufa (sinter, limestone)

This is a full record for a style:

Record Type: concept
Term: Mannerist
Preference: preferred
Term Type: descriptor **Language:** English
Term Source: *Art & Architecture Thesaurus* (1990–)
Term: Mannerism
Preference: variant
Term Type: used for term
Term Source: *Art & Architecture Thesaurus* (1990–)
Term: Maniera
Preference: variant
Term Type: descriptor **Language:** Italian
Term Source: *Art & Architecture Thesaurus* (1990–)
Broader Context: Renaissance-Baroque style
Styles and Periods
<styles and periods by region>
European
<Renaissance-Baroque styles and periods>
Mannerist
Relationship Type: usage overlaps with
Related Generic Concept: Late Renaissance
Scope Note: Refers to a style and a period in evidence approximately from the 1520s to 1590, developing chiefly in Rome and spreading elsewhere in Europe. The style is characterized by a

distancing from the Classical ideal of the Renaissance to create a sense of fantasy, experimentation with color and materials, and a new human form of elongated, pallid, exaggerated elegance.
  Note Source: *Art & Architecture Thesaurus* (1990–)

This is a full record for an animal species:

Record Type: concept
Term: Canis lupus **Qualifier:** species name
  Preference: preferred
  Term Type: descriptor
  Term Source: *Art & Architecture Thesaurus* (1990–)
Term: gray wolf
  Preference: variant
  Term Type: alternate descriptor
  Term Source: *Art & Architecture Thesaurus* (1990–)
Term: timber wolf
  Preference: variant
  Term Source: *Art & Architecture Thesaurus* (1990–)
Term: grey wolf
  Preference: variant
  Term Source: *Art & Architecture Thesaurus* (1990–)
Broader Context: Canidae (Animals)
  Animal Kingdom
    Vertebrates (subphylum)
      Mammalia (class)
        Carnivora (order)
          Canidae (family)
            Canis lupus
Scope Note: The best-known of the three species of wild doglike carnivores known as wolves. It is the largest nondomestic member of the dog family (Canidae) and inhabits vast areas of the Northern Hemisphere. It once ranged over all of North America from Alaska and Arctic Canada southward to central Mexico and throughout Europe and Asia above 20 degrees N latitude. There are at least five subspecies of gray wolf. Most domestic dogs are probably descended from gray wolves. Pervasive in human mythology, folklore, and language, the gray wolf has had an impact on the human imagination in mythology, legends, literature, and art.
  Note Source: "Wolf." *Encyclopedia Britannica online*
  Page: accessed 25 May 2005

Note Source: *Animal Diversity Web.* University of Michigan Museum of Zoology, 1995–2002. http://animaldiversity.ummz.umich.edu/ **Page:** accessed 25 May 2005

6.7. Subject Authority

The Subject Authority includes iconographical subjects and other named subject matter of works of art (sometimes referred to as *content*); this is the narrative, iconic, or nonobjective meaning conveyed by an abstract or figurative composition. It is what is depicted in and by a work of art or architecture. This authority is used for the Subject field of the work record.

Note that the Subject field of the work record is linked not only to the Subject Authority but also to other authorities; subjects described with the names of places or people should be taken from the Person/Corporate Body Authority and the Place/Location Authority (e.g., *Rome, Italy*). Subjects described by generic terms that are not proper nouns should be taken from the Generic Concept Authority (e.g., *cathedral, still life, landscape*). If a particular term or name is recorded in one of these other authorities, it does not need to be repeated in the Subject Authority.

Iconography: The Subject Authority may be used to record *iconography,* which is the narrative content of a figurative work depicted in terms of characters, situations, and images that are related to a specific religious, social, or historical context. Themes from religion (e.g., *Ganesha* or *Life of Jesus Christ*) and mythology (e.g., *Herakles* or *Quetzalcóatl (Feathered Serpent)*) are within the scope of this authority. Themes from literature (e.g., *Jane Eyre* or *Lohengrin*) are also included.

Events: This authority may include records for historical events (e.g., *Coronation of Charlemagne* or *U.S. Westward Expansion*).

Built works: This authority may include the proper names of buildings. Note, however, that if built works are the focus of a cataloging effort, they should be recorded as works as described in *CDWA* and *CCO,* rather than in an authority.

Hierarchical relationships: If possible, this authority should be compliant with ISO and NISO standards for thesauri; it should be structured as a hierarchical, relational database. It should be polyhierarchical, because the entities in the Subject Authority often have multiple parents or broader contexts.

Associative relationships: Subjects have associative relationships when they are related nonhierarchically to other subjects.

Other relationships: Entities in the Subject Authority may be linked to records in the other three authorities, referring to the people, places, and generic concepts associated with a particular subject.

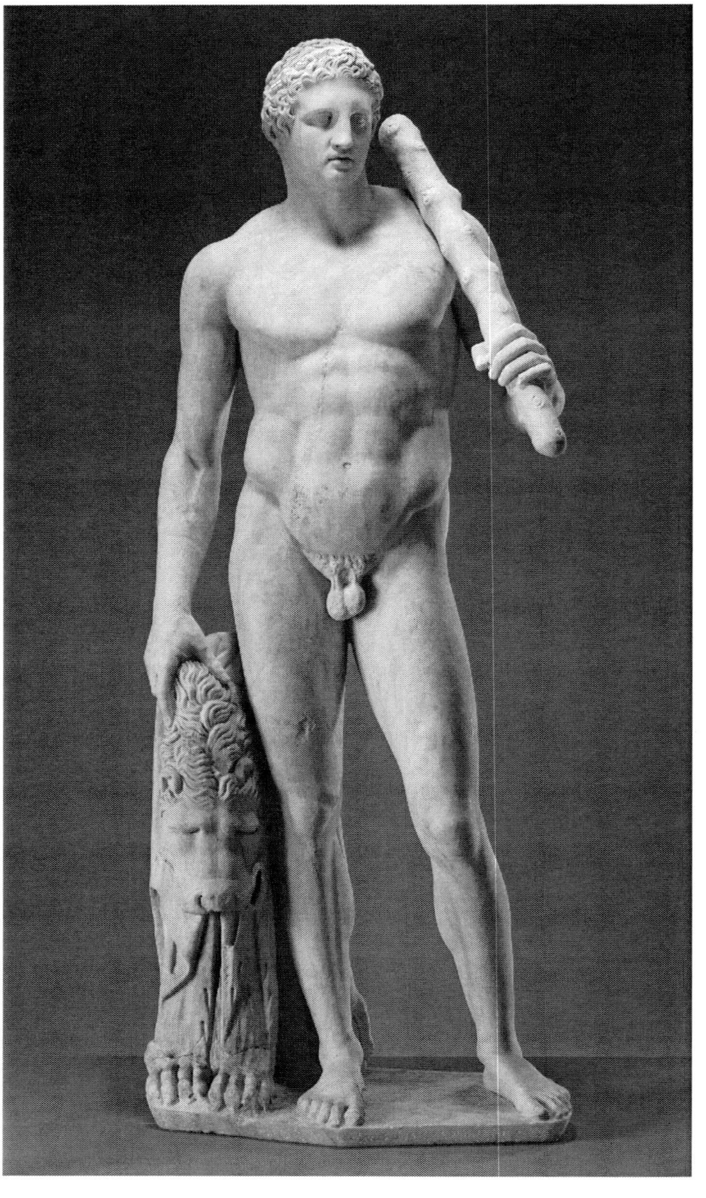

Fig. 41. The iconography of the Greek and Roman hero Herakles (Hercules) may be indexed using a Subject Authority, which may be populated with terminology from *Iconclass* and other sources.

Unknown Roman; *The Lansdowne Herakles;* 125 CE; marble; height: 193.5 cm, weight: 385.5 kg (76 3/16 inches, 850 pounds); J. Paul Getty Museum (Los Angeles, California); 70.AA.109.

6.7.1. Sources for Terminology

All information in the authority record should be derived from published sources, where possible. A short list of sources appears below. Variant names from all sources consulted should be included, with preference given to the most authoritative, up-to-date sources available, which may include the following, arranged in a general descending order of preference:

Standard general reference sources

- major authoritative dictionaries and encyclopedias
- *Library of Congress Subject Headings* (*LCSH*)

Other authoritative sources

- other authoritative subject thesauri and controlled vocabularies (e.g., *Iconclass*)
- textbooks on art history, history, or other relevant topics

Other material on pertinent topics

- books, journal articles, and newspaper articles
- archives, historical documents, and other original sources (for historical terms only)

Other sources

- articles or databases on museum or university Web sites

Sources for iconographic themes

- François Garnier's *Thesaurus iconographique*
- *Iconclass*
- *Index of Jewish Art*
- Helene Roberts's *Encyclopedia of Comparative Iconography*
- Margaret Stutley's *Illustrated Dictionary of Hindu Iconography*

Sources for fictional characters

- Frank Magill's *Cyclopedia of Literary Characters*
- Martin Seymour-Smith's *Dent Dictionary of Fictional Characters*

Sources for events

- Bernard Grun and Eva Simpson's *Timetables of History*
- *Holidays, Festivals, and Celebrations of the World Dictionary*
- George Kohn's *Dictionary of Wars*
- *Library of Congress Subject Headings* (*LCSH*)
- H. E. L. Mellersh's *Chronology of World History*

Sources for names of buildings

- *Cultural Objects Name Authority* (*CONA,* in development)
- *America Preserved: A Checklist of Historic Buildings, Structures, and Sites*
- *Avery Index to Architectural Periodicals at Columbia University*
- *Grove Art Online*
- Banister Fletcher's *History of Architecture*
- *Library of Congress Subject Headings* (*LCSH*)
- *Macmillan Encyclopedia of Architects*

6.7.2. Suggested Fields

Below is a relatively extensive list of fields that may be used for a Subject Authority, as discussed in *CDWA.* A subset of these fields is discussed in *CCO.* Suggested required fields are flagged *core.* Builders of local authorities may decide to use only the core fields, adding any others that may be useful for their specific needs.

Record Type
Subject Name Core
  Name Preference
  Language
  Historical Flag
  Name Source Core
    Page
Name Type
Name Date
    Earliest Date
    Latest Date
Subject Date
  Earliest Date
  Latest Date
Subject Roles/Attributes
  Preference
  Role/Attribute Date
    Earliest Date
    Latest Date
Related Subject
  Relationship Type
Relationship Date
    Earliest Date
    Latest Date
Broader Context Core
  Broader Context Date
    Earliest Date
    Latest Date
Related Place/Location
  Relationship Type
Related Person/Corporate Body
  Relationship Type
Related Generic Concept
  Relationship Type
Label/Identification
Descriptive Note
  Note Source
    Page
Remarks
Citations
  Page

Below are examples of authority records from *CDWA,* illustrating full records for two mythological characters, an episode in a story, a fictional place, an event, a literary topic, and a built work.

This is a record for a mythological character:

Record Type: religion/mythology, character/person
Subject Name: Hercules
  Preference: preferred
  Name Source: *Iconclass* (1979–)
Subject Name: Herakles
  Preference: variant
  Name Source: *Iconclass* (1979–)
Subject Name: Heracles
  Preference: variant
  Name Source: *Iconclass* (1979–)
Subject Name: Ercole
  Preference: variant
  Language: Italian
  Name Source: *Iconclass* (1979–)
Subject Name: Hercule
  Preference: variant
  Language: French
  Name Source: *Iconclass* (1979–)
Subject Name: Hércules
  Preference: variant
  Name Source: *Iconclass* (1979–)
Subject Roles/Attributes: Greek hero, king, strength, fortitude, perseverance
Broader Context: Story of Hercules (Greek heroic legends, Classical Mythology)
  Classical Mythology
    Greek heroic legends
      Story of Hercules
        Hercules
Citation: *Iconclass.* http://www.*Iconclass*.nl/
Citation: Grant and Hazel, *Gods and Mortals in Classical Mythology* (1973) **Page:** 212 ff.

This is a fuller record for a mythological character:

Record Type: religion/mythology, character/person
Subject Name: Shiva
  Preference: preferred
  Name Source: *Encyclopedia Britannica* online (2002–)
Subject Name: Siva
  Preference: variant
  Name Source: *Encyclopedia Britannica* online (2002–)
Subject Name: Siwa
  Preference: variant
  Name Source: *Encyclopedia Britannica* online (2002–)
Subject Name: Sambhu
  Preference: variant
  Name Source: *Encyclopedia Britannica* online (2002–)
Subject Name: Sankara
  Preference: variant
  Name Source: *Encyclopedia Britannica* online (2002–)
Subject Name: Pasupati
  Preference: variant
  Name Source: Besset, *Divine Shiva* (1997)
Subject Name: Mahesa
  Preference: variant
  Name Source: *Encyclopedia Britannica* online (2002–)
Subject Name: Mahadeva
  Preference: variant
  Name Source: *Encyclopedia Britannica* online (2002–)
Subject Name: Auspicious One
  Preference: variant
  Name Source: *Encyclopedia Britannica* online (2002–)
Subject Roles/Attributes: Hindu deity, androgynous, destroyer, dancer, restorer, mendicant, ascetic, yogin, sensuality, herdsman, avenger
Broader Context: Hindu gods (Hindu Iconography)
  Hindu Iconography
    Hindu gods
      Shiva
Relationship Type: focus of
  Related Generic Concept: Saivism
Relationship Type: manifestation is
  Related Generic Concept: lingus
Relationship Type: manifestation is
  Related Subject: Ardhanarisvara (Hindu Iconography)

Relationship Type: manifestation is
Related Subject: Nataraja (Hindu Iconography)
Relationship Type: consort is
Related Subject: Parvat (Hindu Iconography)
Relationship Type: consort is
Related Subject: Uma (Hindu Iconography)
Relationship Type: consort is
Related Subject: Sati (Hindu Iconography)
Relationship Type: consort is
Related Subject: Durga (Hindu Iconography)
Relationship Type: consort is
Related Subject: Kali (Hindu Iconography)
Relationship Type: consort is
Related Subject: Sakti (Hindu Iconography)
Relationship Type: parent of
Related Subject: Ganesha (Hindu Iconography)
Relationship Type: parent of
Related Subject: Skanda (Hindu Iconography)
Relationship Type: animal image is
Related Subject: Nandi the Bull (Hindu Iconography)
Relationship Type: developed in
Related Place/Location: India (Asia)
Descriptive Note: One of the primary deities of Hinduism. He is the paramount lord of the Shaivite sects of India. Shiva means "Auspicious One" in Sanskrit. He is one of the most complex gods of India, embodying contradictory qualities: both the destroyer and the restorer, the great ascetic and the symbol of sensuality, the benevolent herdsman of souls and the wrathful avenger. He is usually depicted as a graceful male. In painting, he is typically white or ash-colored with a blue neck, hair represented as coil of matted locks, adorned with the crescent moon and the Ganges. He may have three eyes and a garland of skulls. He may have two or four arms and carry skulls, a serpent, a deerskin, trident, a small drum, or a club with a skull on it. He is depicted in art in various manifestations, often with one of his consorts.
Note Source: Toffy, *Gods and Myths: Hinduism* (1976)
Citation: Besset, *Divine Shiva* (1997)
Citation: *Encyclopedia Britannica* online (2002–) **Page:** "Siva," accessed 4 February 2004

This is a record for an episode in a story:

Record Type: religion/mythology, literature
Subject Name: Marriage of the Virgin
  Preference: preferred
  Name Source: *Iconclass* (1979–)
Subject Name: Sposalizio
  Type: variant **Language:** Italian
  Name Source: *Iconclass (*1979–)
Subject Name: Betrothal of the Virgin
  Preference: variant
  Name Source: *Iconclass* (1979–)
Subject Name: Marriage of Mary and Joseph
  Preference: variant
  Name Source: *Iconclass* (1979–)
Broader Context: Life of the Virgin Mary (New Testament, Christian Iconography)
  Christian Iconography
    New Testament
      Life of the Virgin Mary
        Marriage of the Virgin
Subject Roles/Attributes: betrothal, high priest, marriage, temple
Relationship Type: actor is
  Related Subject: Mary (Biblical characters, New Testament, Christian Iconography)
Relationship Type: actor is
  Related Subject: Joseph (Biblical characters, New Testament, Christian Iconography)
Descriptive Note: Mary and Joseph are married by the high priest (*Iconclass*). The story is not in the canonical Bible; it comes from the apocryphal Book of James (or Protoevangelium, Infancy Gospel 8–9) and the Golden Legend by Jacobus de Voragine. The "marriage" scene is technically a betrothal. It generally takes place in or outside the temple. Mary and Joseph typically stand to either side of the priest, who joins their hands in betrothal. Joseph may be depicted as an older man. He has been chosen from a group of suitors, all of whom had been asked by the high priest to bring a rod (a branch or twig) to the altar; the rod of Joseph bloomed miraculously by intervention of the Holy Spirit, thus designating him as the man chosen by God to be the spouse of Mary.
  Note Source: *Golden Legend of Jacobus de Voragine* (1969)

Citation: *Iconclass* (1979–) **Page:** Notation: 73A42
Citation: *Oxford Companion to Art* (1996) **Page:** 1195 ff.
Citation: Testuz, *Protoevangelium Jacobi: Apocryphal Books* (1958)

This is a record for a fictional place:

Record Type: fictional place
Subject Name: Niflheim **Preference:** preferred
  Name Source: *Encyclopedia Britannica* online (2002–)
Subject Name: Niflheimr **Preference:** variant
  Name Source: *Encyclopedia Britannica* online (2002–)
Subject Name: House of Mists **Preference:** variant
  Name Source: *Encyclopedia Britannica* online (2002–)
Broader Context: Creation story (Norse Mythology)
  Norse Mythology
    Creation story
      Niflheim
Subject Roles/Attributes: underworld, creation, death, mist, cold, dark
Relationship Type: ruled by
  Related Subject: Hel (Norse goddess)
Descriptive Note: In the Norse creation story, Niflheim was the misty region north of the void (Ginnungagap) in which the world was created. It was also the cold, dark, misty world of the dead, ruled by the goddess Hel. In some accounts it was the last of nine worlds, a place into which evil men passed after reaching the region of death (Hel). It was situated below one of the roots of the world tree (Yggdrasill). Niflheim contained a well (Hvergelmir) from which many rivers flowed.
  Note Source: *Encyclopedia Britannica* online (2002–)
  Page: "Niflheim," accessed 13 June 2005

This is a record for an event:

Record Type: event
Subject Name: First Battle of Bull Run **Preference:** preferred
  Name Source: *Encyclopedia Britannica* online (2002–)
Subject Name: First Battle of Manassas **Preference:** variant
  Name Source: *Encyclopedia Britannica* online (2002–)
Subject Date: 21 July 1861
  Earliest: 1861 **Latest:** 1861
Broader Context: American Civil War (American History, Historical Events)

Historical Events
American History
American Civil War
First Battle of Bull Run
Subject Roles/Attributes: battle, invasion, casualties
Relationship Type: predecessor was
Related Subject: First Shenandoah Valley Campaign
Relationship Type: participant
Related Person/Corporate Body: General Irvin McDowell (American Union general, 1818–1885)
Relationship Type: participant
Related Person/Corporate Body: General P. G. T. Beauregard (American Confederate general, 1818–1893)
Relationship Type: location
Related Place/Location: Manassas (Virginia, United States)
Descriptive Note: One of two battles fought a few miles north of the crucial railroad junction of Manassas, Virginia. The First Battle of Bull Run (called First Manassas by the South) was fought on July 21, 1861, at a very early stage of the Civil War. Both armies were ill-prepared, but political pressures forced the Northern General Irvin McDowell to advance to a small stream named Bull Run near Manassas in northern Virginia, southwest of Washington; this was a move against the Southern city of Richmond, Virginia.
Note Source: *Antietam National Battlefield* [online] (2003)
Page: accessed 5 February 2004
Citation: Kohn, *Dictionary of Wars* (2000)

This is a record for a literary topic:

Record Type: literature
Subject Name: Wuthering Heights **Preference:** preferred
Name Source: Brontë, *Wuthering Heights,* edited by Sale and Dunn (1990)
Page: title
Broader Context: British Literature
Literary Themes
British Literature
Subject Roles/Attributes: love, romance
Relationship Type: author
Related Person/Corporate Body: Emily Brontë (English novelist, 1818–1848)

Relationship Type: character
  Related Subject: Catherine Earnshaw
Relationship Type: character
  Related Subject: Heathcliff
Relationship Type: location
  Related Place/Location: Yorkshire (England, United Kingdom)
Descriptive Note: An emotional story of heartbreak and mystery surrounding a doomed romance. The novel was written between October 1845 and June 1846; it first appeared in print in December 1847. The work did not receive critical recognition until after Emily Brontë's death from consumption in 1848.
Citation: Brontë, *Wuthering Heights,* edited by Sale and Dunn (1990)
Citation: Brontë, *Wuthering Heights,* prefaces by Emily and Anne and Charlotte Brontë and H. W. Garrod (1950)

This is a record for a built work, but some institutions will wish to catalog built works as works in their own right rather than recording them only in their local Subject Authority:

Record Type: built work
Subject Name: Eiffel Tower **Preference:** preferred
  Language: English
  Name Source: *Encyclopedia Britannica* online (2002–)
Subject Name: Tour Eiffel **Preference:** alternate preferred
  Language: French
  Name Source: *Encyclopedia Britannica* online (2002–)
Subject Name: Three-Hundred-Metre Tower **Preference:** variant
  Historical Flag: historical
  Name Source: *Encyclopedia Britannica* online (2002–)
Broader Context: Built Works
  Built Works
    Eiffel Tower
Subject Roles/Attributes: industrial exposition, tower
Relationship Type: location
  Related Place/Location: Paris (France)
Relationship Type: event
  Related Subject: International Exposition (Paris, 1889)
Citation: Harriss, *The Tallest Tower: Eiffel and the Belle Epoque* (1975)

6.8. Source Authority

It is critical to record sources for cultural heritage information. The reliability and authoritativeness of work records and the controlled vocabularies associated with them are dependent upon the information in these records having been well researched, with the sources of information cited. Given that one publication may be the source for numerous pieces of information in a vocabulary or catalog record, it is recommended to maintain a Source Authority.

The Source Authority contains information about published bibliographic materials, Web sites, archival documents, unpublished manuscripts, and references to verbal opinions expressed by scholars or subject experts. While libraries typically prefer to use the MARC format for recording citations, museums and other institutions may wish to record sources in a Source Authority that uses a relational tables format or another format familiar to them.

6.8.1. Sources for Terminology

The information to construct a bibliographic citation is generally found on the title page of the source. If the source is not physically in hand, *copy cataloging* may be employed, which is preparing a bibliographic record by using or adapting one already prepared by someone else. Citations may be copied from the Library of Congress online catalog or another library catalog.

6.8.2. Suggested Fields

Below is a list of fields that may be used for a Source Authority. Suggested required fields are flagged *core*. Builders of local authorities may decide to use only the core fields, adding any others that may be useful for their specific needs.

- Type
- Brief Citation **Core**
- Full Citation **Core**
  - Title
  - Broader Title
  - Author
  - Editor/Compiler
  - Publication Place
  - Publisher
  - Publication Year
  - Edition Statement
- Remarks

Below are examples of Source Authority records from *CDWA*.

The following are examples of brief authority records:

> **Brief Citation:** Higgins, *Minoan and Mycenaean Art* (1967)
> **Full Citation:** Higgins, Reynold. *Minoan and Mycenaean Art.* New York: Praeger Publishers, 1967.
>
> **Brief Citation:** *Dictionary of Architecture and Construction* (2000)
> **Full Citation:** *Dictionary of Architecture and Construction.* 3rd ed. Edited by Cyril M. Harris. New York: McGraw-Hill, 2000.
>
> **Brief Citation:** *Oxford Concise Dictionary of Art and Artists* (1996)
> **Full Citation:** *Concise Oxford Dictionary of Art and Artists.* Ian Chilvers, ed. Oxford: Oxford University Press, 1996.
>
> **Brief Citation:** Cole, *Sienese Painting* (1980)
> **Full Citation:** Cole, Bruce. *Sienese Painting: From Its Origins to the Fifteenth Century.* New York: Harper & Row, 1980.
>
> **Brief Citation:** Janson, *History of Art* (1971)
> **Full Citation:** Janson, H. W. *History of Art.* New York: Harry N. Abrams, Inc., 1971.
>
> **Brief Citation:** Pope-Hennessy, *Raphael* (1970)
> **Full Citation:** Pope-Hennessy, John. *Raphael.* New York: Harper & Row, Publishers, 1970.
>
> **Brief Citation:** Adkins and Adkins, *Thesaurus of British Archaeology* (1982)
> **Full Citation:** Adkins, Lesley, and Roy A. Adkins. *Thesaurus of British Archaeology.* Newton Abbot, England: David & Charles, 1982.

The following are fuller authority records:

> **Type:** catalog
> **Brief Citation:** Trubner et al., *Asiatic Art* (1973)
> **Full Citation:** Trubner, Henry, William J. Rathbun, and Catherine A. Kaputa. *Asiatic Art in the Seattle Art Museum.* Seattle: Seattle Art Museum, 1973.
> > **Title:** *Asiatic Art in the Seattle Art Museum*
> > **Author:** Trubner, Henry
> > **Author:** Rathbun, William J.
> > **Author:** Kaputa, Catherine A.

Publication Place: Seattle (Washington, United States)
Publisher: Seattle Art Museum
Publication Year: 1973

Type: reference
Brief Citation: Smith, *Egypt* (1981)
Full Citation: Smith, W. Stevenson. *Art and Architecture of Ancient Egypt.* 2nd ed., revised with additions by William Kelly Simpson. Pelican History of Art. New Haven and New York: Yale University Press, 1981.
Title: *Art and Architecture of Ancient Egypt*
Author: Smith, W. Stevenson
Publication Place: New Haven (Connecticut, United States)
Publication Place: New York (New York, United States)
Publisher: Yale University Press
Publication Year: 1981
Edition Statement: 2nd edition

7. Constructing a Vocabulary or Authority

Constructing a rich and complex controlled vocabulary or authority is a time-consuming and labor-intensive process. However, the benefits are worth the cost, because the resulting vocabulary helps to ensure consistency in indexing and facilitates successful retrieval. It also saves labor, because catalogers do not have to repeatedly record the same information. The issues discussed in this chapter concern both the construction of a local authority and the construction of a new vocabulary for broader use. Further information is found in **Chapter 6: Local Authorities.** Given that an authority in this context is also a kind of vocabulary, both are intended by the use of the term *vocabulary* below.

7.1. General Criteria for the Vocabulary

Before beginning the project, the creators of the vocabulary must agree upon and document the intended compliance with standards, construction methods, plans for maintenance, desired structure, types of relationships, display formats, and policies regarding compound terms, true synonymy, and types of acceptable warrant. A first step in resolving these issues is to determine the purpose, scope, and audience of the vocabulary.

7.1.1. Local or Broader Use

Is the vocabulary intended strictly for local use or to be shared in a broader environment? Local authorities should be customized so that they work well with the specific situation and the specific collection or collections at hand. Each institution should develop a strategy for creating local authorities customized for their specific collections.

However, if the collection is or will be queried in consortial or *federated* environments, controlled vocabularies should be customized for retrieval across different collections; depending upon the particular situation, the requirements are different and the terminology is broader or narrower in scope.

In today's automated environment and with the growing tendency to share data, it can generally be assumed that a vocabulary will someday be shared with others or incorporated into a larger context, even if this is not an immediate goal of the project. Thus, it is wise to create a vocabulary that is compliant with national and international standards. Furthermore, the vocabulary should use the structure and editorial rules of existing standard vocabularies in order to make it easier to achieve interoperability in the future.

Builders of local vocabularies should investigate the possibility of contributing new terms to an existing standard vocabulary, such as the *AAT* or the *Library of Congress Authorities.* Contributing to a common resource allows an institution and others in the academic or professional community to effectively share terminology, thus avoiding redundant efforts and enhancing interoperability.

7.1.2. Purpose of the Vocabulary

What is the purpose and intended audience of the new vocabulary or local authority? Vocabularies and authorities are typically used for cataloging, retrieval, or navigation.

In an ideal situation, separate—although closely related—vocabularies are used for cataloging and for retrieval. A vocabulary primarily designed for cataloging contains expert terminology. At the same time, it is designed to encourage the greatest possible consistency among catalogers by limiting choices of terminology according to the scope of the collection and the focus of the field being indexed. In contrast, a vocabulary for retrieval is typically broader in scope and contains more nonexpert and even *wrong* terminology (e.g., misspelled names or incorrect, but commonly used, terms).

In a structured vocabulary intended for cataloging, equivalence relationships should be made only between terms and names that have *true synonymy* (identical meanings) in order to allow accuracy and precision in indexing and retrieval. However, a vocabulary for retrieval may link terms and names that have *near synonymy* (similar meanings) in order to broaden the results. In fact, due to limited resources, many institutions use the same vocabulary for both cataloging and retrieval, thus requiring a compromise between the two approaches.

If the vocabulary is to be used for navigation or browsing on a Web site, it should be very simple and aimed at the nonexpert audience rather than at specialists. Typically, such a vocabulary is not used for cataloging or retrieval beyond navigation.

7.1.3. Scope of the Vocabulary

No vocabulary can contain all terminology. Boundaries for the vocabulary should be set, and the realm of knowledge encompassed should be precisely defined. Will it have a broad scope but shallow depth? Or will it have narrow or specific scope, but deep depth? An example of the latter is the *AAT,* for which the scope is limited to art and architecture, but the depth of hierarchies within this realm may be very extensive.

If the vocabulary is complex, as when the scope is broad or the hierarchies are deep, facets and other divisions should be established in order to divide the terms in a logical and consistent way throughout the vocabulary. The vocabulary may grow and change over time, which will affect the continuing need for divisions within the hierarchies. The levels of granularity and specificity that will be needed by the users of the vocabulary should be carefully considered. This issue is further discussed in **Chapter 8: Indexing with Controlled Vocabularies.**

7.1.4. Maintaining the Vocabulary

Terminology for art and material culture may change over time; vocabularies must be living, growing tools. What methodology will be used for keeping up with changing terminology? If it is possible to contribute terminology to a published vocabulary (such as the Getty vocabularies or the *Library of Congress Authorities*), a plan and methodology should be developed to submit new terms; this will of course have an impact on workflow, so that must be taken into consideration.

7.2. Data Model and Rules

The following basic issues related to the data model, minimum records, editorial rules, and other topics should be resolved before beginning work on a new vocabulary.

7.2.1. Established Standards

When populating the authority, use established authoritative standards and vocabulary resources for models, rules, and values. In order to avoid duplication of effort and to allow future interoperability, developers of a new vocabulary should attempt to incorporate existing authoritative standards and vocabularies in whole or in part, if they overlap with the scope of the intended new vocabulary. Whenever possible, the vocabulary should be populated with terminology from existing controlled vocabularies, such as the Getty vocabularies and the *Library of Congress Authorities*, rather than inventing terms from scratch. The unique numeric or alphanumeric identifiers of incorporated records should be included so that information may be exchanged with others and updates from the original vocabulary sources may be received.

Standard, published sources for terms or names and other information should be used when it is necessary to make new vocabulary records. Appropriate sources are discussed in **Chapter 6: Local Authorities.** The sources for information in the authority record should be systematically cited. If the name or term does not exist in a published source, it should be constructed according to *CDWA, CCO,* the *Editorial Guidelines* of the Getty Vocabulary Program, *AACR2,* or other appropriate rules.

Among synonyms, one of the terms or names should be flagged as the *preferred* term/name and chosen according to established rules and standards.

7.2.2. Logical Focus of the Record

Establish the logical focus of each vocabulary record. The scope of the vocabulary should be defined by determining what will be included and omitted from the vocabulary. Will there be limitations of time period, geographical extent, or topical subjects? How will each record be circumscribed? For the purpose of this discussion, a *record* is defined as a grouping of data that includes the terms that have an equivalence relationship to each other; links to related records; broader contexts; the scope note; and other information as required.

If only a small number of terms are needed for an application, perhaps all terminology may be included in a single vocabulary, with distinctions between broad types made through the use of facets. However, for medium-sized and large vocabularies, it is generally more efficient to create separate vocabularies for different types of data. A primary criterion for judging when to make separate vocabularies or a single vocabulary is to consider how similar the data is for various records. For example, a vocabulary for people's names requires information that is quite different from information about geographic names: people have biographies and very shallow hierarchies (if any), while geographic places have coordinates and a position in an administrative hierarchy. Based on these differences, it is more efficient to create separate vocabularies for people and geographic places.

7.2.3. Data Structure

Establish the entity-relationship model and data structure. After the scope is defined, the relationships between various types of data should be established. The following should be determined: Which data needs to have controlled terminology? Which elements must be a text field? Where multiple values may exist for a field, which fields must be grouped together? How are various types of information otherwise related? When designing the data model, a standard such as *CDWA* or *CCO* should be consulted, as should existing vocabulary data models such as those used for the Getty vocabularies. The model advocated in these standards is a relational model, which allows maximum versatility, power, and linking for complex, large data sets and intensive editorial requirements.

However, implementers may decide on another data model if their needs are different.

In addition to the issues outlined here, there will be dozens of other technical decisions that must be made before constructing the vocabulary. What technology will be used? How will authority files, lists, and other controlled vocabularies be integrated into the rest of the system? These are critical questions that depend upon local needs and resources. If an institution is tied to a particular software, a vocabulary that operates within the parameters of that software may have to be designed, and compromises relative to the standards should be made as necessary.

7.2.4. Controlled Fields vs. Free-Text Fields

Accommodate both controlled fields and free-text fields. *Controlled* fields contain data values drawn from controlled terms and are formatted to allow for successful retrieval. *Free-text* fields communicate nuance, uncertainty, and ambiguity to end users.

The primary function of an indexed field is to facilitate end-user access. Access is improved when controlled terms are used to populate database fields. Fields in one controlled vocabulary may be controlled by terms in another controlled vocabulary; for example, the place names in a personal name vocabulary may be controlled by a geographic place name vocabulary.

Consistency is less important for a free-text field than for a controlled field, but it is still desirable. Although free-text fields by definition contain uncontrolled terminology, the use of terminology that is consistent with the terms in controlled fields is recommended for the sake of clarity. Using a consistent style, grammar, and sentence structure is also recommended.

7.2.5. Minimum Information

Establish the minimum required information for each record by determining which information in the data model is required and which is optional. The standards and vocabularies listed above may provide guidance. The data that is needed in order to use and display the vocabulary must be decided upon and supplied for every record. For example, the use of preferred terms and hierarchical placement is required for every record. Other data may be desirable but not required; a strategy may be adopted for data to be supplied incrementally over time. For example, developers of the vocabulary could work in phases, beginning with a set of minimal records and then, at a later date, filling out and supplementing the records.

7.2.6. Editorial Rules

Identify and adopt appropriate editorial rules for building the vocabulary to ensure consistent data. If an existing set of standard rules must be altered due to local requirements, the local rules should be thoroughly documented. Once the rules are in place, they should be applied consistently and without fail. To avoid altering established rules on a case-by-case basis when existing rules do not work in a given situation, a system should be in place whereby an authorized individual or team may update the rules and distribute the revisions to all users of the vocabulary.

What do editorial rules comprise? They include the following: a list of which fields are required; how to choose a preferred term for each record; which variant terms to include; the required parameters for choosing hierarchical positions for new records and how to construct new branches of the hierarchies; how to establish other relationships between terms and records; the format and syntax used to fill in each field; the language allowed for each field (is the data in English only or multilingual?); character sets; the authorized sources for each field; and decision trees regarding how to choose which information is preferred when sources disagree. Ideally, the rules should include many examples illustrating how to enter the data and make decisions.

References to a computer system should be as generic as possible in the editorial rules, so that they do not have to be entirely rewritten when new systems are adopted over time. Training or documentation on the functionality of a specific computer system should be separate from the editorial rules, so far as is practical.

7.3. Imprecise Information

For vocabularies covering art and cultural heritage, developers should take into account that information in this field of study is often imprecise or ambiguous. There is often no one established fact, date, or opinion. Systems that catalog this information must allow for the expression of multiple possibilities and the flagging of information as *possibly* or *probably.* The following examples show some of the complex issues involved.

The name and identity of a person may be unknown. A work of art may have been created by an anonymous artist who has a known oeuvre (body of artistic works) from which approximate life dates and loci of activity may be surmised. When an artist's name is not known, scholars and museums devise appellations based on various attributes: the name of an artwork (e.g., *Master of the Ovile Madonna*); a client (e.g., the *Beardsley Limner*—a combination of the word *limner,* referring to a painter of portraits or miniatures, and a sitter's name, Mrs.

Hezekiah Beardsley); a location (e.g., *Frankfurt Master*); a stylistic attribute (e.g., *Master of the Mountain-like Clouds*); the artist's initials, if known (e.g., *Master E.L.G.*); or a relationship to a known artist (e.g., *Pseudo Pier Francesco Fiorentino*). Most anonymous artists have multiple appellations, in different languages and formats. All these appellations must be associated with the identity. If there is a suspicion that the anonymous artist may be identified with a named individual, a relationship must be established between the two entities. For example, the Master of the Parlement de Paris worked during the fifteenth century, and the style of the works and their locations would probably make him a French or Flemish artist. A vocabulary such as the *ULAN* provides a record for such anonymous artists, listing the appellations and all variations on them and recording approximate dates and loci of activity.

Even with named artists, biographical information may be uncertain. Uncertain dates may be expressed as *ca.* (circa) or *possibly* or in terms of a century or the reign of a ruler. The loci of activity may be uncertain (e.g., either France or Flanders), and relationships to other artists may be presumed but not documented.

In an example for geographic information, as in the *TGN,* the exact location of a documented historic place may be uncertain; thus, a lost settlement must be accommodated in the hierarchy.

In an example for a vocabulary of generic terms, such as the *AAT,* there may be multiple logical hierarchical placements for the term within the vocabulary. There may be disagreement among scholars regarding whether a concept is a period or a culture and when and where it started or ended.

Vocabularies may track such uncertain or ambiguous information in several ways, often all used together in one vocabulary. Ambiguous information may be accommodated via repeatable fields to allow indexing of multiple possible values. For example, if there are multiple possible nationalities or loci of activity for an artist, all of them should be indexed to provide access (e.g., El Greco was a Greek artist who worked in Spain). Where uncertainty or variability may exist in the hierarchical context, polyhierarchical links allow multiple parents to be recorded. Finally, note fields may be used throughout the record to allow expression and explanation of ambiguity; important information in such notes should be indexed to allow retrieval. For example, an artist's life dates for display may be *born ca. 532 BCE, died before 490 BCE.* This uncertain information could then be indexed as *birth date:–542, death date:–490,* with rules provided for estimating uncertain life spans when precise dates of birth and death are unknown.

7.4. Rules for Constructing a Vocabulary

Devise consistent editorial rules for the establishment of warrant, choice of terms, placement in the hierarchy, and writing of scope notes and other data. Where possible, existing rules should be consulted, including the *Editorial Guidelines* of the Getty vocabularies, the *CCO* and *CDWA* chapters on authorities, *AACR2,* or other standard guidelines. A brief discussion of some important principles is included below.

7.4.1. Establishing Terms

Terms should be included based on how closely they represent concepts included in the vocabulary. For persons, places, iconography, etc., the name must be proven to represent the person, place, or subject intended by a given vocabulary record. For terms in a Generic Concept Authority, the terms representing a given concept should be true synonyms for the concept, established through literary warrant.

Criteria in choosing terms should include the elimination of ambiguity and the control of synonyms. Vocabularies should eliminate the ambiguity that occurs in natural language, including the ambiguity surrounding homographs. Homographs are words or terms that share the same spelling. A homograph may be a homonym or a polyseme. Homonyms have different meanings and unrelated origins, whereas polysemes are usually considered to have multiple meanings.

For each term, it is necessary to provide descriptors, alternate descriptors, and other variant terms (*used for* terms) based on the principle of true synonymy. Terms that represent variant spellings, current and historical usage, various languages, and various forms of speech should be included.

The preferred term and other descriptors should be flagged. The *preferred* term is the term or name that should be automatically designated as the default term by algorithm in displays. The preferred term should be the one most commonly used in scholarly literature in the language of the catalog record. If sources disagree on the preferred form of the name or term, the source highest in the list of prioritized preferred sources should determine which name or term to use.

It is important to develop a methodology for establishing authoritative terms already in use or a means to test and validate emerging terms through usage. The use of literary warrant is recommended for validating terms and distinguishing them from a word or words used in a casual sense. To establish literary warrant, the term should be found in scholarly authoritative literature or reference sources; the usage of the term should consistently refer to the same concept in the sources. Use these sources to establish both descriptors and variants based on common usage.

For less formal vocabularies, as in a local online retrieval system, terms may be based on *user warrant,* which takes into account the language of users. For such vocabularies, developers should look at searches in search and retrieval systems to help devise nonexpert paths to the more formal expert terminology and associated materials. *Organizational warrant* may be another informal means of establishing vocabulary terms for local use, based on the needs and conventions of the organization for which the vocabulary is being developed.

7.4.1.1. Capitalization

The controlled vocabulary should serve as an orthographic authority in addition to noting preferred terminology. An appropriate combination of capitals and lowercase letters should therefore be used in terms, as dictated by usage. Generic terms should be expressed in lowercase (e.g., *cathedral*). Proper names should be capitalized as in standard usage (e.g., *Henry de Gower*). Acronyms and initialisms are generally all uppercase (e.g., *USA*); however, common usage may dictate only an initial capital, a mixture of upper and lowercase letters (e.g., *MoMA*), or letters and numbers.

7.4.2. Regulating Hierarchical Relationships

Hierarchical relationships should be recorded consistently and with an overall logic throughout the vocabulary. Some of the most important considerations are listed below.

In order for a record to be a child of a given parent, the relationships must be logical all the way up the tree. A child that is part of a given parent must also be a narrower context for its grandparent; for example, *Luxor* is part of its parent, *Qinā* governorate; its grandparent, *Upper Egypt* region; and its great-grandparent, *Egypt.* The relationships should be logical when traversing down the tree as well.

Each subset of narrower terms clustered under a broader term should be independent and mutually exclusive in meaning. Occasionally, meanings may overlap (although they are not identical) among siblings, but this should be avoided when possible. For example, the two children of *municipal buildings, moot halls* and *town halls,* are sometimes considered synonymous, so their meanings overlap. Ideally, this overlap should be captured in an associative relationship.

All records in the same branch of the hierarchy should refer to the same class of things, actions, properties, or other topics. That is, every *subordinate* term should refer to the same kind of concept as its *superordinate* term. For example, *photographs* are objects, and subordinate terms to photographs should be objects as well (e.g., *aerial photographs*). A term for a photographic technique such as *dye toning* should not be under the object term *photographs;* instead, *dye toning* would be better placed under *photographic techniques.* Associative relationships may be used to link objects such as *photographs* to related processes and techniques, but the object and the technique should be organized separately in the hierarchical structure.

7.4.2.1. Mixing Relationships

Ideally, a given vocabulary uses predominantly one type of hierarchical relationship throughout: whole/part, genus/species, or instance. If relationships are mixed in a single vocabulary, the relationship should be flagged for clarity, using codes prescribed in the ISO and NISO standards for thesaurus construction (BTP and NTP for partitive, BTG and NTG for generic, and BTI and NTI for instance relationships). The following is an example of mixed hierarchical relationships, with corresponding codes:

dresses
  BTG main garments
  NTP bodices
  NTP skirts
  NTG gowns
  NTG sheath dresses

7.4.2.2. Incorporating Facets and Guide Terms

One way to achieve a consistent and harmonious arrangement in a medium-sized or large vocabulary is to structure the hierarchies using facets and guide terms.

Facets, also known as *faceted displays,* group the records into broad classes according to various criteria that make sense for the vocabulary. For example, the *AAT* includes facets for activities, objects, materials, agents (people), styles, physical attributes, and abstract concepts. A facet contains a homogeneous class of concepts, the members of which share characteristics that distinguish them from members of other classes. For example, in the *AAT, marble* refers to a substance used in the creation of art and architecture and is placed in the Materials Facet. *Impressionist* denotes a visually distinctive style of art and is placed in the Styles and Periods Facet. Rather than using facets with this type of topic designation, vocabularies sometimes use geographic or temporal facets.

The tree structure of hierarchical vocabularies often descends from the *root,* which is the single highest level of the hierarchical structure. The facets are located directly below the root, as with the Objects

Fig. 42. Partial display of *photographs* in the *AAT* Objects Facet, illustrating the various levels of hierarchical display, including facets and guide terms (in angled brackets).

Top of the AAT hierarchies
.... Objects Facet
.... Visual and Verbal Communication
.... Visual Works (Hierarchy Name)
.... <visual works (Guide Term)>
.... <visual works by medium or technique>
.... photographs
.... <photographs by form>
.... negatives (photographic)
.... positives (photographs)
.... <photographs by form: color>
.... <photographs by form: format>
.... <photographs by function>
.... documentary photographs
.... forensic photographs
.... identification photographs
.... news photographs
.... <photographs by technique>
.... <photographs by picture-taking technique>
.... <photographs by processing or presentation technique>
.... <photographs by subject type>
.... astrophotographs
.... fashion photographs
.... film stills
.... frame enlargements
.... psychic photographs
.... spirit photographs
.... studio portraits

Facet in the example from the *AAT* above. Each facet may have one or more additional levels, known as *subfacets* or *hierarchies.* In the example above, Visual Works is a subfacet.

Guide terms, also known as *node labels,* are levels that collocate similar sets or classes of records as necessary (illustrated in the example above with angled brackets). They should logically illustrate the principles of division among a set of sibling terms, as with levels dividing a long list of types of photographs by form, function, technique, and subject in the example above. They should be consistent with other divisions in the same or a similar hierarchy. Guide terms may represent the instance relationship in a vocabulary that otherwise comprises either whole/part or genus/species relationships.

It is advisable to avoid making overly complex divisions that cause unnecessary complexity in the structure; such divisions hinder the ability of end users to access the data through browsing the hierarchies, in addition to making parent strings (hierarchical context displayed in horizontal format) unwieldy and difficult to read. In the example above, the *AAT* has used a large number of guide terms in the hierarchy to provide an orderly arrangement of a large number of types of photographs. If the number of types of photographs had been small, the guide term subdivisions would have been unnecessary.

Guide terms should not be used for indexing or cataloging. In displays, they should be enclosed in angled brackets (e.g., *<photographs by technique>*), italicized, or otherwise visually distinguished from terms that are intended for indexing.

7.5. Displaying a Controlled Vocabulary

Display issues relate to the choice of fields or subfields and how data is presented to different users. Issues of display relate to how vocabulary terms and other controlled information are displayed in a work record (i.e., the record containing information for the object being described) for certain groups of end users. A separate issue, discussed here, concerns how to display data in the controlled vocabulary itself.

7.5.1. Display for Various Types of Users

The display of a controlled vocabulary should anticipate the requirements of various types of users. Controlled vocabulary developers should ideally create different views of the vocabulary for different classes of users.

Creators: Vocabulary creators and those responsible for the maintenance of the vocabulary require access to complete information about each term and the ability to edit and add terms, relationships, and other information. They are typically experts in the subject domain of the controlled vocabulary. They require access to the revision history of the records and other administrative information that is not displayed to other users of a controlled vocabulary.

Indexers: Indexers and expert searchers typically have expertise in the subject domain of the controlled vocabulary. They require the ability to search and view equivalence, hierarchical, and associative relationships as well as definitions, dates, and notes for terms. They must have a way of suggesting or adding new terminology when the existing terms do not meet their needs.

End users: End users of the controlled vocabulary are typically unfamiliar with the jargon and complexities of thesaurus construction and online information retrieval. They probably do not understand the conventions of controlled vocabulary notation (e.g., BT, NT, UF, AD). They may have expertise in the subject area and understand its terminology. In other cases, end users are the general public, who do not have subject expertise and may need to come to the pertinent vocabulary terms for their queries through more common language or by browsing through hierarchies.

The types of displays and documentation available to indexers can be useful to end users as well, when designed with their needs in mind. End users may benefit from on-screen instructions in addition to any printed documentation that may exist.

7.5.2. Technical Considerations

The information in controlled fields is not always user-friendly, because it may need to be structured in a way that facilitates retrieval or machine manipulation (required for sorting, arithmetic calculations, etc.). Information intended for display, however, should be in a format that is easily read and understood by users.

Information for display may, in some cases, be expressed in a free-text field; in other cases, it may be concatenated or otherwise displayed from controlled fields. If the controlled terms are self-explanatory, they can be displayed as they are or concatenated with other terms. For example, a preferred geographic name and the broader hierarchical contexts for the place may be drawn from hierarchically linked records and concatenated for display.

7.5.2.1. Display Independent of Database Design

As far as possible, display or technical constraints should not drive the database design. When planning a database design and the rules for data entry, immediate display demands should not dictate database structure or data entry practice. How information displays in one context should be secondary to consistent and accurate compiling of data. Allowing local display issues or the limitations of a particular computer system to drive how a database is designed or how information is inputted may offer short-term solutions to some problems but will make it more difficult to migrate and share vocabulary data in the long term.

When vocabularies are used in an application for indexing or retrieval, the application must deal with issues surrounding how to gain access to the vocabulary data itself, how to display vocabulary data, and how to apply vocabulary data in a query across target resources. In applications that provide access to the vocabularies, users should be allowed to find the names and other information associated with a concept by either spelling a term or browsing through hierarchies and alphabetical lists.

7.5.3. Characteristics of Displays

Designing a good display is critical. Catalogers' or other users' willingness and ability to use the vocabulary are dependent upon how well they can understand and find terms. There are several types of possible displays, ranging from simple alphabetical listings to complex graphical displays. It is often desirable to provide multiple views of the vocabulary, including hierarchical displays, full record displays, and search results displays. Various methods of display, typography, capitalization, sorting, and arrangement of the data on the page or screen can be used to make terms easy to find and understand.

Usability and accessibility standards should be applied rigorously to all controlled vocabulary display designs. User interface design should take into consideration accessibility issues for people with disabilities, which is a growing area of research and standardization.

7.5.3.1. Format of Display

Controlled vocabularies may be delivered in print or electronic formats. Electronic formats allow greater versatility in searching and displays, including Web functionalities such as hyperlinking that are not available in print format.

7.5.3.2. Documentation

Vocabulary creators should provide user documentation for the controlled vocabulary, explaining the scope, development process, structure, basic rules for construction, and how to use the vocabulary.

Separate documentation may be desirable for vocabulary creators, indexers, and searchers. With controlled vocabularies that are published in print form, this documentation should be part of the introductory material. If the controlled vocabulary is available online, the user documentation should also be available online, with the possibility to download and print it. In software applications, the documentation may be available as in-context online help.

Comprehensive supporting documentation should include the following: the purpose of the controlled vocabulary; its scope, including the subject area covered and what is excluded; the meaning of conventions, abbreviations, and any punctuation marks used in nonstandard ways; and the rules and authorities to be used in selecting the preferred forms of terms and in establishing their relationships. The following should be noted: if the vocabulary complies with a national or international standard for controlled vocabulary construction; the total number of terms and records; the dates and policy for releasing updates; the contact information of the responsible organization to which comments and suggestions should be sent; and any special online navigation conventions or searching options.

7.5.3.3. Displaying Hierarchies

Thesauri, taxonomies, and any vocabularies with established relationships between records should include a hierarchical display that illustrates the relationships. A primary consideration for displays includes how to represent the relationships, whether through notation codes, indentation, or other graphical displays.

7.5.3.3.1. Indentation vs. Notations

In a flat display, which is often used in printed publications, the hierarchical relationships of thesauri may be indicated with relationship notations, such as BT (broader term), NT (narrower term), and UF (*used for* term), as in the examples below.

bobbin lace
BT lace
NT Antwerp lace
NT Brussels lace
NT Chantilly lace
NT duchesse lace

Fig. 43. *Chantilly lace* (detail), the subject of this print, is a type of *bobbin lace*. This parent/child relationship must be clear in a thesaural display.

William Henry Fox Talbot (English, 1800–1877); *Lace*; 1841/1846; salt print from a photogenic drawing negative; image (irregular): 22.7 × 18.7 cm ($8\frac{15}{16} \times 7\frac{3}{8}$ inches), sheet (irregular): 22.9 × 18.9 cm ($9 \times 7\frac{7}{16}$ inches); J. Paul Getty Museum (Los Angeles, California); 2003.495.

The flat format has the disadvantage of typically allowing only one level of narrower terms and broader terms to be shown with clarity. This means that if any of the narrower terms have further levels of narrower terms, they are not displayed under the ancestor broader term, making the full extent of relationships difficult to visualize. In some notational displays, multiple levels of narrower terms are displayed with traditional notations and rudimentary indentation as well as numbers to list multiple levels of narrower terms, as in the example below.

lace (needlework)
UF lacework
UF dentelle (lace)
BT needlework (visual works)
  NT1 bobbin lace
    NT2 Antwerp lace
    NT2 Brussels lace (bobbin lace)
    NT2 Chantilly lace
    NT2 duchesse lace
  NT1 needle lace
    NT2 Armenian lace
    NT2 Battenberg lace
    NT2 Brussels lace (needlepoint)
    NT2 Venetian lace
      NT3 Alençon lace
      NT3 Burano lace
      NT3 point de neige
      NT3 point plat de Venise
      NT3 punto a relievo
      NT3 rose point

The fully realized indented hierarchy tree display as shown in the example on the opposite page is more user-friendly than relationship notation codes, because the significance of indentation as a broader/narrower context indicator is familiar to most end users and requires no knowledge of specialized jargon. Even for expert users, indentation is often clearer and more easily understood at a glance.

Broader/narrower relationships may be indicated with indentation representing a tree structure. In an automated presentation, levels may be expanded or collapsed by using a file folder symbol or another sign (such as the hierarchy tree sign in the example). It is recommended to always display the top of the hierarchy and all levels of ancestors so that the user has a clear notion of where the terms are placed in the full hierarchy.

Fig. 44. Example of the *AAT* indented hierarchical display for *bobbin lace.*

```
Top of the AAT hierarchies
.... Objects Facet
........ Visual and Verbal Communication
............ Visual Works (Hierarchy Name)
................ <visual works (Guide Term)>
.................... <visual works by medium or technique>
........................ needlework (visual works)
............................ lace (needlework)
................................ bobbin lace
.................................... Antwerp lace
.................................... Brussels lace (bobbin lace)
........................................ Angleterre lace
.................................... Chantilly lace
.................................... duchesse lace
.................................... Lille lace
.................................... Torchon lace
.................................... Valenciennes
```

7.5.3.3.2. Alternative Hierarchical Displays

Algorithms may be established to allow display of the hierarchy by different languages or by other alternative displays. For example, if the language or other information is flagged in the data, this data may be used to establish alternative displays for the hierarchy. In the examples on the following page, the *TGN* is displayed with English names as the default (when there is an English name; otherwise it defaults to the vernacular), and the alternate display includes the vernacular name (local language of the place, transliterated into the Roman alphabet) for all places below the continent. The user may toggle back and forth between English or vernacular displays. The base language of the *TGN* is English, but terms and scope notes may be expressed and flagged in any language.

7.5.3.3.3. Display of Polyhierarchy

If a record has multiple parents, and if that record also has children, the children must display with the parent in all hierarchical views. Thus, these children must fit logically with not only their immediate parent but also logically belong to all of their grandparents.

When there are multiple parents, one of the parents should be flagged as a *preferred parent* to facilitate default displays and other technical requirements. When a record is displayed with a nonpreferred parent, there should be an indication alerting the end user to its status. In the *chocolate pots* example on the following pages, the nonpreferred parent relationship is indicated with an *N* in brackets, and in the second display, by a heading called *additional parents.*

Fig. 45. Examples of *TGN* displays: in one, the English name (if any) is displayed (e.g., *Cairo*); in the other, the vernacular name is displayed (e.g., *Al-Qāhirah*) for all levels below the continent.

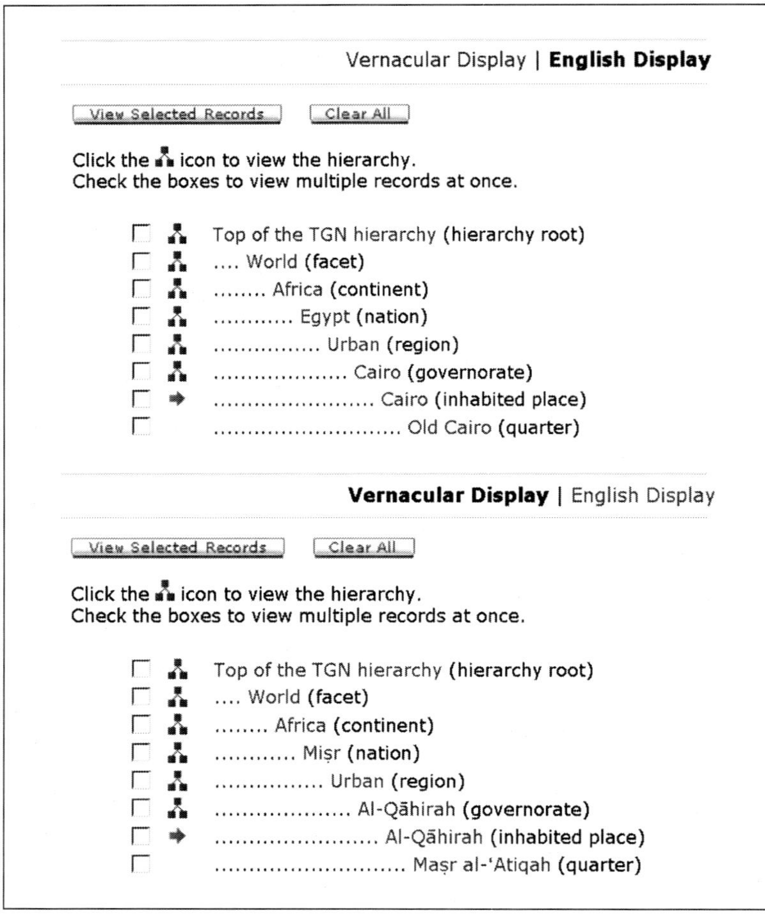

Fig. 46. Examples of *AAT* displays for *chocolate pots* with multiple parents. At the top of the figure, there is a full hierarchical display with the children displayed beside an "[N]" under a nonpreferred parent; at the bottom, there are two abbreviated hierarchical displays, with nonpreferred parents labeled *Additional Parents*.

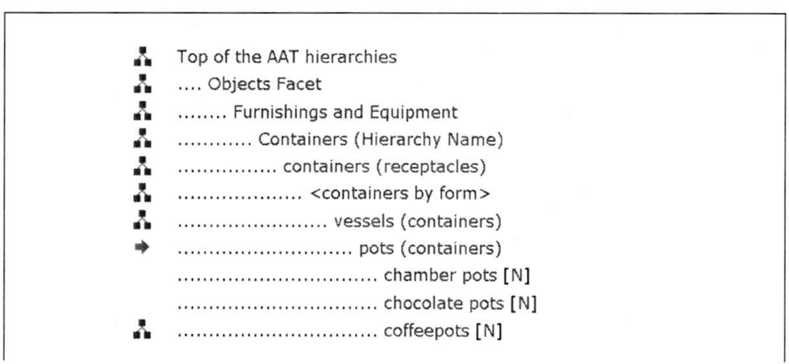

Fig. 46. (continued)

Hierarchical Position:

Objects Facet
.... Furnishings and Equipment
.... Containers (Hierarchy Name)
.... containers (receptacles)
.... <containers by function or context>
.... <culinary containers>
.... <containers for serving and consuming food>
.... <vessels for serving and consuming food>
.... <vessels for serving drinks>
.... chocolate pots

Additional Parents:

Objects Facet
.... Furnishings and Equipment
.... Containers (Hierarchy Name)
.... containers (receptacles)
.... <containers by form>
.... vessels (containers)
.... pots (containers)
.... chocolate pots

Fig. 47. Examples of the *TGN* hierarchical displays of *Azincourt,* with both current and historical parents.

Top of the TGN hierarchy **(hierarchy root)**
.... World **(facet)**
.... Europe **(continent)**
.... Flanders **(former nation/state/empire)**
.... Aalst **(inhabited place)** [N]
.... Amiens **(inhabited place)** [N]
.... Antwerp **(inhabited place)** [N]
.... Arlon **(inhabited place)** [N]
.... Arnhem **(inhabited place)** [N]
.... Arras **(inhabited place)** [N]
.... Artois **(historical region)** [N]
.... Avesnes-sur-Helpe **(inhabited place)** [N]
.... Azincourt **(inhabited place)** [N]
.... Bastogne **(inhabited place)** [N]
.... Besançon **(inhabited place)** [N]
.... Blankenberge **(inhabited place)** [N]
.... Boulogne **(inhabited place)** [N]
.... Bouvines **(inhabited place)** [N]
.... Bruges **(inhabited place)** [N]

Hierarchical Position:

World (facet)
.... Europe (continent)
.... France (nation)
.... Nord-Pas-de-Calais (region)
.... Pas-de-Calais (department)
.... Azincourt (inhabited place)

Additional Parents:

World (facet)
.... Europe (continent)
.... Flanders (former nation/state/empire) (H)
.... Azincourt (inhabited place) (H)

...... to Flanders at various times during medieval period; was part of the area ceded to France in the 17th and 18th centuries

Historical relationships may be included; dates may be used to circumscribe the duration of the relationship. In the example from the *TGN* on the previous page, a historical flag (indicated by the letter *H*) and a natural-language display date (*to Flanders at various times*) appear in the hierarchical display. See **Chapter 4: Vocabularies for Cultural Objects** for more information about dates for relationships.

7.5.3.3.4. Sorting of Siblings

Siblings in hierarchical displays are generally arranged alphabetically. They may also be arranged chronologically or in another logical order, if it is deemed to be more intuitive for the user.

Special coding of siblings may be necessary to enforce a special sorting order. In the example below, a sort order number is included to force sorting in an order other than alphabetical. The sort order was established manually by an editor, who used a chronological sequence to guide the ordering.

Fig. 48. Examples of various methods for sorting siblings in the *AAT* and *TGN*, including alphabetically, chronologically, and spacially (by distance from the sun).

AAT sorted alphabetically

- engineering
  - aerospace engineering
    - aeronautical engineering
  - bioengineering
    - biomedical engineering
  - ceramic engineering
  - chemical engineering
  - civil engineering
    - environmental engineering
    - hydraulic engineering
    - structural engineering
    - traffic engineering
    - transportation engineering (civil engineering)
  - computer-aided engineering
  - electrical engineering
    - electrochemistry [N]
    - electronic engineering
  - industrial engineering

AAT sorted chronologically

- Imperial (Roman)
  - Early Imperial
  - Augustan
  - Julio-Claudian
  - Flavian
  - Trajanic
  - Hadrianic
  - Antonine
  - Severan
  - Tetrarchic [N]
  - Constantinian [N]

Fig. 48. (continued)

***TGN* sorted spatially**

.... Solar System (solar system)
.... Sun (star)
.... Mercury (planet)
.... Venus (planet)
.... Earth (planet)
.... Mars (planet)
.... Jupiter (planet)
.... Saturn (planet)
.... Uranus (planet)
.... Neptune (planet)
.... Pluto (dwarf planet)
.... Ceres (dwarf planet)
.... Eris (dwarf planet)
.... Quaoar (planetary body)
.... Sedna (planetary body)

Fig. 49. Nonalphabetical order for selected siblings is created through Sort Order numbers in the *AAT* editorial system.

<ancient Italian periods> 300107305
Roman (ancient Italian
Republican
Sullan
Caesarian
Late Republican

Subject Sort Order for Republican

Subject ID	Sort Order	Term
300107343	1	Sullan
300107341	2	Caesarian
300020540	3	Late Republican

7.5.3.3.5. Faceted Displays and Guide Terms

The display of records may be organized according to the broad categories or facets. Facets may have a further hierarchical arrangement as well so that narrower facets are arranged within broader categories.

Top of the AAT hierarchies
  Styles and Periods Facet
    Styles and Periods
      <styles and periods by region>
        <The Americas>
          <American regions>
            Central American
            Caribbean
            North American
            South American
          Pre-Columbian

Guide terms (*node labels*) are used to group both narrower and related terms into categories. Guide terms are not used for indexing but only for collocation of terms within a controlled vocabulary. They should be displayed in a way to distinguish them from terms representing concepts (*postable terms*). The recommended method for distinguishing guide terms is placing them in angled brackets.

7.5.3.3.6. Classification Notation or Line Number

In a tree structure, each term may be assigned a classification notation or line number, often built from the top down. When a hierarchical classification scheme is applied to such a tree structure, the notation may be inhospitable to interpolation at any level. A notation scheme consisting entirely of either letters or numbers is less versatile than a mixed alphanumeric notation. Computer-generated or human-assigned line numbers may be easily revised when terms are added, but the notation will not reflect the levels of hierarchy. See also **Chapter 4: Vocabularies for Cultural Objects** for a discussion of *Iconclass,* which is an example of an alphanumeric classification system that can be displayed as a hierarchy.

Fig. 50. Example from the *AAT* where guide terms under *paint* are distinguished from concepts (postable terms) by angled brackets.

.... paint
.... <paint by composition or origin>
.... aluminum paint
.... enamel paint
.... encaustic paint
.... metallic paint
.... oil paint (pigmented coating)
.... red oxide (paint)
.... silicate paint
.... synthetic resin paint
.... water-base paint
.... <paint by function>
.... artist's color
.... concrete paint
.... deck paint
.... house paint
.... industrial paint
.... <paint by property>
.... antifouling paint
.... chemical-resistant paint
.... fire-retardant paint

Fig. 51. Examples of classification notations (e.g., V.RD) for the upper levels of the *AAT* hierarchical structure.

V	**OBJECTS FACET**	
	Built Environment	
V.RD		Settlements and Landscapes
V.RG		Built Complexes and Districts
V.RK		Single Built Works
V.RM		Open Spaces and Site Elements
	Furnishings and Equipment	
V.TC		Furnishings
V.TE		Costume
V.TH		Tools and Equipment
V.TK		Weapons and Ammunition
V.TN		Measuring Devices
V.TQ		Containers
V.TT		Sound Devices
V.TV		Recreational Artifacts
V.TX		Transportation Vehicles

7.5.3.4. Full Record Display

Full record displays (also called *term detail displays*) include complete details for each record, including equivalence, associative, and hierarchical relationships as well as scope notes, sources, and other related information. In print formats, the term detail display is typically incorporated into the hierarchical display. In electronic formats, users should be able to select a term from any display type and see an expanded view of the detail for that record. Web implementations of controlled vocabularies may include a hyperlink from the term, wherever it appears, to the full term detail display. The user should be able to mark multiple records and view them together for comparison.

7.5.3.5. Displaying Equivalence and Associative Relationships

Relationships between terms in a record (equivalence relationships) and between records (associative relationships, or nonhierarchical relationships) should be clearly designated to users. It should be obvious to the user which terms are descriptors, as distinguished from alternate descriptors and other variant terms (called *used for* terms). The types and number of associative relationships should be evident.

Many controlled vocabularies use standard thesaural notations to express relationships between synonyms and related terms. Equivalence relationships may be expressed in a list, using notations for term type (e.g., *D, AD, UF*). In printed indexes, *see references* may be used. The standard thesaural notation for associative relationships is *RT,* for *related term* (*term* actually refers to a record, not just a single term).

aerial perspective
SEE **atmospheric perspective**

aerial photographs
AD aerial photograph
UF air photographs
UF air photos
RT bird's-eye views
BT <photographs by picture-taking technique>

aerials
SEE **antennas**

As is true for hierarchical relationships, displays that use the standard thesaural notations illustrated above for equivalence and associative relationships will likely be difficult for nonexperts to use. A more user-friendly display labels information in a way that both experts and nonexperts can understand. In the examples below, indications of term type are still included, but in a display that is easier for nonexperts to interpret (e.g., users can click on the hyperlink for a definition of *used for* term), along with language and other information about the term.

Terms
aerial photographs *(preferred, descriptor, English-preferred)*
aerial photograph *(alternate descriptor, English)*
air photographs *(used for term, English)*
air photos *(used for term, English)*
photographs, aerial *(used for term, English)*
photographies aériennes *(descriptor, French-preferred)*
photographie aérienne *(alternate descriptor, French)*

Related concepts
distinguished from. . . . aerial views
. . . . (<views by vantage point or orientation>, views (visual works), . . . Visual and Verbal Communication) [300015527]
distinguished from. . . . astrophotographs
. . . . (<photographs by subject type>, photographs, . . . Visual and Verbal Communication) [300134468]
distinguished from. . . . bird's-eye views
. . . . (<views by vantage point or orientation>, views (visual works), . . . Visual and Verbal Communication) [300015529]

distinguished from. . . . space photographs . . . . (<photographs by picture-taking technique>, <photographs by technique>, . . . Visual and Verbal Communication) [300246214]

7.5.3.5.1. Permuted Lists and Inverted Forms

Some controlled vocabularies include an auxiliary permuted or rotated list that gives access to every word in all the terms. In other words, a permuted display lists each compound term multiple times in the alphabetic sequence of the controlled vocabulary, once for each of the words in the term. A permuted listing is often useful in a printed product, but it is not needed for online displays, given that the terms may be found by keyword searching and other searching utilities. Furthermore, caution must be taken because automatically generated permuted displays may result in combinations that are misleading and incorrect. For example, the term *library science* appears as *science—library* in a permuted list, which may easily be misconstrued as a different concept.

Useful term inversions differ from a simple permuted list in that editors create the term inversions based on the need and appropriateness of such terms. Useful inversions should be included as *used for* terms, whereas a full permuted listing should not.

7.5.3.5.2. Displaying Homographs

Homographs are terms or names that are spelled alike but have different meanings. Homographs must be distinguished in displays.

One method is to disambiguate the term with a *qualifier*, which is a word or brief phrase. In many thesauri, the qualifier is included in the same field as the term, distinguished from the term by punctuation or formatting. A more versatile implementation is to put the qualifier in a separate field, as in the example below. If the term field

Fig. 52. Examples of qualifiers for *drums* in the *AAT*. The qualifiers are recorded in separate fields in the editorial system and presented in parentheses adjacent to the terms for end-user display.

***AAT* editorial system**

#	P	H	T	V	Terms/Names	Qualifier
1	P	C	D	U	drums	walls
2	V	C	AD	U	drum	wall

***AAT* end-user-display**

Terms:

drums (walls) (**preferred**,C,D,U,English-P)
drum (wall) (C,AD,U,English)

is dedicated to the term only, it allows implementers to decide whether or not to include the qualifier in retrieval. The qualifier should, however, be displayed with the term for end users (as in the second example on the previous page). It is customary to display the qualifier in parentheses following the term (e.g., *drums (walls)*).

7.5.3.5.3. Sorting and Alphabetizing Terms

Terms consisting of alphabetic characters may be sorted *word-by-word* or *letter-by-letter*. Word-by-word sorting is familiar to users from alphabetized telephone directories. In word-by-word sorting, a space is significant (it is also called *nothing before something filing*); it keeps together terms that begin with the same word.

However, a disadvantage of word-by-word filing is that it separates compound words (e.g., *bookbinding*) from compound terms, which are terms consisting of two words (e.g., *book jackets*). Letter-by-letter sorting alleviates this problem. At its most effective, letter-by-letter sorting is performed on terms that have been normalized so that spaces, punctuation, diacritics, and capitalization are ignored (the normalized terms are stored in a table separate from the exact term strings and are generally not seen by end users). Letter-by-letter sorting is familiar to users from dictionaries. With either method, parenthetical qualifiers should be ignored in sorting; that is, terms with qualifiers should not be sorted in the same way as compound terms.

Below is an example of word-by-word sorting:

> book catalogs
> book cloth (textile material)
> book cupboards
> bookbinding
> bookcases
> bookends

Below is an example of letter-by-letter sorting:

> bookbinding
> bookcases
> book catalogs
> book cloth (textile material)
> book cupboards
> bookends

Resources such as the *American Library Association Filing Rules, Library of Congress Filing Rules,* and *British Standard Alphabetical Arrangement and the Filing Order of Numerals and Symbols* (*BS 1749*) contain rules for sorting and filing. However, these standards are not always compatible with each other. Electronic systems may enforce pre-established sorting rules and handling of nonalphabetic characters, while other systems provide options for developers to select the sorting rules.

7.5.3.5.4. Diacritics in Sorting

A typical database requires implementers to identify one—and only one—language for the data; the system applies pre-established sorting algorithms based on that language. However, the vocabularies discussed in this book include terms and names in many languages. Even when limiting the discussion to only the Roman alphabet, different languages have different rules for sorting characters with diacritics.

Since it is impossible to create a sorting rule that recognizes diacritics while still obeying rules of alphabetization for all languages, and since most Web users are accustomed to seeing terms and names sorted by standard ASCII characters without special weighting of diacritics, normalized diacritics should be used for sorting. For example, users expect to see all words beginning with the letter *A* sorted together in alphabetic displays—not those with accents or umlauts sorted before or after the rest of the *A*s.

Normalization of diacritics by mapping them to ASCII characters in the Roman alphabet is the most practical way to deal with diacritics in sorting. If multiple alphabets are used in Unicode or another encoding scheme, the issues are even more complex. Normalization of diacritics for retrieval and sorting is discussed in **Chapter 9: Retrieval Using Controlled Vocabularies.**

Fig. 53. Example of a results list in which diacritics, spaces, punctuation, case, and qualifiers are ignored in the sorting of *AAT* terms.

1. **Alā'-ad-Dīn Khalīl**
   (Qaramanid, <Anatolian Islamic styles and periods after Manzikert>, .
2. **Alabama limestone**
   (oolitic limestone, <limestone by composition: aggregate type>, ... M
3. **alabaster (mineral)**
   (gypsum, mineral, ... Materials) [300011101]
4. **alabastra**
   (<containers for personal grooming and hygiene>, <containers for pe
5. **alae**
   (alcoves, <rooms and spaces by form>, ... Components (Hierarchy N
6. **Alago**
   (<Benue River region styles>, <Niger-Congo language groups styles
7. **Alamannic**
   (Germanic, <Migration period styles>, ... Styles and Periods) [300019
8. **alamedas**
   (promenades (walkways), walkways, ... Built Environment (Hierarchy
9. **Alani**
   (Sarmatian, <Northern Steppe early historic styles and periods>, ... S
10. **à la poupée**
    (<printing surface preparation techniques>, <printing techniques>, ..
11. **<Alaskan Native styles>**
    (<Arctic Native American styles>, <Arctic and Subarctic Native Ame
12. **almanacs**
    (reference sources, <document genres by function>, ... Visual and V

7.5.3.5.5. Display of Diacritics

The display of diacritics may necessarily differ in systems for creators and for end users of vocabularies. Full diacritics or diacritical codes should display in the system used by creators of vocabularies and indexers. Some Web applications may not be able to display all diacritics, because certain diacritics in certain fonts may not display correctly. For this reason, creators of vocabularies and indexers should avoid such applications.

It may be unavoidable to expose end users to missing diacritics, because they typically do not have access to the native data in the editorial system. If end users are using a Web interface, implementers should make sure that it displays as many of the vocabulary's diacritics as possible. Some Unicode values are specific to certain fonts, so this should guide the choice of font.

For diacritics that cannot display on the Web, one solution for end users is to display the plain ASCII character that is equivalent to the diacritic. The disadvantage of this method is that the end user cannot tell that the word is missing a diacritic, the word without a diacritic is incorrect, and this practice may result in unintentional homographs being displayed in a single record. The alternative solution is to display the terms with whatever internal symbol appears in place of the diacritic, because this at least alerts the user that a diacritic is displaying incorrectly. As Web interfaces become increasingly more sophisticated in displaying Unicode, this problem is diminishing over time.

Note that diacritics may appear not only in the term field but also in display dates, notes, and several other fields of the data.

7.5.3.6. Search Results Displays

Results of search queries should display both the terms that met the criteria of the search and an indication of the hierarchy and other context of the terms. Display of results lists is further discussed in **Chapter 9: Retrieval Using Controlled Vocabularies.**

7.5.3.6.1. Headings or Labels

Headings or labels are used in search results displays and in other displays where a brief listing of the vocabulary record is required. The heading or label is a short display that identifies the vocabulary concept, combining the term or name with additional information. Ideally, the information is recorded in separate fields and concatenated with the name or term for heading displays. In the examples on the opposite page, biographical information is used to disambiguate people with homographic names, while the broader contexts and place types (terms describing the type of place) are used to disambiguate homographic place names.

Fig. 54. Examples of headings in results list displays. At the top, an illustration of how the Library of Congress results list is generated from a MARC authority record using subfields of the 100 field. Below are *ULAN* names displaying with a short biography and *TGN* names displaying with a place type and hierarchical context.

LC Authorities

Authorized Heading 9	0	Smith, William, 1654-1705
Authorized Heading 10	1	Smith, William, 1697-1769
Authorized Heading 11	0	Smith, William, 1707-1764
Authorized Heading 12	0	Smith, William, 1711-1787
Authorized Heading 13	0	Smith, William, 1722?-1791

LC Control Number: n 91053529
HEADING: Smith, William, 1707-1764
100 10 |**a** Smith, William, |**d** 1707-1764
670 __ |**a** The Smith brothers of Chichester, c1986: |**b** p. 9 (William Smith)
670 __ |**a** BLAISE 8/90 |**b** (Smith, William, 1707-1764)
953 __ |**a** nf20

ULAN

1. **Smith, William**
(British painter, active in London 1813-1859) [500005046]

2. **Smith, William**
(English architect, 1661-1724) [500007409]

3. **Smith, William**
(English painter and printmaker, 1707-1764) [500020690]

4. **Smith, William**
(American printmaker, 1919-2000) [500122224]

5. **Smith, William**
(British artist, active 1889-1919) [500172789]

6. **Smith, William**
(British architect, 1705-1747) [500187145]

TGN

1. **Black Forest** .... (woods)
(World, Europe, Germany, Baden-Württemberg) [7005963]
Vernacular: Schwarzwald

2. **Black Forest** .... (mountain)
(World, Europe, Germany, Baden-Württemberg, Freiburg dis
Vernacular: Schwarzwald

3. **Black Forest** .... (woods)
(World, North and Central America, United States, Arizona,

4. **Black Forest** .... (inhabited place)
(World, North and Central America, United States, Colorado,

5. **Black Forest** .... (forest)
(World, North and Central America, United States, Colorado,

6. **Black Forest** .... (inhabited place)
(World, North and Central America, United States, Georgia,

7.5.3.6.2. Ascending or Descending Order of Parents

Ascending order refers to the display of hierarchical entities in a heading from smallest to largest, familiar to users in the U.S. from mailing addresses. Descending order refers to the display of hierarchical entities in a heading from largest to smallest. This display may be familiar to users from back-of-book indexes.

For the horizontal displays of hierarchical information in headings or labels, it is most user-friendly to display the parents in ascending order (e.g., *Black Forest (Paulding county, Georgia, United States)*), because this is how most users are accustomed to referring to such broader contexts in speech and print.

However, listing the parent string in descending order is useful in results lists or other displays that require meaningful sorting among homographs, because the homographs can be sorted alphabetically by parent string. In the example below, the records for *Springfield* in Africa and Europe sort alphabetically above the records in North America, with records in Canada above the records in the United States; among the subset of records in the United States, sorting is by state, then by county.

Fig. 55. Results list for the homographs *Springfield* in the *TGN* illustrating parent strings arranged in descending order to allow sorting by the parent string.

7.5.3.6.3. Displaying the User's Search Term

The results list should clearly demonstrate to the user why the results were returned. The users' search string may not necessarily match the preferred term; regardless, the term that made the match should be included in the results. It is recommended that the preferred term, the terms that matched the query, and other information (such as parent strings) be displayed to provide context.

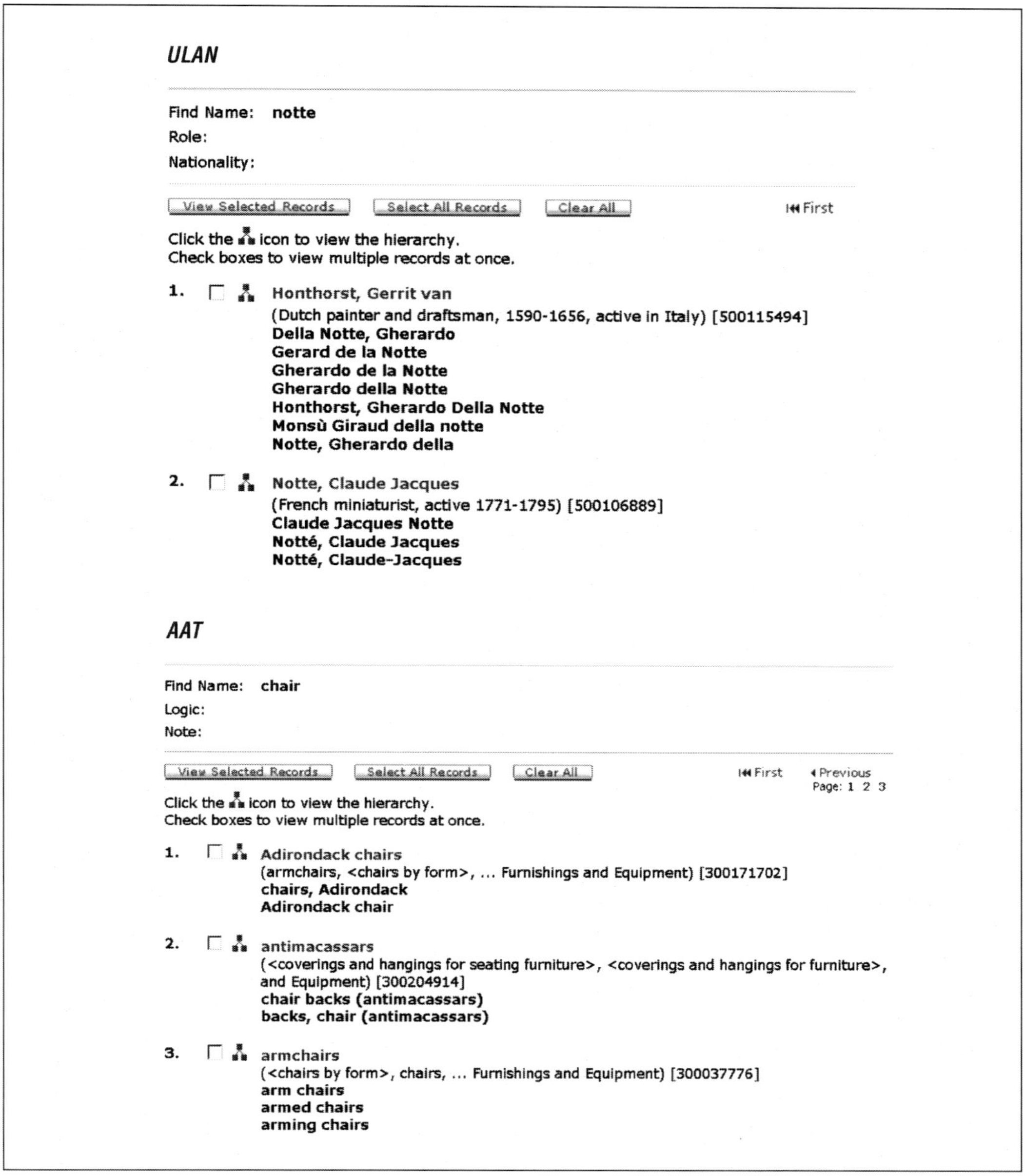

Fig. 56. Results lists from the *ULAN* and *AAT* illustrating how the terms that matched the user query for keywords—*notte* and *chair*—are displayed even when those terms are not the preferred term for the vocabulary record.

7.5.3.7. Pick Lists

Some electronic implementations of controlled vocabularies use pick lists as a way to lead users to a small set of choices of terms for a given field. These are often implemented as drop-down lists. When the user comes to a particular controlled field, a full list of choices for terminology is displayed for users to select when indexing or constructing a query. Typically, pick lists do not include synonyms, although they could be tied to larger vocabularies that include synonyms and other information for the concepts.

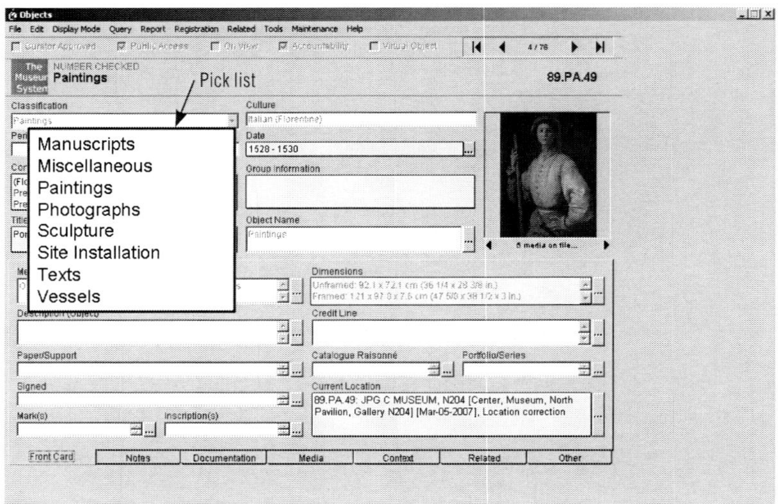

Fig. 57. Example of a pick list from The Museum System (TMS) application for the J. Paul Getty Museum.

8. Indexing with Controlled Vocabularies

In the context of this book, *indexing* is the process of evaluating information and designating indexing terms by using a controlled vocabulary that aids in finding and accessing the cultural work record. This indexing is done by human labor, as opposed to indexing resulting from the automatic parsing of data (*automatic indexing*) into a *database index*, which is used by a system to speed up search and retrieval. Indexing as described in this book is a conscious activity performed by knowledgeable catalogers who consider retrieval implications when assigning indexing terms.

8.1. Technical Issues of Indexing

When building a database and in the process of cataloging, it is important to employ the best design and editorial practice possible. However, if a cataloging or retrieval system is less than ideal, it will be necessary to adjust cataloging rules to accommodate the shortcomings of an information system or software, particularly concerning the application of controlled vocabularies and authorities.

As discussed in **Chapter 7: Constructing a Vocabulary or Authority**, it is critical to invest in both the data structure and the data used to populate the data elements in that structure; the data should survive through a succession of computer systems over time. However, in the real world of cataloging, technical concerns may limit or enhance cataloging in various ways. Ideally, the technical environment will not dictate limitations on good cataloging practice, but practice must sometimes be adjusted nonetheless. For example, if it is not possible to link to hierarchical authorities, it may be necessary for catalogers to index both specific terms and their broader contexts in each record to allow access.

8.1.1. Availability of Indexing Terms to the Cataloger

Ensuring successful indexing using a controlled vocabulary is determined in part by how the vocabulary is expressed to the cataloger or indexer. If possible, terminology should be customized for each particular field in the work record. For example, when filling in values for the Materials field, ideally, catalogers should *not* have access to the Styles and Periods terms from the *AAT*, because excluding access to extraneous terms reduces the possibility for errors in indexing. However, access to terms should not be limited too narrowly. For example, a collage or other such work may be made of other works, so terminology generally reserved for Work Type (e.g., *photograph*) may be considered a Material in a collage.

Methods for applying vocabulary in the cataloging system may range from copying and pasting from online vocabulary sources to a thorough integration of one or more vocabularies in an information system. The copy-and-paste method is easy and typically inexpensive; however, there are caveats associated with it. Most notably, by copying and pasting terms, the link to the original vocabulary record and all of its variant terms and associated information is lost. In addition, it is not possible to automatically update the records in the future as the vocabulary changes over time. Integrating a controlled vocabulary into the editorial or cataloging system is a much more efficient way of incorporating vocabularies, either through the use of local authorities or by including the published controlled vocabularies in their entirety. Incorporating the vocabularies in the software allows access to variant terms and the unique numeric identifiers of the vocabulary, which accommodate updates to the terms in the system when the published controlled vocabularies issue updates.

Ideally, the system should allow the cataloger to use the preferred or any variant term in the same authority record to refer to the concept. In order to facilitate this, unique identifiers may be assigned to the individual terms, in addition to the unique identifier for the overall concept record.

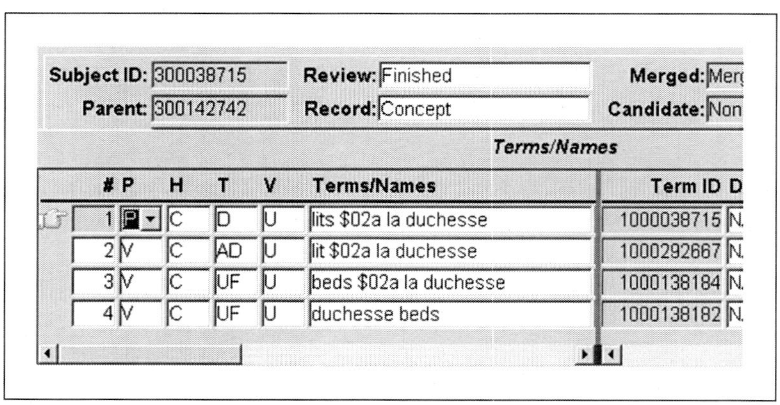

Fig. 58. *AAT* terms in an editorial system illustrating how there are unique numeric identifiers for the overall record (Subject ID) and for each term (Term ID).

8.2. Methodologies for Indexing

Institutions should adopt rules and methodologies for indexing work records that are appropriate to their collections and priorities.

8.2.1. Indexing Display Information

Retrieval issues should be considered when assigning terms and values to controlled fields. All important information contained in a free-text display field should be indexed in a controlled field to provide good access to the information. Display fields should generally utilize the preferred terms listed in index fields for consistency, especially if both are visible to end users. Display and indexing issues are defined in **Chapter 2: What Are Controlled Vocabularies?**

Display materials/technique (free-text):
brown ink and brown wash over black chalk underdrawing on white laid paper, with squaring, for an engraving

Indexing fields (repeating, controlled):
Material Names:
ink **Role:** medium
wash **Role:** medium
black chalk **Role:** medium
laid paper **Role:** support
Technique Names:
drawing
squaring
underdrawing

8.2.2. When Fields Do Not Display to End Users

Any field that contains a controlled number (e.g., Start Date), values controlled by pick lists (e.g., Preferred flag), or controlled values linked to authorities are indexing fields. Such indexing fields may or may not display to end users. If an indexing field in a work record will be displayed to end users, values that will not confuse or mislead the user should be used, not guesses or estimates based on incomplete data. For example, if a writing table seems to be constructed of a dark wood that the cataloger guesses may be walnut, the cataloger should not index the material as *walnut* without technical verification from the repository. Instead, the cataloger should index only what he or she knows, perhaps using the broad term *wood*.

Other fields may be used for searching but do not display to end users. For example, dates may be expressed in a free-text display field for end users, and indexed with Start Date and End Date fields, which do not display to end users. If fields do not display to end users but are used behind the scenes for retrieval, indexing may be done more broadly or liberally without fear of confusion. For example, for Start and End Dates, a broad span of time should be estimated, because estimating too narrowly will result in failed retrieval; however, estimating too broadly will result in some false hits in retrieval.

Display Date: ca. 1730–ca. 1750
Start: 1725 **End:** 1755

Display Date: 17th century
Start: 1600 **End:** 1699

Display Date: New Kingdom, 18th dynasty (1404–1365 BCE)
Start:–1404 **End:**–1365

8.2.3. Specificity and Exhaustivity

Applying indexing terms involves consideration of the precision and quantity of terms applied to a particular field in the work record; in cataloging, these characteristics are known as *specificity* and *exhaustivity. Specificity* refers to the degree of precision, or *granularity,* used in assigning terms. For example, the cataloger would ideally choose the most specific term to describe a work type, such as *amphora,* rather than the more general term, *storage vessel. Exhaustivity* refers to the degree of depth and breadth that the cataloger uses in description, typically expressed by using a larger number of indexing terms.

In order to ensure consistent indexing by catalogers, guidelines should be established regarding the number of terms to be assigned and the method to be used for analyzing a work to determine indexing terms for each field.

Catalog records are more valuable to researchers if they are indexed with a greater level of specificity and exhaustivity. However, practical considerations often limit the ability of cataloging institutions in assigning large numbers of terms to each field of every work record. Is it useful to index every aspect of the work? If not, where do you draw the limit?

8.2.3.1. Specificity Related to the Authority Records

Do specific details of the authority record need to be included in a work record if those topics are already part of the authority record? Generally, those aspects that are apparent, important, unusual, or particular in the work being cataloged should be indexed, even if they are also in the authority record.

One consideration is whether the particular information system being used will link a specific term to its broader context and synonyms in an authority. One primary purpose of the authority is to reduce the cataloger's labor in linking all variant names and broader contexts for a concept to every work record. However, if the authority does not do this, the broader context and synonyms in the work record should be included.

Assuming that the authority is linked to the work record, there is no need to repeat basic information, such as names. The issue is complicated by the fact that not all aspects of a given authority record will necessarily apply to the work being indexed. Even though the authority record for the subject *Adoration of the Magi* may include the names of the magi, the names of the gifts, the types of animals generally present at the scene, the symbolic significance of the scene, etc., not every depiction of the *Adoration of the Magi* will include all of these topics. Therefore, the indexing of this subject for a particular work should focus on the major aspects of the subject as portrayed in that specific work.

8.2.3.2. General and Specific Terms

In certain fields, it is advantageous to include both general and specific indexing terms, particularly when the general and specific terms are not linked hierarchically in the authorities. For example, with subject indexing, it is useful to label a general subject (e.g., *landscape* or *portrait*) for overall access, in addition to specific terms that name the location or person depicted. For example, an authority record for a geographic place is usually linked to the broader geographic contexts of that place but not to the concept of *landscape.* Without this general designation, the work cannot be retrieved in a search by general subject classification.

Subject:
- landscape
- poetry
- Longqiu Waterfall, Yandang Mountain (Zhejiang province, China)
- waterfalls
- pool
- human figures
- mountains
- clouds
- pine trees
- literati (Chinese scholars-artists)

8.2.3.3. Preferred or Variant Terms

The term that best fits the characteristic being indexed should be used. Ideally, system constraints do not require the use of only the preferred term or descriptor for indexing. This is particularly important when end users can see the terms. In some cases, a singular term may be appropriate, while in others the plural makes more sense. In other cases, the cataloger may wish to index with a *used for* term, a historical term, or a descriptor in another language. So long as all of these terms are linked to the same vocabulary concept record, the cataloger should be able to use any that fits the situation at hand.

8.2.3.4. How Many Terms

Rules regarding the number of terms to assign and the method of analysis that is most appropriate to local needs should be established. Strategies should be devised that allow catalogers to be thorough, without expending more time than necessary, so that production quotas can be met.

To ensure that the entire work is indexed evenly and consistently with other works in the collection, guidelines should be set for the catalogers to treat the work systematically. Catalogers should index by whatever is most appropriate to a given field in the work record, whether that be by moving front to back, top to bottom, most important to least important, or chronologically. For instance, they could index materials according to the level of importance of the materials or the order in which the media were applied. For example, for a table, the mahogany used as the primary material would be more important than the brass fittings on the feet; for a design drawing, the squaring in pencil would be applied before chalk outlines of figures, with the white highlighting applied last. For the subject of the work, assigning indexing terms according to the following three levels of subject analysis is appropriate: description of the generic subject, identification of the specific subject, and interpretation of symbolic meaning contained in the subject. See *CDWA* and *CCO* for further suggestions regarding how to index specific fields in the work record.

8.2.3.4.1. How to Establish Core Elements

How much information should a catalog record contain? Standards such as *CCO, CDWA,* and *VRA Core 4.0* can provide guidance for core data. Not every field in the work record needs be filled with the maximum number of indexing terms. The focus of cataloging should be twofold: promoting good access to the works, and providing clear, accurate descriptions that users will understand. This can be achieved with either a full or a minimal cataloging record, so long as the cataloger follows standards and the descriptive cataloging and indexing is consistent from one record to another.

8.2.3.4.2. Minimal Records

Minimal records contain the minimum amount of information in the minimum set of elements, as defined by the cataloging institution. What comprises a minimal work record for the institution must be decided; this includes which fields are required, which are required if known, and which are optional. All required fields must be included for every record. Even when it appears that two fields overlap, if they are both required, values should be included in both. For example, if the Subject of a utilitarian work is the same as the Work Type or Title, the term should be repeated in all required fields. Noting the values in fields or metadata elements dedicated specifically to certain content elements ensures that the data is consistently recorded and indexed in the same place, using the same conventions for all works in the database.

8.2.3.4.3. Missing Information

What should the cataloger do if core information is limited or unavailable? Occasionally, data for any element may be missing during the cataloging process. It is up to the cataloging institution to determine how to deal with missing data. Default values should be established to index unavailable but required fields, so that it is apparent to users that the data is unavailable for a particular record (as opposed to the field having simply been skipped).

Possibilities for dealing with missing data include the following: (1) using a value such as *unavailable, unknown, not applicable, destroyed;* (2) making the value NULL on the database side; or (3) leaving the field blank entirely and supplying data for missing values at the public access end (e.g., if the creator is unknown, rather than filling in the value *unknown Celtic* in the Creator field, it could be left blank in the local database but filled with the value *Celtic* from the Culture field in displays). How these defaults are implemented is a local decision that may vary from institution to institution. See also the discussion in **8.2.3.5.5. Expertise of Catalogers and Indexers.**

> **Descriptive Note:** Location unknown; formerly at Aghia Triadha (Iraklion department, Crete, Greece)
>
> **Current Location:** unknown
>
> **Former Location:** Aghia Triadha (Iraklion department, Crete, Greece)

Descriptive Note: Destroyed in 1966; formerly Gabinetto Disegni e Stampe (Uffizi, Florence, Italy)

Current Location: destroyed

Former Location: Gabinetto Disegni e Stampe (Uffizi, Florence, Italy)

8.2.3.5. Size and Focus of the Collection

The level of homogeneity of a collection may influence the specificity and exhaustivity of indexing. The more similarity there is among items in the collection, the more specific indexing terms need to be and the more granularity should be used in indexing the vocabulary or vocabularies. For example, to make meaningful distinctions between items in a specialized collection of tapestries, the terminology used to index them should be much more specific than that used for a few tapestries in a more general collection.

The size of the collection may play a role in limiting the levels of specificity and exhaustivity employed by any given institution. An institution that is cataloging a large collection may not have the need or resources to record extensive and specific information for every work. On the other hand, a small institution may be constrained by not having access to specific information; for example, a repository may not have a conservation laboratory to supply accurate analysis of materials.

8.2.3.5.1. Different Works Require Different Indexing

Different levels of specificity and exhaustivity may be dictated by the works themselves. For example, one sculpture may have been cast of a single material, so simply stating the material is sufficient (e.g., *bronze*), while another sculpture may be composed of various materials that should be indexed (e.g., *fiberglass and resin on wire mesh*).

8.2.3.5.2. Cataloging in Phases

Cataloging in phases may influence the way in which terms are assigned. An institution may index a few broad or important elements in minimal records to gain control of a collection and then go back in a second pass to add more specificity and greater numbers of terms.

8.2.3.5.3. Indexing Groups vs. Items

An archival group (or *record group*) is an aggregate of items that share a common provenance. Group-level cataloging focuses on the description of coherent, collective bodies of works. Indexing should emphasize the characteristics of the group as a whole, highlighting the unique and distinctive characteristics of the most important works in the group.

If an institution is cataloging groups of works rather than individual items, an appropriate methodology of assigning indexing terms must be established. The two most common methods are to assign terms that refer to all items in the group, or to assign terms that refer to only the most important items in the group. If the items will eventually be cataloged individually, broad terms or a miscellaneous term applicable to the group, such as *various materials,* should be assigned, and as a second step, narrower terms appropriate to individual items should be assigned in the individual item records.

Title: Group of Points from Bannerstone Site
Work Types:
arrowheads
kirk points
netting
Materials and Techniques: flint, vitric tuff, and rhyolite
Indexing Materials:
flint
tuff
rhyolite

Description: 152 design drawings and models for the East Building project that I. M. Pei & Partners gave to the archives of the National Gallery of Art in 1986.
Work Types:
design drawings
models
Materials and Techniques: various materials
Indexing Materials:
various

8.2.3.5.4. Expertise of End Users

What types of terms will the intended end users be familiar with? A major challenge for catalogers is that indexing terms should accommodate the expectations and knowledge of the intended users of the information system. Many institutions must satisfy a wide range of users, from the scholarly expert to the novice visitor to a museum Web site. Ideally, separate—but related—vocabularies would be used for indexing and retrieval; however, this is not possible for most institutions. If end users will be exposed to the original specialist vocabulary terms, rather than utilizing an intermediary vocabulary designed to bridge the gap between nonexpert and expert users, nonexpert terms should be included along with expert terms in indexing.

A collection may someday be retrieved in a consortial environment, for which the indexing terms may need to be broader or narrower than in a local environment. Indexing terms will need to be specific enough to allow the records to remain meaningful in the context of a larger information repository.

8.2.3.5.5. Expertise of Catalogers and Indexers

The indexing and other content of work records necessarily reflect the level of subject expertise of the catalogers. Catalogers may not be experts on the works being cataloged. In general, catalogers of visual resources collections and others who are cataloging works not held in their own institution do not have access to some information about the work.

8.2.4. Indexing Uncertain Information

It is desirable to be specific, so a good general rule is, if you know something, include it. However, an equally important axiom is this: if you do not know, do not guess.

Data should only be indexed when authoritative sources for the information are available. It is important to consider the reliability and idiosyncrasies of the sources and to analyze what is true and what is only possibly or probably true. When important information is described as uncertain by reliable sources, the information may still be recorded, but with an indication of uncertainty or approximation in a Descriptive (Scope) Note or Display Date field (e.g., *ca.* or *probably*).

Materials/Techniques Description: probably soft paste porcelain
Indexing Material Name: soft paste porcelain

Catalogers should never use a specific term unless they have the research, documentation, or expertise to support that use. A broader but accurate term should be used in place of an incorrect specific term. It is better to be general and correct than specific and incorrect. For example, a cataloger should index the broader material *stone* rather than the specific *banded slate* if he or she is unsure of the specific material. Rules should be established regarding default values for required elements for which no information is available.

Another option is to index multiple values for uncertain information, explaining any ambiguity and nuance in display fields. For example, if scholarly opinion is divided regarding whether a figure represents *Zeus* or *Poseidon,* the names of both gods should be indexed as subjects for retrieval, and the situation should be explained in a note. If sources disagree about whether an artist was French or Flemish, index both nationalities and explain the discrepancy in a note.

Display biography: French or Flemish draftsman, active by 1423, died 1464
Nationalities:
French
Flemish

Descriptive Note: It is uncertain if the work was used as a table or a stool.
Work Type:
furniture
table
stool

Fig. 59. If the cataloger is uncertain of information, such as the composition of the upholstery fabric of a piece of furniture, it is better to choose an indexing term that is broad and correct than to use a specific term that is wrong (e.g., use *cloth* rather than *silk*). For the chair illustrated here, the repository has done analysis, and the specific material is indeed known.

Frames: attributed to François-Honoré-Georges-Jacob-Desmalter (French, 1770–1841); upholstery: Beauvais Tapestry Manufactory (French, founded 1664); *Armchair (Bergère);* ca. 1810; mahogany and beech, with gilt-bronze mounts, silk and wool tapestry upholstery; J. Paul Getty Museum (Los Angeles, California); 67.DA.6.

8.2.4.1. Knowable vs. Unknowable Information

There is a difference between *knowable* and *unknowable* information: one refers to information that is simply unknown to the cataloger due to lack of expertise or access to research and publications, while the other refers to information that is debated among scholars or unknown despite expert analysis. To maintain high-quality, reliable, and professional catalog records that are in keeping with standard art historical practice, this distinction should be kept clearly in mind during indexing.

8.2.4.1.1. Knowable Information

For information that is *knowable* but simply unknown by the cataloger, a more general term should be used or the information should be omitted. Most catalogers are not experts on all the works they catalog, but information in a catalog record should only be supplied by experts and authoritative sources. When a lack of knowledge is due to ignorance regarding a particular issue, the cataloger's assumptions should not be indexed. In such cases, terms such as *probably* or *perhaps* should not be used, because this would imply that scholars or other experts are uncertain.

For example, if a source describes the material of a Louis XVI chair as *gilded beechwood* but does not identify the material of the upholstery, the upholstery should not be indexed as *silk* or even described as *probably silk,* even if it appears to be so. The fiber content of that upholstery is knowable by technical analysis and perhaps may even be published in other sources. If an end user were to read *probably silk,* he or she should be able to assume that technical analysis was inconclusive or impossible, not that a cataloger was making a guess. In this case, it would be best to index *gilding* and *beechwood* but avoid indexing or describing the upholstery at all, because there is no source of information for the upholstery.

8.2.4.1.2. Debated Information

For information that is *unknowable* because current authoritative sources indicate that scholars disagree, the historical or archaeological information is incomplete, or interpretation of the information differs in reliable sources, multiple possibilities should be indexed with words such as *probably* or *perhaps* in a note explaining the ambiguity or uncertainty of prevailing authoritative sources.

When sources are in disagreement, the preferred information is that which is supported by general scholarly opinion or found in the most recent authoritative sources. If scholarly opinion is evenly split or both sources are equally reliable, neither view can be preferred; the debate should be explained in a note and both possibilities should be indexed.

9. Retrieval Using Controlled Vocabularies

Vocabulary resources, with their synonyms, hierarchical structures, and other conceptual relationships, can provide extremely powerful tools for retrieval across disparate data resources residing in different places and even in different languages, enabling users to obtain meaningful results in their online searches. It only remains for those whose mission is to deliver high-quality information to tap the vocabularies' immense potential.

Of all the information in a catalog record for an art object, the fields for the names of people, places, and things are the most obvious targets where vocabularies should be used in retrieval. Terms and names used to index art and cultural heritage information can vary widely, even when the same concept is being referenced.

In retrieval, users do not always know what a person, place, or thing is called. Nonexpert users often do not know the term used by a specialist to index a work. For example, an expert would call a particular vessel a *rhyton,* but a nonexpert would call it a *drinking horn* or even a generic *vessel* (if they did not know the purpose of the vessel). A controlled vocabulary allows such users to browse or search for data using familiar terms or other criteria in order to discover relevant information. Expert users will know the specialized terms for a work, but different specialists may use different terms to refer to the same person, place, or thing. Thus, no matter who the user is, vocabularies are critical in gathering these equivalent terms, relationships, and other information together and using them to launch searches across disparate data sets or even within a single database.

9.1. Identifying the Focus of Retrieval

The discussion of retrieval with and of controlled vocabularies covers two activities: retrieval using vocabularies versus retrieval of vocabulary terms themselves.

The primary end-user activity is retrieving work records or other content objects using vocabularies. In this activity, the user searches across content objects, often by typing a search term. The vocabulary is used, often behind the scenes—for example, to broaden the search by adding synonyms to the query. How to employ vocabularies to broaden retrieval and how to display content objects as results to end users are topics that have been extensively studied and written about for several decades.

However, another activity often involves searching a controlled vocabulary itself. In this case, a user first approaches a controlled vocabulary in order to locate desired terms for use in searching or indexing. This activity involves retrieving the vocabulary records themselves, with the goal of either finding vocabulary records as an end or using the retrieved vocabulary records to in turn retrieve or index content objects. How to retrieve and display the controlled vocabularies themselves is a field of study in itself, discussed in ISO, NISO, and other thesaurus standards.

Given that these two activities are so intimately connected and overlapping, they are discussed together in this chapter. Issues surrounding interoperability of multiple vocabularies in retrieval are discussed in **Chapter 5: Using Multiple Vocabularies.**

9.2. User Intervention or Behind the Scenes

How end users will conduct searches using vocabularies is an important issue. The end users may be guided in their searches by showing them the expert terminology from which to choose, in a process known as *user intervention* or *mediation.* If searchers are offered nearest equivalents for their search term and, preferably, also broader and narrower terms, they can choose those that best match their retrieval requirements.

Another approach is to apply vocabulary terms to a user's query entirely *behind the scenes,* with no overt user intervention. In interfaces where users are the general public, this approach is often likely to be less confusing and more satisfying to most users. However, this approach limits the ability of the user to control the search criteria, which can be frustrating to more technically sophisticated users and content experts.

Ideally, a vocabulary designed specifically for retrieval (separate from the indexing vocabulary) accommodates nonexpert searches. End users should be provided with a vocabulary designed specifically for nonexperts, which is linked to the specialist vocabulary that was used for indexing. In the example on the opposite page, users are presented with a short browsing list of nonexpert terms, which allow access to records that were indexed with expert terminology.

9.2.1. Retrieval by Browsing

In online retrieval, *browsing* refers to the activity of looking through various entries to make a selection, such as a list of terms or hypertext links. Browsing should allow users to follow links on a Web page and explore the content as if they were scanning titles on the shelves of a library or thumbing through an encyclopedia. Entries may be arranged

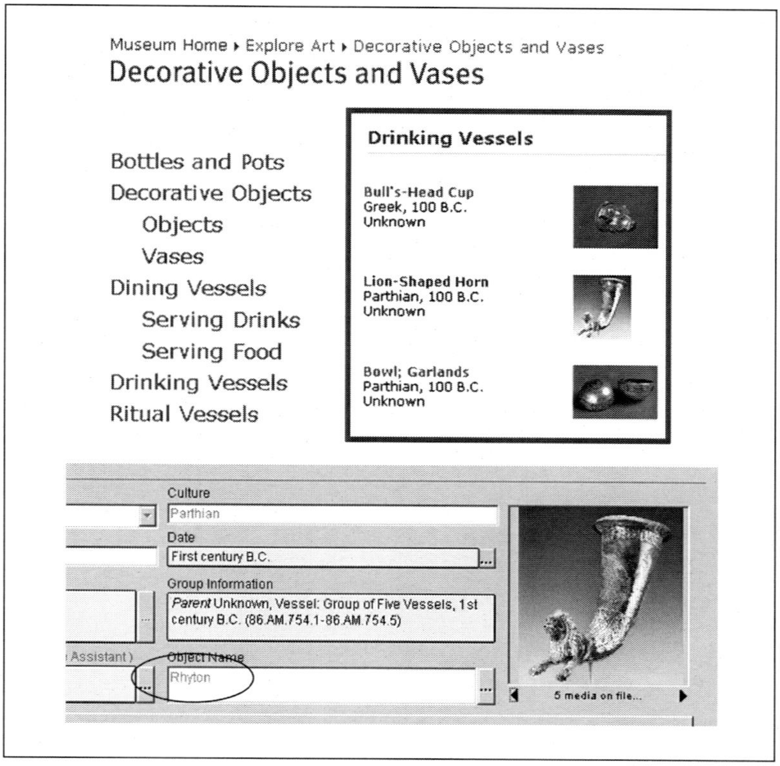

Fig. 60. Examples of an end-user browser display and the editing screen for a rhyton in the J. Paul Getty Museum. In the upper image, nonexpert terms such as *Bottles and Pots* provide access to the general public. In the lower image, what the public has seen as a *Lion-Shaped Horn* is indexed with the expert vocabulary term *rhyton* in the cataloging database.

by alphabetical lists, short pull-down lists, or in other arrangements. In the example on the following page, both pull-down lists and a more extensive alphabetical display are provided.

The lists of terms in a browsing interface and their organization may be derived from the indexing terms that have been used to catalog the works or other content objects. With browsing, retrieval is generally not accomplished by variant names; authorized terms or names must be located in the provided lists. Occasionally, such lists may have *see references,* but typically they do not. If users do not know how to spell the name, they will have difficulty in finding the content they seek. Thus many art-information sites allow retrieval via search boxes in addition to via browsing. The most successful use of browsing allows discovery by users who wish to have the broadest of overviews of the collection, generally helpful to those who do not know enough about the content to search for particular artists or works.

The term *browsing* may also refer to other examples of lists in a system or on the Web, as where users scan a results lists for the desired content or move through a hierarchical display scanning for appropriate terms.

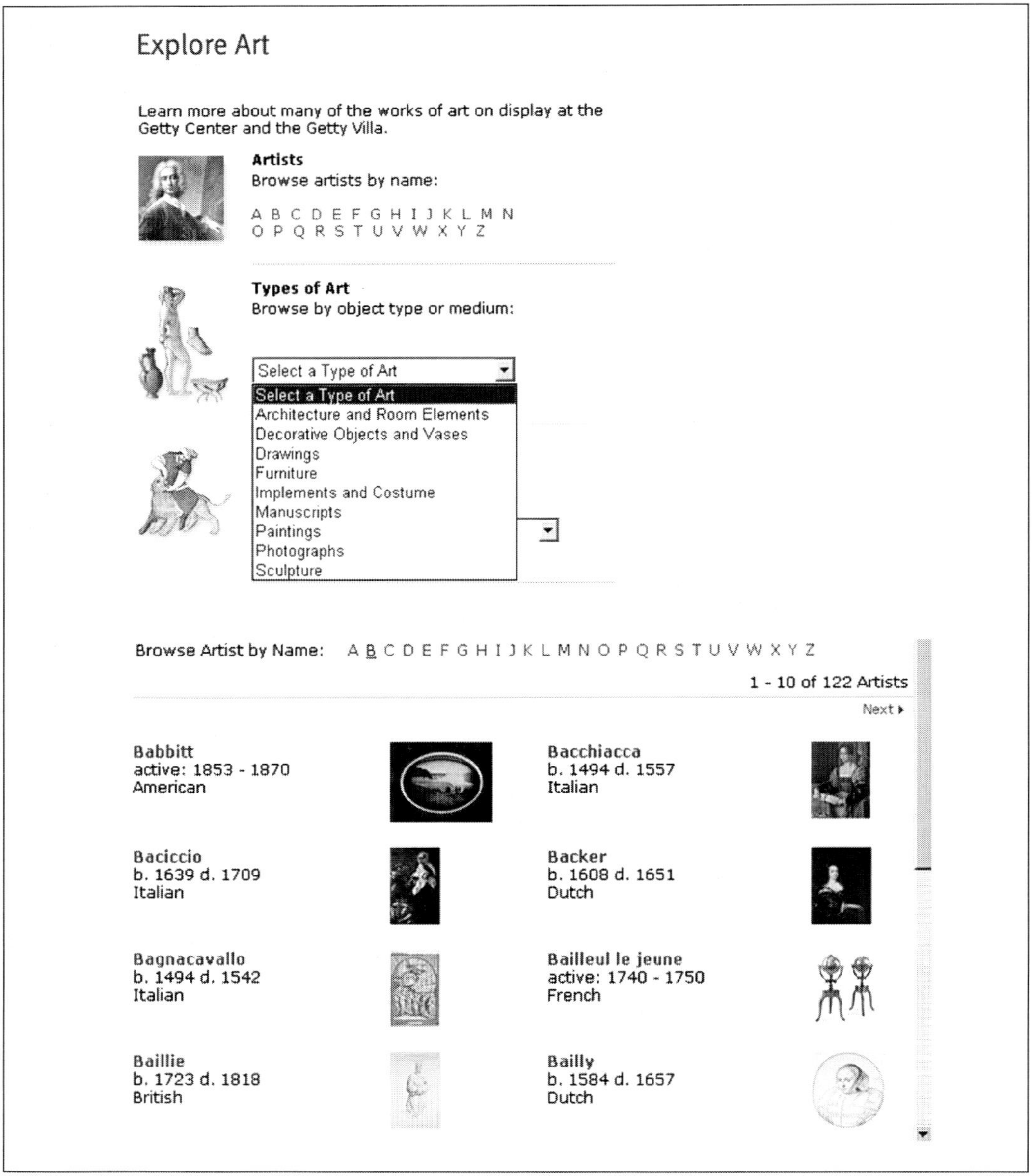

Fig. 61. Examples of browser displays from the J. Paul Getty Museum Web site. The upper image illustrates how users may browse alphabetical lists and pull-down lists. The second image illustrates a detail of the alphabetical listing for artist names beginning with *B*.

9.2.2. Retrieval via Search Box

A search box is a field or other method by which users can enter terms and compose searches. When they search for a term, they expect to retrieve all occurrences of the term (and its synonyms) throughout the database or site. Ideally, the searching interface would use a vocabulary behind the scenes to provide users with alternate terminology choices when their search is unsuccessful or the results are ambiguous.

In the example below, the user typed a term that retrieved no results on the pages searched; however, the user's term was found in a vocabulary (the *ULAN*) used for retrieval behind the scenes. Based on the matches in the vocabulary, the user is offered two choices for terminology that meet the criteria and bring back results on the site.

Ideally, the search engine will not offer the user choices of terms from the vocabulary that would retrieve zero results from the target data being searched (called *blind references*). In the example below, the term *breugel* was actually found in several vocabulary records, but only two of the artists were represented on the target site; therefore, the vocabulary terms that would have brought back no hits were suppressed from the user in this view.

If the search term does not match any preferred or variant term in the vocabulary, the system could offer the user additional options by displaying the terms that are alphabetically close to the search term. For example, the system could display a list of terms from the vocabularies that alphabetically would precede and follow the search term entered by the user, as is common in online dictionaries.

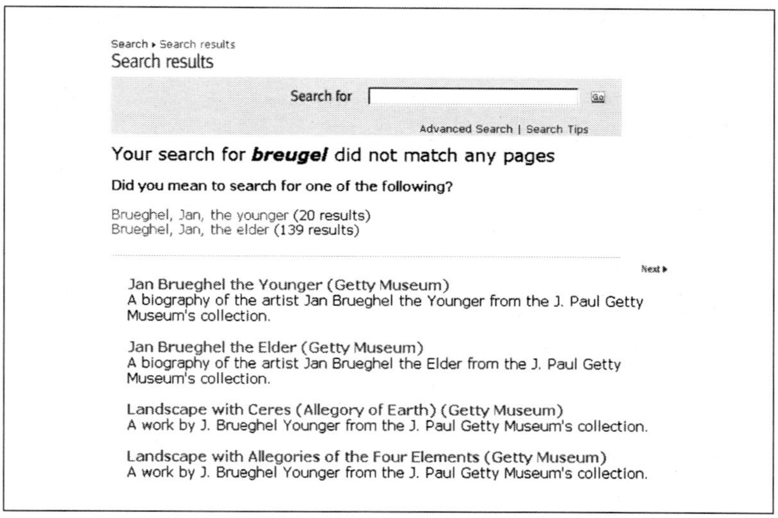

Fig. 62. Example of a search box that allows minimal user interaction. The retrieval results are displayed along with a prompt allowing the user to narrow the results by one of the two available artists named *Jan Brueghel* on this site.

9.2.3. Retrieval by Querying in a Database

Which is better for the users, a simple search or an expanded query? Users may be offered the choice of a simple search across the entire data set or a fielded query, which is a search on individual fields in a database. In the example of a simple search on the previous page, the search terms were gathered from the vocabulary and used across all Web pages available on the site. This approach provides a simple searching interface typically suitable as a default search option for most members of the general public. They receive the benefit of vocabulary-assisted searching without having to worry about the difference between types of information; they may search for the artist's name in the same search box as they would for the medium of the work.

However, a more technically sophisticated user or a content expert will probably be dissatisfied with such a broad search. An alternative method is to use vocabulary to search individual fields of a database. The terminology made available for each field should be appropriate for that field (e.g., fields for artists' names should be linked to vocabulary for artists' names, fields for materials should be linked to vocabularies appropriate for materials, etc.). The results of searching data fields is more accurate and more precise than with a simple search across all content.

In the example below, pull-down lists for some fields are combined with search boxes that allow users to type in the artist's name and the title of the work. The *artist's last name* search box is linked to a

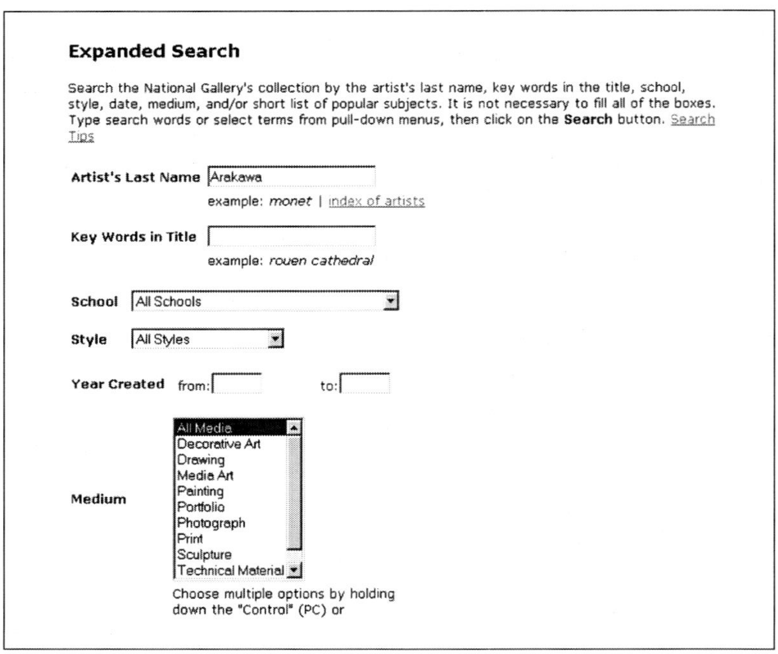
Expanded Search

Search the National Gallery's collection by the artist's last name, key words in the title, school, style, date, medium, and/or short list of popular subjects. It is not necessary to fill all of the boxes. Type search words or select terms from pull-down menus, then click on the **Search** button. Search Tips

Artist's Last Name Arakawa
example: *monet* | index of artists

Key Words in Title
example: *rouen cathedral*

School All Schools

Style All Styles

Year Created from: to:

Medium All Media
Decorative Art
Drawing
Media Art
Painting
Portfolio
Photograph
Print
Sculpture
Technical Material

Choose multiple options by holding down the "Control" (PC) or

Fig. 63. Example of an expanded query form for the National Gallery of Art Web site, which allows the user to choose values for several specific fields, including artist, title, and medium.

Name Authority, allowing the user to access works by that artist via his or her preferred name or any variant name.

Search boxes for retrieval are also utilized in systems used for cataloging artworks. Catalogers must be able to retrieve sets of work records for editing, comparison, and other purposes. In a search for work records, the cataloging system (typically a *collection management system*) should allow catalogers to incorporate variant terms and hierarchical

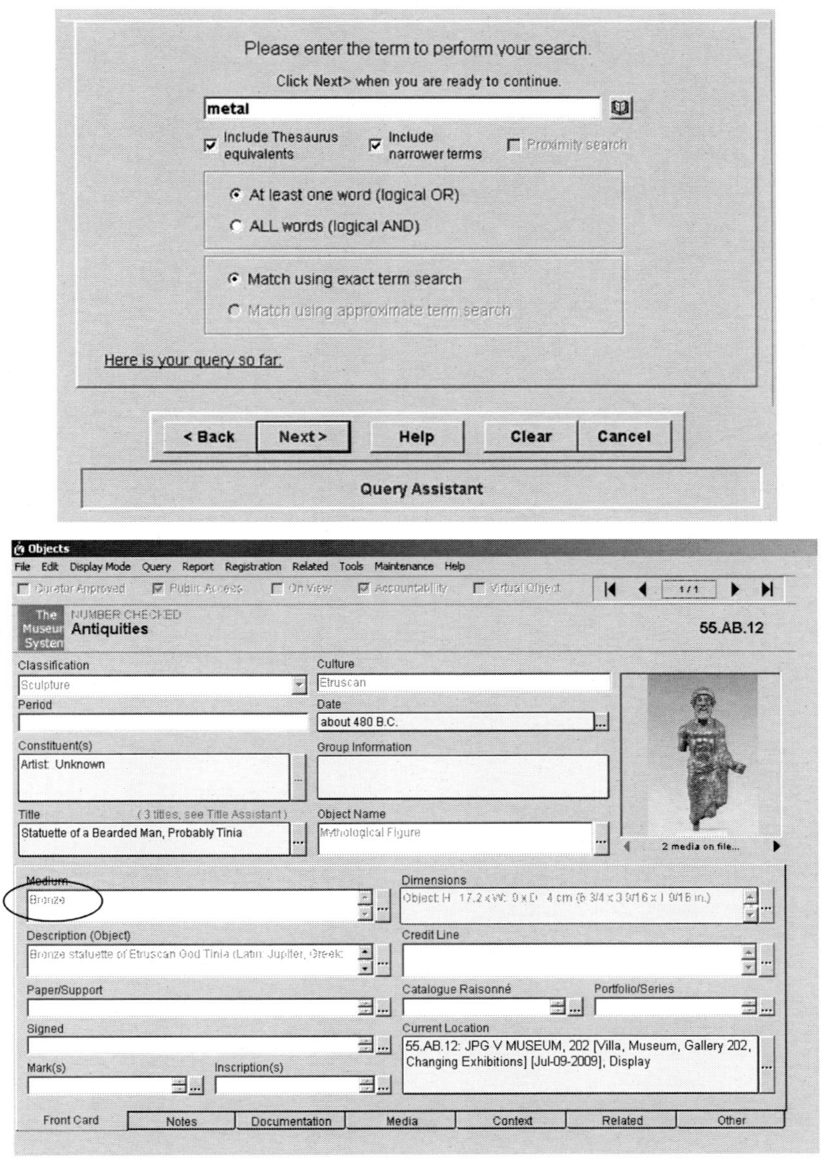

Fig. 64. A search screen and results from the J. Paul Getty Museum cataloging system illustrating how a query may be formulated using equivalents and narrower terms from a thesaurus. The query for works with the medium *metal* returned a work record with the medium *bronze*, for which *metal* is the broader context in the thesaurus.

relationships from the controlled vocabularies. In the example on the previous page, the collection management system gives users the option of including terms from the thesaurus and narrower concepts in the query.

Search boxes may be combined with the ability to truncate terms or to add Boolean operators and other facilities to allow users to make versatile and powerful searches. In the example below, an advanced search interface allows term truncation, Boolean operators, and searching for ranges of dates.

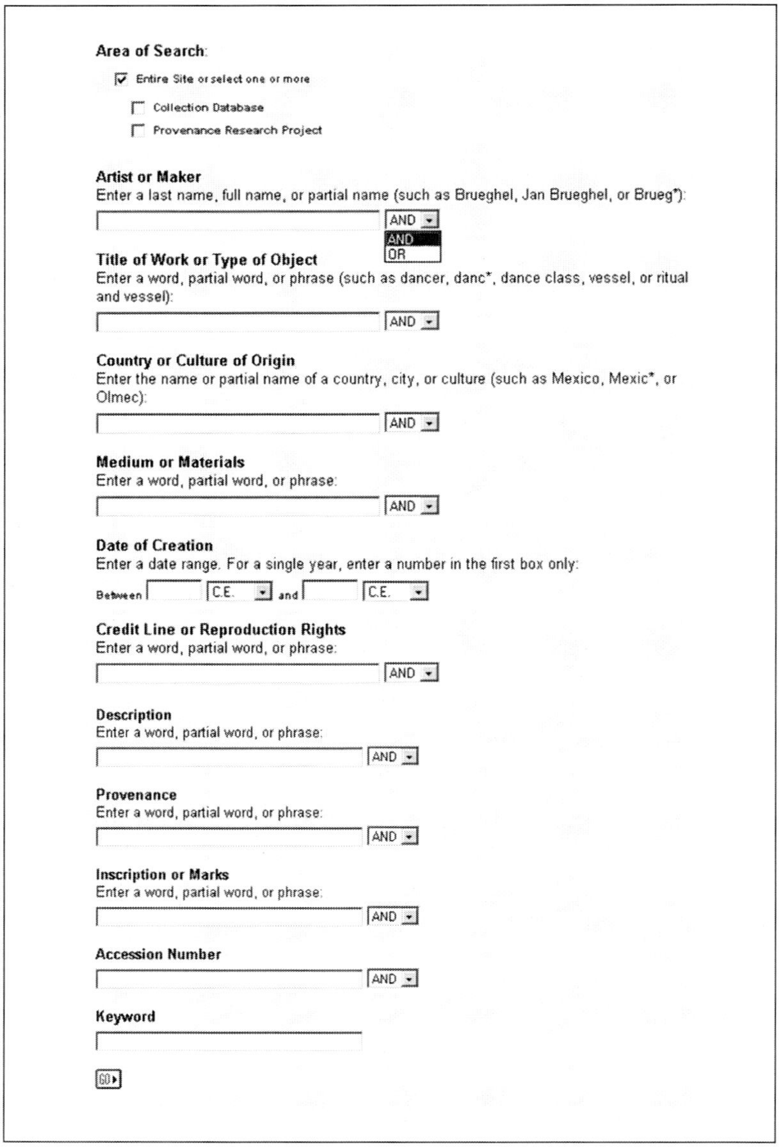

Fig. 65. An advanced search screen formerly used on the Metropolitan Museum of Art Web site illustrating how the user may narrow the query to a particular database (the collection or the provenance research project) as well as query an extensive list of fields, including artist, title, country of origin, and others. The Boolean operators AND and OR are available. The Metropolitan Museum of Art, www.metmuseum.org. Copyright © 2000–2009 The Metropolitan Museum of Art. All rights reserved.

9.2.3.1. Reports and Ad Hoc Queries of the Database

For maintainers of the vocabulary data and other authorized advanced users, predefined reports must be supplied and ad hoc queries on the database must be allowed. A *predefined report* is a query and a format for output that has been written in advance and is used for queries that are asked frequently. This type of report may or may not have variables that can be changed by the user. An *ad hoc query* allows a qualified user to use a query language to access all of the underlying data tables without going through a user interface that limits access to only certain fields and predefined query logic. In the examples below, users construct queries targeting various data tables and columns in a relational database.

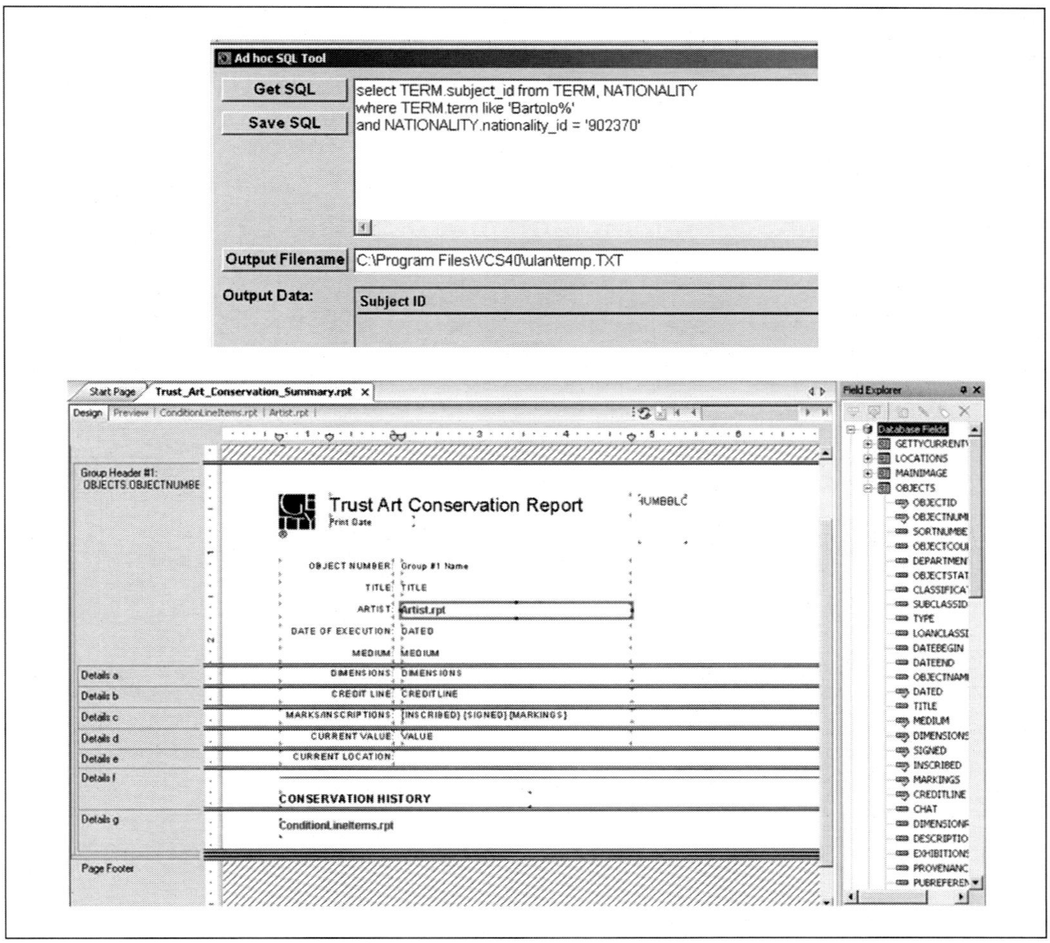

Fig. 66. Examples of query screens for constructing reports in VCS (the Getty Vocabulary Program's editorial system) and TMS (The Museum System). The upper image illustrates an ad hoc query in VCS, where the editor has constructed an SQL (Structured Query Language) query based on values in the relational database of vocabulary data. The lower image illustrates a query under construction in a report writer in TMS.

9.2.4. Querying across Multiple Databases

When querying across multiple databases, implementers must resolve several issues having to do with target data and vocabularies. Data located on the surface Web (or *visible Web*), even if it is derived from multiple databases, may be rendered accessible to local search engines and public retrieval tools, including Google. However, other data can be hard to retrieve in concert across multiple databases. The various databases may be located at different institutions or even at the same institution, but they may be on different servers, different platforms, they may have different interfaces, and the data fields, rules, and data values may not be compatible. Such data may be visible on the Web in certain views, but if it is located in the deep Web (or *invisible Web*), the information is hidden or generally inaccessible through traditional search methods.

As a first step in resolving these issues, disparate databases must be mapped to each other or to a separate standard set of fields. In addition, deep Web data generally must be made accessible to a common search engine, either by copying all the data onto a common location or somehow making the data available from its native environments. If both of these criteria are met, controlled vocabularies may be applied during searching to minimize retrieval problems caused by the original data having been cataloged using different vocabularies. For issues surrounding the use of multiple vocabularies for retrieval, see **Chapter 5: Using Multiple Vocabularies.** For a set of fields for exchanging work data, see the *CDWA Lite* XML schema.

9.2.5. Seeding Tags with Vocabulary Terms

Another way in which vocabularies can improve retrieval of Web content is by seeding *meta tags* located in the source code of a Web page with synonyms and broader contexts. HTML (Hypertext Markup Language) is a programming and markup language used to create documents for display on the World Wide Web. These Web documents are presented in a specific tagging language, where the data values, formatting, and other information necessary to display the page appear between opening and closing tags in angled brackets.

In the example below, variant names for an artist have been taken from a vocabulary and added to the keywords for a Web page. This allows the page to be retrieved by search engines by any of the variant names for this artist.

> <META NAME="keywords" CONTENT="**El Lissitzky, Lissitsky, Lisickij, Lisitski, Lisitskii, Lisitsky, Lissickij**, avant-

garde art, avantgarde, book design, Yiddish book design, children's books, Futurism, Futurist Art, Modernism, Modernist, Modernists, Proun, Russian art, Soviet art">

9.3. Processing Vocabulary Data for Retrieval

Retrieval of vocabularies must accommodate the special needs of the vocabulary data; it should not necessarily be limited by the functionality of off-the-shelf software and standard search algorithms. Efficient retrieval of vocabulary terms and names requires processing and algorithms suited to the unique characteristics of the data, which is unlike natural language. Vocabulary data includes proper names, generic terms, compound terms, historical terms, term inversions, and variations representing all possible languages. Standard searching methods are optimized for uncontrolled free text and often do not work well with terminology from a controlled vocabulary. The methods discussed in this chapter are primarily intended for thesauri. For a discussion of other types of vocabularies that may be optimized for retrieval, including synonym ring lists and ontologies, see **Chapter 2: What Are Controlled Vocabularies?**

As discussed earlier, the requirements of vocabularies intended for indexing generally differ from those of vocabularies intended for retrieval. A vocabulary for indexing focuses on warrant, correct usage, and authorized spellings of terms, while a vocabulary for retrieval allows less strict parameters to accomplish broader retrieval. However, in many institutions, the same vocabularies must be used for both purposes. This issue may be largely resolved by processing or preprocessing the indexing vocabulary for optimal use in retrieval.

In this context, *data preprocessing* may refer to any type of processing performed on data to prepare it for a processing procedure different from that for which it was originally compiled. Preprocessing of vocabulary terms translates the data into a format that is more easily and effectively processed for the use of the search engine or end-user displays.

Terms and other data may be preprocessed and stored in indexes or tables specific to the retrieval application, or the terms and data may be processed for retrieval as needed on the fly. For large and complex data sets, it is typically more efficient to store the preprocessed terms and other data, rather than constructing them on the fly. For example, data in a complex relational database designed for an editorial system could be packaged so that it could be displayed faster and more easily on the Web for end users. The packaging could include the precoordination of parent strings from the hierarchical structure, preconcatenating them so they do not need to be constructed on the fly in the Web interface for end users.

9.3.1. Know Your Audience

Defining the user audience is critical to most issues discussed in this book, but it is particularly relevant in the context of retrieving, processing, and sorting names or terms. In this book, the audience is assumed to be an international audience familiar with English, which is the common default language of the computing community and the Web. It is necessary to have a default language because the vocabularies discussed here are often multilingual; thus one language must be preferred as a base language because it is impractical to have dozens of alternative sets of rules in a single vocabulary to deal with all possible languages. The scenarios and rules discussed here are generic, intended for a multilingual vocabulary accessible to an international audience.

However, if the audience is restricted to a particular location and language, and if it is certain that the data will never be shared with the broader user community, rules for normalization, processing, and sorting terms may differ from those described here. For example, if a vocabulary contains only German terms and the audience is and always will be restricted to speakers of German, then rules can be established that are applicable specifically to the German alphabet, keyboards, etc. Characteristics of Unicode and other issues are discussed below.

9.3.2. Using Names for Retrieval

Although the hierarchy and other information in a vocabulary record may sometimes be used in queries, querying by name or term is the method used most often to access records in a controlled vocabulary. Basic access by all terms or names for a given vocabulary record is critical. The main purpose of adding variant names and synonyms is to allow access to the vocabulary data by any linked term. Any retrieval system should search for any and all variant terms and names for the person, place, thing, or concept. In the example below, if the user searches for *ushabti* (small ancient Egyptian funerary figures), all work records, pages, or other content objects in the target database that contain *shawtabys* and the other synonyms should also be retrieved.

ushabti *(preferred, descriptor)*
ushabtis *(used for term)*
shabti *(used for term)*
shawabti *(used for term)*
shawtaby *(used for term)*

shawtabys *(used for term)*
ushabtiu *(used for term)*
ushabty *(used for term)*
ushabtys *(used for term)*

Access must be allowed through official and correct names as well as through nicknames, pseudonyms, and other unofficial names. These names will probably be included in the authoritative vocabulary used for indexing. For example, the twentieth-century architect *Charles Édouard Jeanneret-Gris* was known by his pseudonym *Le Corbusier;* both names should be included in a vocabulary record for this artist. Even common misspellings may be included in the indexing vocabulary to improve access, particularly when these misspellings are published. For example, the twentieth-century painter *Georgia O'Keeffe* is frequently if incorrectly listed as *O'Keefe* (with only one *f*). This common published misspelling should be included in the vocabulary and used to aid retrieval.

On the retrieval side, consideration should also be given to additional misspellings and name variations, even if they are not found in a published source. These misspellings would not be appropriate for the authoritative indexing vocabulary, but they should be used behind the scenes for retrieval, hidden from the end user to prevent confusion. For example, by using a hidden index or other method, it may be advantageous to allow end users who enter *Richard Meyer* to retrieve information about the contemporary architect *Richard Meier,* even though the users have misspelled his name.

9.3.3. Truncating Names

Users should be able to access terms and names by *truncation:* truncation involves the user employing a wildcard symbol (often an asterisk, question mark, or percent sign, or another method) to search for a string of characters regardless of what other characters follow (or sometimes, precede) that string. *Right-hand* truncation is used to match terms starting with the same letters; for example, searching for *arch** retrieves *arch, arches, architrave, architecture, architectural history,* etc.

For names and terms, querying must allow, at minimum, right-hand truncation on strings and on key words. Truncation should be allowed in combination with Boolean operators, as in the following example.

Edinburg*
Jan Cornel*
gar* AND eldon

The employment of the wildcard symbol at the middle or left-hand side of the string is helpful as well, allowing retrieval when exact spelling is unknown. However, due to the impact on processing, left-hand and middle character truncation are often impractical when querying large sets of terms.

> Pyeitawinzu Myanm* Nain*
> *durrahim

9.3.4. Keyword Searching

Keyword searching is a method of computer searching ultimately based on natural language texts rather than controlled vocabulary; however, it should be adapted to searching vocabularies. Keyword searching refers to searching for individual words or combinations of words; this is useful for searching vocabularies that may contain names and terms comprising multiple words. In standard retrieval, keywords are often determined on the fly during a search; however, creating indexes that contain normalized keywords and other normalized strings is a recommended strategy for vocabulary data (see also **9.3.5. Normalizing Terms**).

Electronic controlled vocabularies should provide keyword access to all words of all the terms in the vocabulary. Keyword searching

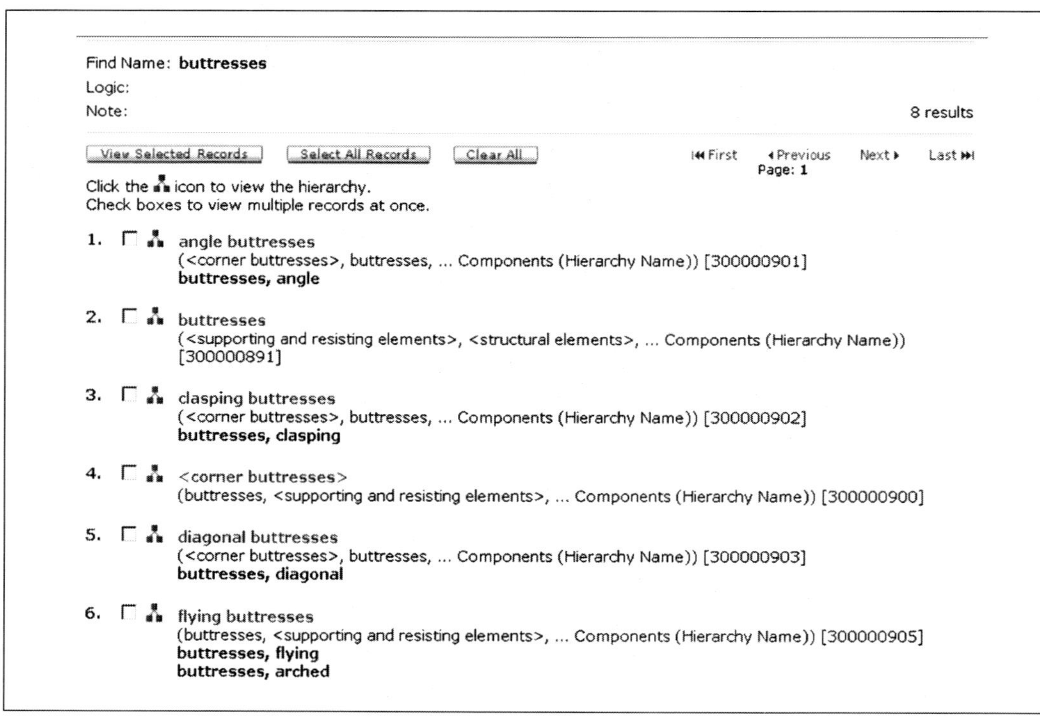

Fig. 67. Example of a results list for a keyword search on *buttresses* in the *AAT*.

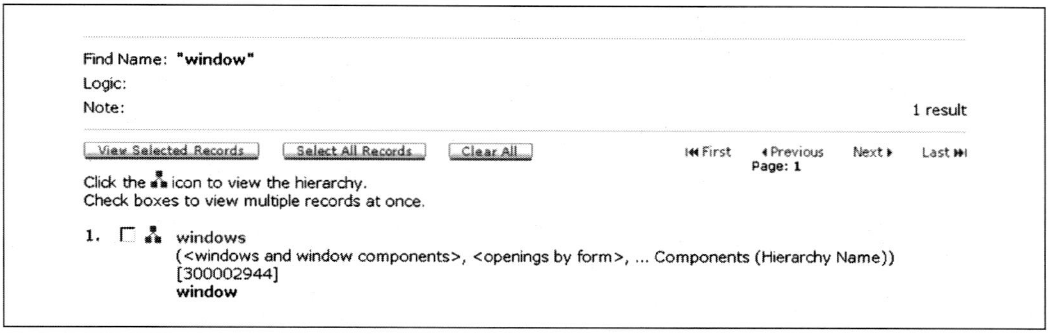

Fig. 68. Example of the results for an exact string match on the term *window* in the *AAT*. In this application, the user has placed quotes around *window* to search for the exact term rather than for keywords; searching for the keyword *window* would have returned over ninety results.

thus serves the same purpose as the permuted and rotated indexes that are common in print formats.

The process of keyword searching typically uses spaces and punctuation between words to determine which elements of a term are separate words. For the term *flying buttresses,* the space would be used to identify *flying* and *buttresses* as separate keywords. If a user searched for the keyword *buttresses,* this term and any others with the word *buttresses* would be returned.

While keyword searching is useful as a default search strategy for end users, the user must be able to search for the full normalized string instead of the keywords when necessary. A common way of designating the string as opposed to keywords in searches is to enclose the string in quotes (e.g., *"flying buttresses"*).

For example, it must be possible to find the exact term *window* without returning the dozens of other terms that have *window* as a keyword.

9.3.5. Normalizing Terms

This section discusses the normalization of terms in the context of vocabulary retrieval. This differs from *database normalization,* which is the process of organizing data in a database by reducing a complex data structure into its simplest structure, creating tables, establishing relationships between tables based on set rules, eliminating data redundancy, and converting Unicode text into a standardized form, among other things.

In the context of this book, *normalizing terms* refers to the process of removing or ignoring spaces, punctuation, diacritics, and case sensitivity in terms. The purpose of such normalization is to allow comparison of terms on the basic character strings, regardless of minor or superficial differences.

Data storage and searching methods typically differ between the editorial system used to create and maintain the vocabulary and the system optimized for end-user access. Maintainers and creators of the vocabulary data need to search by normalized terms, but they also require the option of searching for an exact match on the full name string, with diacritics, punctuation, and capitalization remaining intact. However, searches for normalized strings and keywords are typically the preferred and only methods required for indexers and end users.

Data should be stored in a way that allows its translation into other encoding schemes. One way to match on normalized terms is to establish normalization routines or create automated indexes of normalized terms. Normalization should be done on the user's query string, on the terms and names in the target vocabulary, and possibly in the database or Web pages being queried. In the example below, the terms have been normalized to all capitals, although normalizing to all lowercase would work equally well.

> **Name:** Atakora, Chaîne de l'
> **Normalized string:** ATAKORACHAINEDEL
>
> **Name:** Carlos María de Borbón
> **Normalized string:** CARLOSMARIADEBORBON
>
> **Term:** Ayios Onouphrios ware
> **Normalized string:** AYIOSONOUPHRIOSWARE

The suggestions in this section refer to the preprocessing and normalization of terms in an index to be used for retrieval; both normalized keywords and normalized strings would be stored together for use in searching. In the example below, the name *d'Or, Castel* has been normalized to create six separate entries in the index. The methods used to create these entries are discussed below.

> The following are normalized keywords and strings for *d'Or, Castel:*
>
> DORCASTEL
> D
> OR
> CASTEL
> DOR
> CASTELDOR

9.3.5.1. Case Insensitivity in Retrieval

A retrieval system should accommodate end-user queries, no matter what case they use. For example, if an end user searches for *Bartolo Di Fredi* or *BARTOLO DI FREDI,* he or she should retrieve records containing the name *Bartolo di Fredi.*

9.3.5.2. Compound Terms and Names in Retrieval

A retrieval system should accommodate compound terms and names that may be spelled with or without a space. For example, an end user's search for *Le Duc* should retrieve records for both *Charles Leduc* and *Johan le Duc;* a search for *Westwood* should retrieve the record for *West Wood.*

9.3.5.3. Diacritics and Punctuation in Retrieval

A retrieval system should accommodate both the end user's *use* of diacritics and punctuation and his or her *omission* of diacritics and punctuation. For example, if the end user searches for *Jean Simeon Chardin* (without the hyphen and diacritic), he or she should retrieve records containing the name *Jean-Siméon Chardin.*

Given that end users may use a variety of codes or alphabets in searching, and given that most users expect results to sort in a particular way (ignoring diacritics), diacritics should be stripped or mapped to normalized strings in order to achieve adequate retrieval and satisfactory sorting in the results.

A user may type a search string containing a character encoding set different from the one used by the native vocabulary data, or with the diacritics stripped (e.g., typing an *o* when the character in the data against which the query is run contains an *o* with circumflex, *ô*). One way to allow retrieval is to map diacritics or Unicode characters to the corresponding nondiacritic ASCII character, no matter which diacritics are typed by the user.

Possible keyword queries from users:
Amazônica
Amazónica
amazonica

Keyword values in the vocabulary data base:
Amazónica
Amazônica

Keywords in the normalized table omit the diacritics:
AMAZONICA
AMAZONICA

Terms retrieved in the query:

Región Amazónica
Amazônica Brasileira
Amazônica, Região
Hoya Amazónica
Bacia Amazônica

Various issues surround the retrieval and display of diacritics, particularly those outside the Latin 1 character set. More and more art institutions are using Unicode, which is a set of codes for diacritics and characters in various alphabets. The Unicode Standard is maintained by the Unicode Consortium in cooperation with the World Wide Web Consortium (W3C) and ISO, the latter of which controls the character set defined in *ISO/IEC 10646:2003: Information Technology—Universal Multiple-Octet Coded Character Set (UCS).*

Outstanding issues include the following: Unicode is still an evolving standard subject to occasional changes in encoding and protocol of usage. In addition, some art institutions are still using technology that cannot accommodate Unicode, meaning their data needs to be mapped to the Unicode character set in a common environment of data sharing. Furthermore, using Unicode in a multilingual environment presents challenges simply because most systems will expect to be told to use one particular language, not many languages simultaneously.

It is not necessary to store data in Unicode. However, it is very important that data is stored in a way that allows it to be translated to UTF-8 (8-bit UCS/Unicode Transformation Format) or any other relevant encoding scheme.

9.3.5.4. Phonetic Matching

Phonetic matching involves retrieval based on the matching of two words that presumably sound alike. It is common in many search engines. However, rather than using standard phonetic matching for art terminology, specialized normalization and searching algorithms are recommended. Although standard phonetic matching is not very useful for art information, it is discussed here so that readers will understand what it is and why it does not work well in multilingual controlled vocabularies.

A *phonetic algorithm* is an algorithm used to index words by their pronunciation. Words with the presumed same pronunciation are encoded to the same code or string so that they can presumably be matched despite minor differences in spelling. Among the best known of the dozens of such phonetic algorithms are Soundex and Metaphone. Soundex is a phonetic algorithm for encoding names by sound as pronounced in English, with the goal of matching names with the same pronunciation despite minor differences in spelling. Metaphone is a similar algorithm, attempting to improve on Soundex.

The primary problem with such phonetic algorithms is that they were developed for use with standard English. They are complex algorithms with many rules and exceptions that attempt to account for irregularities of spelling and pronunciation in English. They do not work well with historical words, words in other languages, or most proper names. For the vocabularies discussed in this book, such algorithms do not work well because historical terms, proper names, and terms and names in all languages (not only English) may be represented; furthermore, name inversions and punctuation idiosyncrasies cause complications not found in standard texts in English.

9.3.5.5. Singulars and Plurals in Retrieval

A retrieval system should accommodate the end user entering either the singular or plural form of the term (or any other grammatical variant), whenever possible. While automating this facility does not produce useful results for all languages, it is useful to target languages that will significantly improve matching in the application.

For example, if an end user searches for the plural *portals,* he or she should retrieve records containing the singular term *portal.* One method of accomplishing this is through automatic *stemming,* a common retrieval feature that retrieves the term and all of its grammatical variants (e.g., stemming on *frame* would also retrieve *frames, framing,* and *framed*). While stemming improves access to natural-language texts in English (which can contain any English word representing all parts of speech), it is less useful for art vocabularies recorded as fielded data (which tend to contain specialized terms, primarily nouns, formulated according to precise rules).

Rather than using off-the-shelf stemming routines, a more efficient method to deal with singulars and plurals is to formulate special algorithms that better suit the content and rules employed in the target vocabulary data. For example, adding and subtracting the letter *s* aids in matching singular and plural terms in English, Spanish, and a few other languages. In the *AAT,* terms may exist in either plural or singular forms. However, due to constraints of practicality, the singular forms have typically not been added for all *used for* terms. Therefore, creating a special routine to subtract and add a final *s* to both the existing *AAT* data and the incoming user queries increases retrieval for many terms. These terms will not be automatically added to the authoritative *AAT* database, but they are used in the special normalized index created for the retrieval process. For example, in a query for *Turkish dome,* the search engine would look to normalized constructed keywords and strings to which *s* has been added or subtracted:

> For the term *domes, Turkish* versions of the normalized strings with the *s* subtracted are included:

DOMES
TURKISH
DOMESTURKISH
TURKISHDOMES
DOME
TURKISHDOME

Another way to improve the retrieval of singular and plural terms would be to automatically truncate words to find a match (e.g., *dome* AND turkish**); this may help with plural forms, but automatic truncation can adversely affect accuracy of retrieval overall.

9.3.5.6. Abbreviations

In cases where the terminology may regularly contain abbreviations, or where users may expect to search using abbreviations, common abbreviations may be mapped to the full word in the term to increase retrieval accuracy. For example, users may expect to retrieve a town by the term *W Lafayette,* but if the value in the vocabulary is *West Lafayette,* the correct record will not be retrieved. An index may be created, mapping words that have common abbreviations to the abbreviation values, in order to add the abbreviated variant (*W Lafayette*) for the purposes of retrieval.

St. Louis
W Lafayette
Mt Everest
Moskovskaya Ob

9.3.5.7. Trunk Names

Some terms or names consist of a core or trunk word or phrase, combined sometimes—but not always—with a modifying word to form a name or term. This happens often with geographic names and certain other classes of terms. Consideration must be given to allow access regardless of whether or not the modifier of the *trunk* or core element of the name is included in the user's query.

For example, depending upon which published atlas or gazetteer the user consults, the name of a particular mountain/volcano can be *Mount Etna, Berg Etna, Monte Etna, Mt Etna,* or simply *Etna,* with the words *Mount, Monte,* or *Berg* omitted as descriptive phrases that are not truly part of the name. Therefore, an efficient retrieval interface would allow users who enter *Berg Etna* to find the correct place, even if the vocabulary includes only the term *Mount Etna.* This could be done by maintaining a table of descriptive words and phrases that could be added or omitted from the trunk name.

9.3.5.8. Form and Syntax of the Name

Names referring to the same concept may be recorded according to a variety of syntactical conventions. The jumble of information on the Web includes texts in which names occur in natural order, along with indexes, catalogs, and other structured data resources in which the standard syntax may be in inverted order. Access should be accommodated no matter what the syntax of the name is in the target data. The retrieval system should accommodate end users' use of terms and names in either natural or inverted order. For example, a search on *Wellesley, Arthur, Duke of Wellington* should retrieve records containing *Arthur Wellesley, Duke of Wellington.*

Searching by keywords accomplishes this to some extent. However, accuracy is increased with the adoption of a routine that creates variant names by pivoting on the comma.

9.3.5.8.1. First and Last Names

Most of the vocabularies discussed in this book do not parse first and last names into separate fields. A single field is used to store the value of the terms and names; commas are used to create inverted forms of the names and terms. The reason for this is that a large percentage of names and terms used for art information could not appropriately be parsed into separate last names and first names, because the use of first and last names is a relatively modern Western custom. Non-Western and early Western artists may not have a first and last name, such as those with qualifiers that are patronymics (as in *Bartolo di Fredi,* meaning "Bartolo son of Fredi") or place name qualifiers (as in *Gentile da Fabriano,* meaning "Gentile from Fabriano").

First and last names do not apply to geographic, generic concept, and subject terminology; however, these names and terms may be inverted in ways similar to people's names. In addition, it is convenient for maintenance and retrieval if all vocabularies used in an institution have the same or very similar data structures.

In all cases, retrieval should not require users to distinguish first and last names. However, retrieval systems must still account for users who may try to look for people by last name and who may look for other vocabularies' terms in similar ways.

9.3.5.8.2. Pivoting on the Comma

Special processing of the terms based on commas is advantageous in retrieval, given the wide variety of possibilities in forming inverted names by using commas and because the vocabulary may contain proper names, generic terms, and words in all languages.

Useful variations of names and terms may be created by establishing algorithms that use the comma as a pivot; this should be used behind the scenes in retrieval only and should not be visible to the end user (because some of the variants created in this way will be nonsense).

Using the comma as a pivot, values are flipped on either side of the comma and other punctuation to create an indexing term. For example, for *Atakora, Chaîne de l',* an algorithm can create the flipped term *Chaîne de l'Atakora*. Both of the terms may then be normalized, removing case sensitivity, spaces, punctuation, and diacritics—for example, *ATAKORACHAINEDEL* and *CHAINEDELATAKORA*.

9.3.5.8.3. Multiple Commas

In cases where a name or term has two or three commas, algorithms should be developed to flip the portions of the term into two or more reasonable formulations. In inverted names, common conventions are not consistent regarding which parts of the name may be at the far right of the inverted phrase containing multiple commas. Even though one string might be nonsense, making variants by pivoting on multiple commas results in useful combinations in half the cases; the strings do not display to end users. The resulting strings would then be normalized, removing punctuation, case sensitivity, spaces, and diacritics.

Fig. 69. Names such as *Jan Brueghel the Elder* may be preprocessed and indexed to allow more satisfactory retrieval.

Jan Brueghel the Elder (Flemish, 1568–1625); *The Entry of the Animals into Noah's Ark;* 1613; oil on panel; 54.6 × 83.8 cm (21½ × 33 inches); J. Paul Getty Museum (Los Angeles, California); 92.PB.82.

Inverted name with two commas:

Brueghel, Jan, the elder

Two indexing strings created by pivoting on the commas:

Jan Brueghel the Elder
the Elder Jan Brueghel

Values added to the normalized index for retrieval of this one name

JAN
BRUEGHEL
THE
ELDER
JANBRUEGHELTHEELDER
THEELDERJANBRUEGHEL

Inverted name with two commas:

Wren, Christopher, Sir

Two indexing strings created by pivoting on the commas:

Sir Christopher Wren
Christopher Wren Sir

Values added to the normalized index for retrieval:

CHRISTOPHER
WREN
SIR
SIRCHRISTOPHERWREN
CHRISTOPHERWRENSIR

9.3.5.9. Articles and Prepositions

Additional normalized combinations of words in names and terms should be created to account for differences in the treatment of articles and prepositions in various languages. For example, processing may involve the construction of additional keywords by an algorithm that grabs any lowercase word to the right of the comma to make a last name to the left of the comma. For instance, even though the name in the vocabulary is inverted *Gogh, Vincent van,* users may consider his last name to be *Van Gogh.* Apostrophes, hyphens, and other designated punctuation may also be considered pivots to create additional last names or joined keywords. Once the additional terms and strings have been compiled, they should be added to the normalized index for retrieval.

Normalized strings and keywords for the name *Gogh, Vincent van:*

GOGHVINCENTVAN
GOGH
VINCENT
VAN
VINCENTVANGOGH
VANGOGHVINCENT
VANGOGH

Normalized strings and keywords for the name *Atakora, Chaîne de l':*

ATAKORA
CHAINE
DE
L
ATAKORACHAINEDEL
CHAINEDELATAKORA
LATAKORA
DELATAKORA

9.3.6. Reserved Character Sets

Certain punctuation and words are used by query languages to designate specific aspects of the underlying logic of formulating queries. When these reserved words and nonalphabetic characters are part of the actual content of the vocabulary, care must be taken that they do not conflict with the same special characters required in search commands. For example, if parentheses, other special characters, or the words *or* and *and* are used in the term field, it should be possible to avoid their being interpreted as nesting indicators or Boolean indicators in a search statement. Where the potential for such ambiguity exists, programming algorithms or another method, such as substituting the problematic characters, should be adopted. For example, the Boolean operators may be expressed in all capitals to distinguish them from terms containing *and* or *or*. In the example below, the term *William and Mary* is a term referring to an English style.

The following search phrase includes the term *William and Mary* and the Boolean *OR:*

William and Mary OR Jacobean

9.3.7. Stop Lists

Stop lists contain words that are ignored in queries. In standard search processing, typical stop lists include articles and prepositions in English. However, for a vocabulary database, these words are not meaningful in a stop list because, unlike in natural language, they do not occur with great frequency in terms and names. In fact, articles and prepositions are critical components of certain names and terms that must not be ignored in searches. For example, the term *clerks of the works* refers to architectural workers and must be retrievable in the *AAT; Master of the Encarnación* must be retrievable in the *ULAN.*

The purpose of stop lists is to avoid retrieving impractically large sets of results, particularly in keyword tables. If it is necessary to devise stop lists in vocabulary databases, words that are appropriate for the terminology should be used. At the same time, users must be able to search for words that are on the stop list if they wish to pursue it. Users should be prompted to use quotes or to narrow their search with additional criteria. For example, in a geographic vocabulary, including the word *lake* in the keyword table could result in too many hits on the tens of thousands of lakes in the database that have the word *lake* in their name. Users would be prompted to use *lake* with another keyword to narrow the search. However, there are towns named simply *Lake,* so it must be possible to retrieve them, even if the word *lake* is on a stop list. One solution is to allow retrieval of *Lake* as an exact phrase (not a keyword), enclosed in quotes.

9.3.8. Boolean Operators

Boolean operators are logical operators used as modifiers to refine the relationship between terms in a search. The three Boolean operators most commonly used are AND, OR, and NOT. For names and terms, a minimum requirement is that complex AND and OR queries must be allowed. They should be used with parentheses and other punctuation to form logical groupings of criteria in queries.

> Bay of Biscay OR Biscay, Bay of
> (Castillo OR Rancho) AND Diego
> Monte AND Oliv*

9.3.9. Context of Terms in Retrieval

In addition to names and terms, other information in the vocabulary can be used to aid in retrieval. Most importantly, the context of the term in the vocabulary is often important in assuring accurate and meaningful retrieval.

9.3.9.1. Qualifiers in Retrieval

In some vocabularies, the qualifier (a word or phrase used to disambiguate homographs) may be recorded in the same field with the term, perhaps separated by parentheses. However, ideally, the qualifier should be located in a separate field, thus allowing qualifiers to be easily processed separately from the terms in retrieval, sorting, and other situations.

Automatically including the qualifier with the term in searching reduces efficiency in retrieval. Qualifiers are intended to disambiguate homographs when the term is displayed, but they can cause a number of problems in retrieval. Consider *drums (column components), drums (membranophones),* and *drums (walls).* In displays, the parenthetical qualifiers distinguish (a) cylinders of stone that form the shaft of a column, from (b) objects with a resonating cavity covered at one or both ends by a membrane, which is sounded by striking, from (c) the vertical walls that carry a dome.

On the one hand, if the qualifiers are automatically included in query phrases across disparate databases, it is unlikely that results will be good, unless the target databases used exactly the same vocabulary resource at the data capture phase. On the other hand, given all the homographs in art information, terms are less meaningful when taken out of context, and retrieving on the name or term alone may result in imprecise results. Qualifiers and broader contexts should then be used with the user's discretion to narrow results as necessary. In the examples below, *Edo* is the name of both an African culture and a Japanese period; *stretcher* is a masonry unit, a furniture component, equipment for mounting and framing, and a conveyance. Allowing users to add the qualifier (or a word from the qualifier) may narrow a search that has returned results that are too large and unwieldy.

Edo *(African culture)*
Edo *(Japanese period)*

stretcher *(masonry unit)*
stretcher *(furniture components)*
stretcher *(framing and mounting equipment)*
stretcher *(conveyances)*

9.3.9.2. Hierarchical Relationships in Retrieval

In addition to qualifiers, hierarchical relationships may also be used to provide context in order to narrow search results. For example, there are many homographs in geographic information; thus, querying on a common name, such as *Paris,* may retrieve too many results. However,

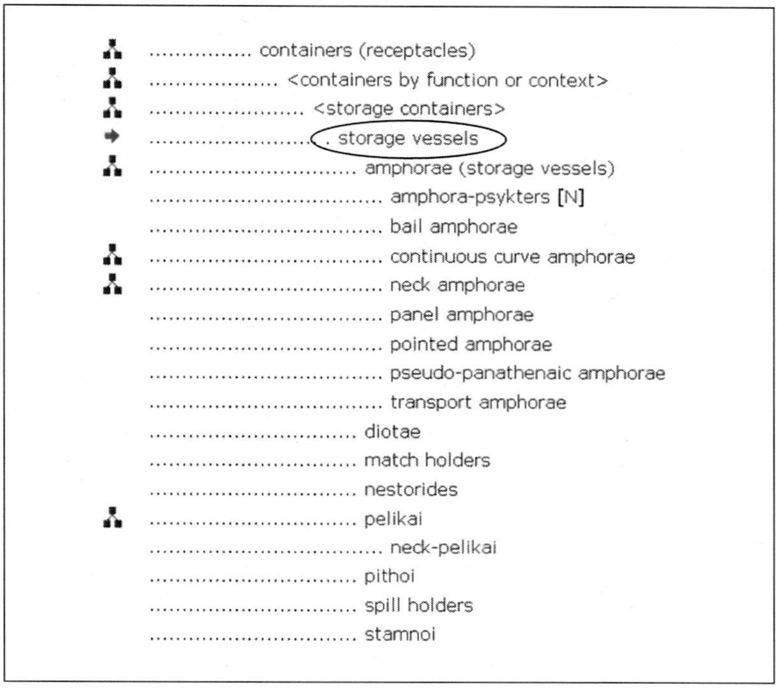

Fig. 70. Example of narrower and broader terms for *storage vessels*. If a user is searching for storage vessels, it may usually be assumed that he or she also wishes to find information for specific types of storage vessels, such as *amphorae* and *pithoi*. However, it should not be assumed that he or she would want information on all broader terms, such as *containers*.

providing a broader context to the query could narrow the results; for example, add one or more of the "parents" of Paris, which are *Europe, France,* and *Île-de-France,* to the search criteria.

Hierarchies are also powerful aids in expanding searches. The rules surrounding construction of thesaural relationships are largely driven by the eventuality of employing hierarchical relationships to enhance retrieval. Retrieving down a hierarchy is highly desirable; if users ask for a term, the search engine should give them the option of also including the terms for all the children of that concept (with their respective descriptors and variant terms) in the query. For example, if a user asks for *storage vessels,* most likely he or she also wants to retrieve all specific types of *storage vessels.* Therefore, the user should have the option of including all the narrower concepts for *storage vessels* in the search, such as *amphorae, diotae,* and *pithoi.* A user interested in Tuscany, Italy, may want to look for data associated with names of any city or town in Tuscany; the hierarchical vocabulary can provide a list of these names to be used in a search.

Retrieving up the hierarchy and retrieving siblings are not typically expected by the user and generally should not be employed. If the user searches specifically for *decanters,* he or she does not expect to additionally receive all other types of serving vessels and their broader contexts. However, allowing the user the option of including broader contexts and siblings may be useful in certain situations.

9.3.9.3. Associative Relationships in Retrieval

Expanding a search with associative relationships may be desirable but should typically be done only when requested by the user. However, the option should be available. For example, a user interested in the wall paintings known as *frescoes* may also be interested in the related concept of *sinopie* (the drawings under a fresco), which would be linked through an associative relationship. A user interested in the French manufactory *Manufacture nationale des Gobelins* (which produced tapestries, furniture, *pietre dure,* and other items) may also be interested in information about the artists of the manufactory. The search engine could offer the user the option of also looking for Gobelins artists linked through associative relationships, including *Marc de Comans* and *François de la Planche,* among others. The following is an example of associative relationships for an architectural firm.

Richard Meier & Partners
Associative relationships:
members are:
Richard Meier
Bernhard Karpf
Michael Palladino
Reynolds Logan
James R. Crawford

9.4. Other Data Used in Retrieval

In addition to queries by names and terms, qualifiers, and hierarchical relationships, additional search criteria can be used to retrieve vocabulary records.

9.4.1. Unique Identifiers as Search Criteria

In a local or controlled environment, the unique numeric identifier for a concept can provide a link between the content being queried and the vocabulary used to aid retrieval (e.g., the seven-digit number *7008038* is the unique identifier of *Paris, France* in the *TGN*). For instance, the identifier for a particular object or concept in a controlled vocabulary could be placed in an object record by a cataloger (presumably in an automatic way aided by the cataloging system) and could thus be linked to the vocabulary to provide extremely accurate retrieval through the use of variants and other data.

This method, of course, does not work when querying across disparate databases that do not all use the numeric identifier or when querying across the Web at large. Generally, in these cases, the vocabularies can be used to suggest terminology to users for queries or to broaden queries automatically behind the scenes; however, they cannot guarantee refined, precise results.

9.4.2. Other Vocabulary Data Used in Retrieval

Controlled descriptive information in the vocabulary record may be used for retrieval. For example, the place type for geographic information or the life roles of people are controlled lists that would be helpful in narrowing searches. The nationality of a person, geographic coordinates of a place, or associated dates would also be useful in retrieval. Such criteria would typically be used in a query in combination with names or other information.

For example, with geographic information, users could find all villages within a certain set of coordinates. With artist information, a user may want to find vocabulary records for all people who were English watercolorists (*English* is the nationality, *watercolorist* is the role); once these records are retrieved, the names in the vocabulary records could be gathered to use in a search against work records or other content objects. On the following page are examples of search interfaces using information in addition to names for retrieval.

9.5. Results Lists

A critical issue related to querying vocabulary data is how to display the information once it is retrieved. Since vocabularies can be very rich and complex, decisions must be made regarding how to display the information without confusing or overwhelming the user. An initial results list should include matches on the terms or names used in the query as well as a brief reference to each concept (e.g., for *TGN*, a preferred name, place type, and hierarchical context). From there, the user can either view the full record for the concept or view the concept in the full hierarchical display. Displays are designed with the goal of presenting as much information as necessary in a clear and coherent way. See **Chapter 7: Constructing a Vocabulary or Authority** for further discussion of displays.

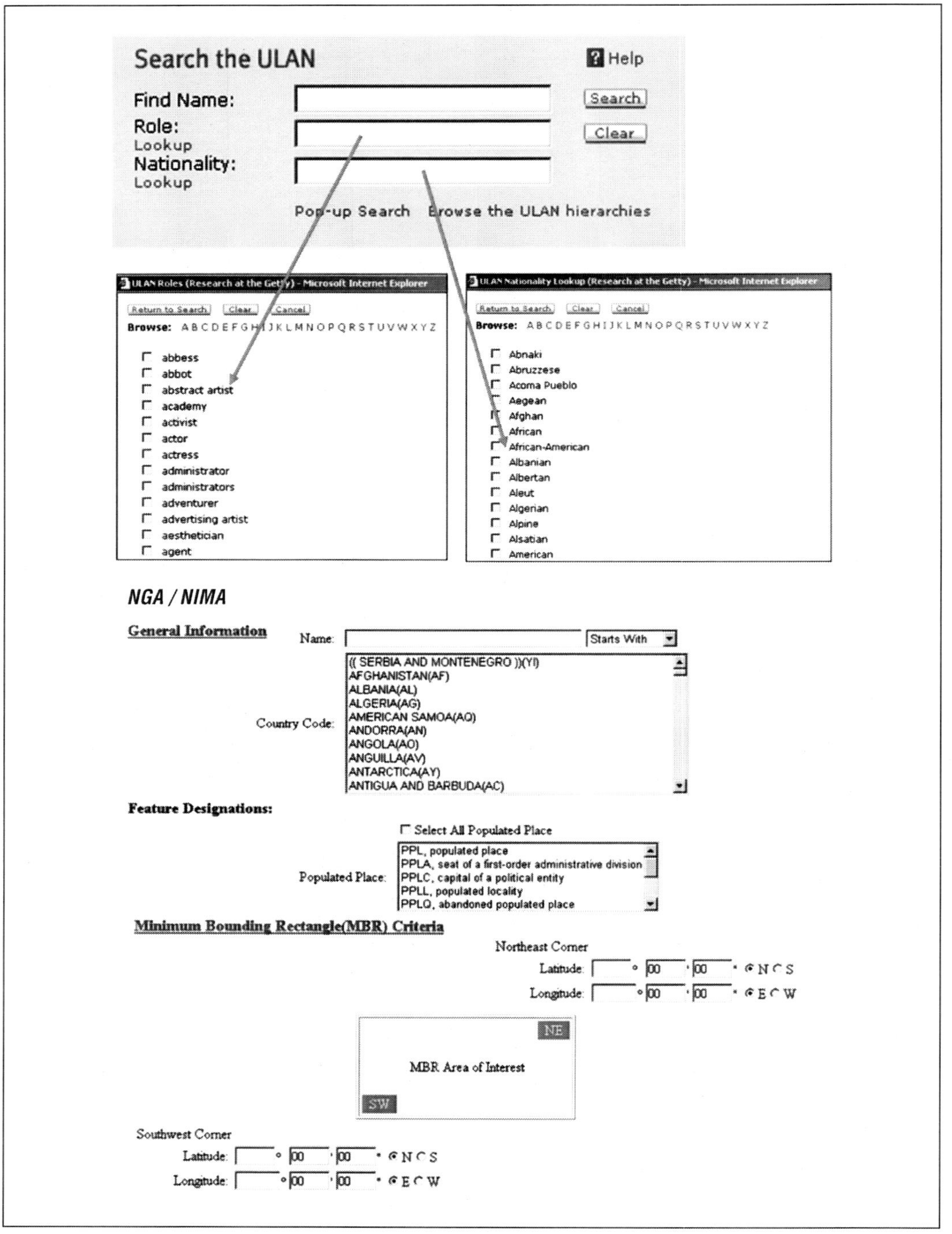

Fig. 71. Examples of search screens with various criteria for queries in the *ULAN* and National Geospatial-Intelligence Agency (NGA) *GEOnet Names Server (GNS)*. In the upper image, criteria for a search in the *ULAN* include the name, nationality, and role (e.g., *abstract artist*). In the lower image, a search on the NGA data includes criteria such as the name, the nation to which the place belongs, place type, and coordinates.

Appendix: Selected Vocabularies and Other Sources for Terminology

Abbey, Cherie D., ed. *Holidays, Festivals, and Celebrations of the World Dictionary.* 4th ed. Detroit: Omnigraphics, 2009.

America Preserved: A Checklist of Historic Buildings, Structures, and Sites. 60th ed. Washington, D.C.: Library of Congress, 1995.

Avery Library. *Avery Index to Architectural Periodicals.* Boston: G. K. Hall, 1994–.

Bénézit, Emmanuel, ed. *Dictionnaire critique et documentaire des peintres, sculpteurs, dessinateurs et graveurs de tous les temps et de tous les pays.* Originally published 1911–23. Paris: Librairie Gründ, 1976.

Bénézit, Emmanuel, Jacques Busse, Christophe Dorny, et al., eds. *Bénézit Dictionary of Artists.* 14 vols. Paris: Librairie Gründ, 2006.

Bibliographic Standards Committee of the Rare Books and Manuscripts Section (ACRL/ALA). *Genre Terms: A Thesaurus for Use in Rare Book and Special Collections Cataloguing.* 2nd ed. Chicago: Association of College and Research Libraries, 1991.

———. *Paper Terms: A Thesaurus for Use in Rare Book and Special Collections Cataloguing.* Chicago: Association of College and Research Libraries, 1990.

Bourcier, Paul. *Nomenclature 3.0 for Museum Cataloging: Third Edition of Robert G. Chenhall's System for Classifying Man-Made Objects.* New York: AltaMira Press, 2009.

Chenhall, Robert G. *Revised Nomenclature for Museum Cataloging: A Revised and Expanded Version of Robert G. Chenhall's System for Classifying Man-Made Objects.* Edited by the Nomenclature Committee. Nashville: AASLH, 1988.

Cohen, Saul B., ed. *Columbia Gazetteer of the World.* 2nd ed. New York: Columbia Univ. Press, 2008.

Fanning, Eileen, ed. *Official Museum Directory, 2009.* New Providence, N.J.: National Register Publishing, 2009.

Fletcher, Banister, and Dan Cruickshank, eds. *History of Architecture.* 20th ed. New York: Architectural, 1996.

Freeman, William. *Dent Dictionary of Fictional Characters.* Revised by Martin Seymour-Smith. London: Dent, 1991.

Gardner, Helen. *Gardner's Art through the Ages.* 12th ed. Edited by Fred S. Kleiner and Christin J. Mamiya. Belmont, Calif.: Thomson/Wadsworth, 2005.

Garnier, François. *Thesaurus iconographique: Système descriptif des représentations.* Paris: Léopard d'or, 1984.

Getty Vocabulary Program. *Art & Architecture Thesaurus (AAT).* Los Angeles: J. Paul Getty Trust, 1990–. http://www.getty.edu/research/conducting_research/vocabularies/aat/.

———. *Cultural Objects Name Authority (CONA)*. Los Angeles: J. Paul Getty Trust, forthcoming.

———. *Getty Thesaurus of Geographic Names (TGN)*. Los Angeles: J. Paul Getty Trust, 1997–. http://www.getty.edu/research/conducting_research/vocabularies/tgn/.

———. *Union List of Artist Names (ULAN)*. Los Angeles: J. Paul Getty Trust, 1990–. http://www.getty.edu/research/conducting_research/vocabularies/ulan/.

Grove Art Online. Oxford Univ. Press, 2008–. http://www.oxfordartonline.com.

Grun, Bernard, and Eva Simpson. *The Timetables of History: A Horizontal Linkage of People and Events*. 4th rev. ed. New York: Touchstone/Simon & Schuster, 2005.

Janson, Anthony F. *Janson's History of Art*. 7th ed. New York: Prentice Hall and Harry N. Abrams, 2006.

Kohn, George Childs. *Dictionary of Wars*. 3rd ed. New York: Facts on File, 2006.

Library of Congress. *Library of Congress Authorities*. Washington, D.C.: Library of Congress, 2002–. http://authorities.loc.gov/.

———. *Thesaurus for Graphic Materials I: Subject Terms*. Washington, D.C.: Library of Congress, 2004–7. http://lcweb.loc.gov/rr/print/tgm1/toc.html.

———. *Thesaurus for Graphic Materials II: Genre and Physical Characteristic Terms*. Washington, D.C.: Library of Congress, 2004–7. http://lcweb.loc.gov/rr/print/tgm2/.

Magill, Frank N. *Cyclopedia of Literary Characters*. Rev. ed. Edited by A. J. Sobczak and Janet Alice Long. Pasadena: Salem, 1998.

Mayer, Ralph. *Artist's Handbook of Materials and Techniques*. 5th ed. Edited by Steven Sheehan. New York: Viking, 1991.

Meissner, Günter, ed. *Allgemeines Künstlerlexikon: Die bildenden Künstler aller Zeiten und Völker*. Munich: Saur, 1992–.

Mellersh, H. E. L., and Neville Williams. *Chronology of World History*. 4 vols. Santa Barbara: ABC-CLIO, 1999.

Merriam-Webster's Geographical Dictionary. 3rd ed. Springfield, Mass.: Merriam-Webster, 2007.

Narkiss, Bezalel, and Gabrielle Sed-Rajna et al., eds. *Index of Jewish Art: Iconographical Index of Hebrew Illuminated Manuscripts*. Jerusalem: Israel Academy of Sciences and Humanities, 1976–.

National Geographic Atlas of the World. 8th ed. Washington, D.C.: National Geographic Society, 2004.

National Geospatial-Intelligence Agency (NGA). *GEOnet Names Server (GNS)*. Washington, D.C.: National Geospatial-Intelligence Agency, 2004–. http://earth-info.nga.mil/gns/html/index.html.

New International Atlas. 25th anniversary ed. Chicago: Rand McNally, 1997.

Osborne, Harold, ed. *Oxford Companion to Art*. Oxford: Clarendon, 1970.

Oxford Atlas of the World. 14th ed. New York: Oxford Univ. Press, 2007.

Placzek, Adolf K., ed. *Macmillan Encyclopedia of Architects*. New York: Free, 1982.

Rijksbureau voor Kunsthistorische Documentatie (RKD). *Iconclass Libertas Browser*. Amsterdam: Koninklijke Nederlandse Akademie van Wetenschappen (KNAW), 2004–6.

The Hague: Rijksbureau voor Kunsthistorische Documentatie, 2006–. http://www.iconclass.nl/libertas/ic?style=index.xsl.

Roberts, Helene E., ed. *Encyclopedia of Comparative Iconography: Themes Depicted in Works of Art.* 2 vols. Chicago: Fitzroy Dearborn, 1998.

Stillwell, Richard, William L. MacDonald, and Marian Holland McAllister, eds. *Princeton Encyclopedia of Classical Sites.* 2nd ed. Princeton: Princeton Univ. Press, 1979.

Stutley, Margaret. *Illustrated Dictionary of Hindu Iconography.* New Delhi: Munshiram Manoharlal, 2003.

Thieme, Ulrich, and Felix Becker, eds. *Allgemeines Lexikon der bildenden Künstler von der Antike bis zur Gegenwart.* 37 vols. Leipzig: Seemann, 1907. Reprint 1980–1986.

Times Comprehensive Atlas of the World. 12th ed. New York: Times, 2008.

Turner, Jane, ed. *Grove Dictionary of Art.* London: Macmillan, 1999–.

U.S. Geological Survey (USGS). *Geographic Names Information System (GNIS).* Reston, Va.: U.S. Geologic Survey and U.S. Board on Geographic Names. http://geonames.usgs.gov/.

Note: All Web sites were accessed on 1 May 2009.

Glossary

abbreviation
A shortened form of a name or term (e.g., *Mr.* for *Mister*). *See also* **acronym** and **initialism.**

access point
An entry point to a systematic arrangement of information, specifically an indexed field or heading in a work record, a vocabulary record, or another content object that is formatted and indexed in order to provide access to the information in the record.

acronym
An abbreviation or word formed from the initial letters of a compound term or phrase (e.g., MoMA, for Museum of Modern Art). *See also* **abbreviation** and **initialism.**

ad hoc query
Also called a **direct query.** A query or report that is constructed when required and that directly accesses data files and fields that are selected only when the query is created. It differs from a **predefined report** or querying a database through a **user interface.**

administrative data
In the context of cataloging art, information having to do with the administrative history and care of the work and the history of the catalog record (e.g., insurance value, conservation history, and revision history of the catalog record). *See also* **descriptive data.**

administrative entity
In the context of a geographic vocabulary, a political or other administrative body defined by administrative boundaries and conditions, including inhabited places, empires, nations, states, districts, and townships. *See also* **physical feature.**

algorithm
In the context of this book, an algorithm is a procedure, a formula, or the rules in a computer program or set of programs, often expressed in algebraic notation, that follow a logical, unambiguous step-by-step process to retrieve a set of results, solve a problem, make a decision, manipulate or alter data, or achieve some other result or state. Although a computer program may be considered one large algorithm, in common usage in computer science, the term typically refers to a small procedure applied recurrently. *See also* **computer program.**

alphanumeric classification scheme
A set of controlled codes (letters or numbers or both) that represent concepts or headings and generally have an implied taxonomy that can be surmised from the codes (e.g., the Dewey Decimal Classification system number 735.942). *See also* **chain indexing.**

alternate descriptor (AD)
A variant form of a descriptor available for use; usually a singular form or a different part of speech than the descriptor (e.g., *lithograph* is an alternate descriptor for the plural descriptor *lithographs*). In thesauri, the relationship indicator for this type of term is AD.

ancestor
In a hierarchy, any record that is a broader context for the record at hand, including parents, grandparents, and all other broader contexts at higher levels; any node in the succession of parent nodes on a path all the way up to the root. *See also* **descendant.**

antonym
A term that is the opposite in meaning of another term (e.g., *roughness* is an antonym for *smoothness*).

application
Also called an **application program.** A software program designed to accomplish a task for an end user (e.g., word processing or project management), as distinguished from the **operating system** program that runs the computer itself.

application programming interface (API)
In the context of this book, an online system, source code, and interface that a data provider (e.g., a vocabulary provider or library) employs to allow users to have access to the data. It may be language dependent (designed for a specific programming language) or language independent (works with multiple programming languages).

architect
A person or firm involved in the design or creation of structures or parts of structures that are the result of conscious construction, are of practical use, are relatively stable and permanent, and are of a size and scale appropriate for—but not limited to—habitable buildings.

architectural work
See **built work.**

architecture
Refers to the built environment that is typically classified as fine art, meaning it is generally considered to have aesthetic value, was designed by an architect, and was constructed with skilled labor. *See also* **built work.**

archival group
See **group.**

art
In the context of this book, refers to the **visual arts** such as painting, sculpture, drawing, printmaking, photography, ceramics, textiles, and decorative arts of the type and caliber generally collected by museums. Performance art is also included, but the performing arts are not. Note that these are works of visual art of the *type* collected by art museums. The objects themselves may actually be held by an ethnographic, anthropological, or other museum, or owned by a private collector.

artist
Any person or group of people involved in the design or production of visual arts that are of the type collected by art museums.

ascending order
In the context of a string of hierarchical parents, refers to the display of parents from narrowest to broadest (e.g., *Columbus (Bartholomew county, Indiana, United States)*). *See also* **descending order.**

ASCII
Acronym for the American Standard Code for Information Interchange, a 7-bit character code defining 128 characters used for information interchange, data processing, and communications systems.

associative relationship
In a thesaurus, the relationship between concepts that are closely related conceptually, but the relationship is not hierarchical because it is not whole/part or genus/species. The relationship indicator for this relationship is RT (for **related term**). *See also* **equivalence relationship** and **hierarchical relationship.**

asymmetric relationship
In the context of a thesaurus, refers to a reciprocal relationship that is different in one direction than it is in the reverse direction—for example, BT/NT (for **broader term/narrower term**). *See also* **symmetric relationship.**

authoritative source
A published source that is based on reliable documentary evidence that is accepted as true by most experts and used as a standard source in a given discipline.

authority file
Also called simply an **authority.** A file, typically electronic, that serves as a source

of standardized forms of names, terms, titles, etc. Authority files should include references or links from variant forms to preferred forms. The main purpose of an authority is to enforce usage, often requiring users to use only the preferred term for a given concept. Any type of vocabulary can be used as an authority. *See also* **controlled vocabulary** and **local authority.**

authority heading
A preferred, authorized heading used in a vocabulary, particularly in a bibliographic authority file that typically includes a string of names or terms, with additional information as necessary to allow disambiguation between identical headings (e.g., *United States—History—Civil War, 1861–1865—Battlefields* and *United States—History—Civil War, 1861–1865—Campaigns*). The types of authority headings used by the Library of Congress are the following: subject, name, title, name/title, and keyword authority headings. *See also* **heading.**

authorization
In the context of vocabularies, the process by which the creators of a vocabulary or an oversight group regulate the selection of terms and establishment of relationships in a controlled vocabulary. *See also* **warrant.**

automatic indexing
In the context of online retrieval, indexing by the analysis of text or other content using computer algorithms. The focus is on automatic methods used behind the scenes with little or no input from individual searchers, with the exception of relevance feedback. The results tend to be broad and imprecise, as contrasted to human **indexing.** *See also* **co-occurrence mapping.**

autoposting
See **up-posting.**

batch load
In the context of populating or contributing to vocabulary systems or other databases, refers to moving or manipulating a group of records as a single unit for the purpose of data processing, typically accomplished by the computer without user interaction, as contrasted to entering records manually, one at a time. *See also* **load** and **processing.**

batch processing
See **processing.**

best match
Also called a **weighted term ranking.** Refers to a variety of electronic term-matching and ranking methods that attempt to predict the potential relevance of query results by assigning relevance scores and ranking based on comparing search terms to the indexing terms of the target database. *See also* **exact match.**

blind reference
In the context of a vocabulary that is being used for indexing or retrieval on a defined data set, refers to a term in the vocabulary that is not linked to any content in the data set. End users should typically not receive blind references in a retrieval situation because they result in a failed search; however, these terms should be retained in structured vocabularies that are used for indexing because they may be needed in the future or in another context.

Boolean operators
Logical operators used as modifiers to refine the relationship between terms in a search. The four most commonly used Boolean operators are AND, OR, NOT, and ADJ (adjacent). They may be used with parentheses and other punctuation to form logical groupings of criteria in queries (e.g., *(Castillo OR Rancho) AND Diego*).

bound term
A compound term representing a single concept, characterized by the fact that the words almost always occur together and the meaning is lost or altered if the term is split into its component words. *See also* **compound term** and **lexical unit.**

brand name
A trade or proprietary name for a thing or process (e.g., *Super Glue*).

broadcast searching
See **federated searching.**

broaden results
To adjust criteria in a search in order to retrieve a larger number of results, typically because the searcher did not find what he or she wanted in an initial narrower search. *See also* **narrow results.**

broader term (BT)
Also called a **broader context.** A vocabulary record to which another record or multiple records are subordinate in a hierarchy. In thesauri, the relationship indicator for this type of term is BT. Variations on the notation include BTG (broader term generic), BTP (broader term partitive), BTI (broader term instance), BT1 (broader term level 1), BT2 (broader term level 2), etc.

browsing
The process whereby a user of a system or Web site visually scans and maneuvers through navigation lists, results lists, hierarchical displays, or other content in order to make a selection, as contrasted to the user entering a search term in a search box. *See also* **searching.**

built work
An instance of architecture, which includes structures or parts of structures that are the result of conscious construction, are of practical use, are relatively stable and permanent, and are of a size and scale appropriate for—but not limited to—habitable buildings. Built works in the context of art information are manifestations of the built environment typically classified as fine art, meaning it is generally considered to have aesthetic value, was designed by an architect (whether or not his or her name is known), and constructed with skilled labor. *See also* **architecture** and **movable work.**

candidate term
Also known as a **provisional term.** A term under consideration for admission into a controlled vocabulary because of its potential usefulness. *See also* **contribution.**

cataloger
In the context of this book, the person who records information in records for works. *See also* **end user** and **indexer.**

cataloging
In the context of this book, the process of describing and indexing a work or image, particularly in a collections management system or other automated system. Cataloging involves the use of prescribed fields of information and rules (e.g., the rules described in *CCO* and *CDWA*).

cataloging rules
See **editorial rules.**

cataloging tool
A system that focuses on content description and labeling output (e.g., wall labels or slide labels), often part of a more complex **collection management system.**

chain indexing
Also called **chain procedure.** A technique for indexing that uses a numeric or **alphanumeric classification scheme**—for example, the Dewey Decimal Classification system—where the entries have meaning beyond simple numeric sequencing (e.g., in Dewey number 735.942, 735 means *sculpture after the year* 1400 CE, 9 means *geographic area,* 4 means *Europe*, and 2 means *England*).

child
See **narrower term.**

classification
In the context of this book, the process of arranging works or other content objects systematically in groups or categories of shared similarity according to established criteria and using terms to identify the classes.

classification notation
In a vocabulary, a numeric, alphabetic, or alphanumeric code in a system of codes used to classify or categorize entries; may be used in a hierarchical arrangement to impose a display or sorting order on the lines or levels in the hierarchy (e.g., V, V.PC, V.PE). *See also* **notation.**

classified display
See **hierarchical display.**

clustering
In the context of automated data, usually refers to the process of grouping or classifying items or data through automatic or algorithmic means rather than incorporating human judgment.

code
See **computer code.**

collection
In the context of cataloging art, refers to multiple works that are physically or conceptually arranged together, including the entire set of objects curated by a given museum or other repository.

collection management system (CMS)
A type of database system that allows an institution to control various aspects of its collections, including description (artist, title, measurements, media, style, subject, etc.) as well as administrative information regarding acquisitions, loans, and conservation information.

complex term
A single phrase denoting more than two distinct concepts, which could be broken out and used independently, as defined by the Library of Congress. *See also* **bound term, compound term,** and **heading.**

component
In the context of cataloging art and architecture, a part of a larger item. A component differs from an item in that an item can stand alone as an independent work, but a component typically cannot or does not stand alone (e.g., a panel of a polyptych or a façade of a basilica). *See also* **group** and **item.**

compound term
A term consisting of two or more words. In the context of this book, mention of compound terms generally refers to bound terms, which are compound terms that represent a single concept (e.g., *flying buttresses*). *See also* **bound term, complex term,** and **lexical unit.**

computer code
Also called **code.** The machine-readable form, arrangement of data, and instructions of a computer program that are created when a computer program, which was written by a human programmer, is converted into binary code that can be read by a computer.

computer program
Also called a **program.** A specific set of instructions for ordered operations that result in the completion of a task by the computer; a computer program consists of **computer code.** While the program is technically a type of data, computer programs are generally considered as separate from the data to which the programs refer (e.g., data would be the terms, scope notes, etc., in a vocabulary record). A program is *interactive* if it acts when prompted by an action or information supplied by a user, or *batch* if it automatically runs at a certain time or under certain conditions and then stops after the task is completed. A program is written in a **programming language.** *See also* **processing.**

computer system
See **system.**

concept
In the context of the *AAT* and other thesauri comprising generic terms, the subject of the vocabulary record (i.e., the concept to which the terms refer), including abstract concepts; physical attributes such as shape, pattern, and color; style or period; activities; terms for performers of activities; materials; objects; and visual and verbal communication forms. *See also* **discrete concept.**

concept record
See **record.**

conceptual data model
An abstract model or representation of data for a particular domain, business enterprise, field of study, etc., independent of

any specific software or information system; usually expressed in terms of entities and relationships. *See also* **logical data model.**

content object
In the context of a database, any entity that contains data. A content object can itself be made up of content objects. For example, a journal is a content object made up of individual journal articles, which are themselves content objects. *See also* **information object.**

contribution
In the context of controlled vocabularies, a term or record that is submitted for admission into a thesaurus or other vocabulary by an agency or individual outside the group responsible for maintaining the vocabulary; contributions are typically made by users of the vocabulary. *See also* **candidate term.**

controlled field
In the context of this book, a field in a record that is not free text, meaning it is specially formatted and often linked to controlled vocabularies (authorities) or controlled lists to allow for successful retrieval. *See also* **free-text field.**

controlled format
Rules applied to the field regarding the types of values that may be included (e.g., a controlled measurement's value field would allow only numbers). Fields may have controlled format in addition to being linked to controlled vocabulary, or the controlled format may exist in the absence of any finite controlled list of valid values.

controlled list
A simple list of terms used to control terminology. In a well-constructed controlled list, terms should be unique, members of the same class, not overlapping in meaning, equal in granularity/specificity, and arranged alphabetically or in another logical order. A type of **controlled vocabulary.**

controlled vocabulary
An organized arrangement of words and phrases used to index content and/or to retrieve content through browsing or searching. A controlled vocabulary typically includes preferred and variant terms and has a limited scope or describes a specific domain.

co-occurrence mapping
Also called **co-occurrence clustering.** An automated method of compiling groups of terms that tend to occur together in certain contexts and are therefore presumed to be related in some way; the resulting groups of terms are considered to be loosely related and may be used to automatically broaden a user's search or to suggest alternative search terms to users in order to improve search results. *See also* **automatic indexing.**

core fields
Also called **core elements.** In the context of this book, the set of fields representing the fundamental or most important information required for a minimal record, whether the record is a work record or a vocabulary record. *See also* **required fields.**

corporate body
In the context of vocabularies discussed in this book, an organized, identifiable group of individuals working together in a particular place and within a defined period of time, whether or not they are legally incorporated (e.g., architectural firms, artist studios, and art repositories).

criteria
In the context of this book, a specific set of limiting conditions used to create a query or select a subset of entries (e.g., a *WHERE statement* in SQL). *See also* **variable.**

cross-database searching
See **federated searching.**

cross-reference links
See **syndetic structure.**

crosswalk
A chart or table (visual or virtual) that represents the semantic or technical mapping of fields or data elements in one database, metadata framework, standard, or schema to fields or data elements that have a

similar function or meaning in one or more other databases, frameworks, standards, or schemas (e.g., the *artist* element in one standard may map to the *creator* element in another). *See also* **mapping.**

cultural heritage
The total corpus of activities and the artifacts of activities that provide a record of the life of a culture. *See also* **material culture.**

cultural works
In the context of this book, art and architectural works and other artifacts of cultural significance, including both physical objects and performance art. In related disciplines, the scope could be broader, also including the performing arts.

data
In common usage in computer science, this term is used as a singular noun to refer to information that exists in a form that may be used by a computer, excluding the program code. In other uses, *datum* is the singular and *data* is the plural, referring to facts or numbers in a general sense.

database
A structured set of data held in computer storage, especially one that incorporates software to make it accessible in a variety of ways. A database is used to store, query, and retrieve information. It typically comprises a logical collection of interrelated information that is managed as a unit, stored in machine-readable form, and organized and structured as records that are presented in a standardized format in order to allow rapid search and retrieval by a computer. *See also* **system.**

database field
Also called a **data field.** A placeholder for a set of one or more adjacent characters comprising a unit of information in a database, forming one of the searchable items in that database. It is a portion of a structured record, especially a machine-readable record, containing a particular category of information (e.g., *term* and *scope note* would be fields included in a vocabulary record). *See also* **field.**

database index
Also called a **data index.** A particular type of data structure that improves the speed of operations in a table by allowing the quick location of particular records based on key column values. Indexes are essential for good database performance. The concept is distinguished from **indexing** (human indexing) and **automatic indexing.**

database normalization
See **normalization.**

database record
See **record.**

data content
The organization and formatting of the words or terms that form **data values.**

data elements
The specific categories or types of information that are collected and aggregated in a database.

data preprocessing
See **preprocessing.**

data processing
See **processing.**

data structure
A given organization of data, particularly the data elements, the logical relationships between data elements, and the storage allocations for the data.

data table
Sets of data that are organized in a grid or matrix comprising rows and columns.

data values
In the context of this book, the terms, words, or numbers used to populate fields in a work or vocabulary record. *See also* **data content.**

decoordination
In the context of a thesaurus, the splitting of a **compound term** into its component words to stand as individual terms. This would typically happen if a compound term

had been added to the thesaurus but was later determined not to be a **bound term.**

deep Web
See **hidden Web.**

derivation
Also called **modeling.** In the context of this book, the process of building a new vocabulary based on an existing vocabulary. In this approach, an appropriate controlled vocabulary is selected as a model for developing controlled terminology for local use, so that the local terms will be interoperable with the larger original vocabulary. *See also* **local authority** and **microcontrolled vocabulary.**

descendant
Also often spelled **descendent** in the disciplines of computer science and thesaurus construction. In a hierarchy, any record that is a narrower context for the record at hand, including children, grandchildren, and all other narrower contexts at all lower levels; any node in the succession of parent nodes on a path all the way down to the tips (leaves) of the hierarchies. *See also* **ancestor.**

descending order
In the context of a string of hierarchical parents, the display of parents from broadest to narrowest (e.g., *Columbus (United States, Indiana, Bartholomew county)*). *See also* **ascending order.**

descriptive data
In the context of cataloging art, data intended to describe and identify a work, as contrasted to information necessary for administrative, technical, or accounting purposes. *See also* **administrative data.**

descriptor (D)
In a thesaurus, the term recommended to represent the concept in displays and indexing. *Also* called the **main term, postable term,** or **preferred term** in a monolingual thesaurus. A multilingual thesaurus may have multiple descriptors (one in each language represented) but may possibly have only one preferred term for use as a default in displays. In thesauri, the relationship indicator for this type of term is D.

diacritics
Also called **diacritical marks.** Signs or accent marks found over, under, or through alphabetic letters in many languages (e.g., the umlaut in German, *München*), used to indicate emphasis or pronunciation, often to distinguish different sounds or values of the same letter or character without the diacritical mark.

digital asset management system (DAMS)
A type of system for organizing digital media assets, such as digital images or video clips, for storage and retrieval. Digital asset management systems sometimes incorporate a descriptive data cataloging component, but they tend to focus on managing workflow for creating digital assets and for managing asset rights, requests, and permissions.

direct mapping
In the context of interoperability of vocabularies, refers to the matching of terms one-to-one in two controlled vocabularies. While the vocabularies need not be the same size or cover exactly the same content, where overlap exists, there should be the same meaning and level of specificity between the two terms in each controlled vocabulary. *See also* **switching.**

direct query
See **ad hoc query.**

disambiguation
In the context of creating and displaying a vocabulary, the use of qualifiers, headings, or other methods to clarify and remove ambiguity between homographs (e.g., *Smith, John (English printmaker, 1654–1742)* and *Smith, John (English architect, 1781–1852)*). *See also* **word sense disambiguation.**

discrete concept
In the context of a generic concept vocabulary, a discrete thing or idea as opposed to

a subject heading, which often concatenates multiple terms or concepts together in a string. *See also* **concept.**

displayed index
An index that is visible and available to end users for browsing. *See also* **nondisplayed index.**

display field
In the context of this book, a field intended for viewing by the end user, typically showing data in natural language that is easily read and understood and that can convey nuance and ambiguity. Display information may, in some cases, be concatenated from controlled fields; in other cases, this information is best recorded in free-text fields. *See also* **indexing.**

document
In the context of search and retrieval, the combination of a defined, primarily self-contained, machine-readable text or other information and the format in which it is housed.

dominant language
In the context of multilingual vocabularies, the more prominent or original language to which terms in other languages are mapped and in which other fields in the record (e.g., scope notes or date notes) are written. In a purely multilingual vocabulary, no language is dominant, but in a rich and complex vocabulary (e.g., the *AAT*), a dominant language may be required for practical purposes.

download
See **load.**

editorial rules
In the context of this book, written rules and guidelines for creators or editors of vocabulary records that dictate how to populate fields and choose or interpret data. They should include which fields are required, how to choose appropriate values for various fields (e.g., how to choose a preferred term), how to choose hierarchical positions, the format and syntax for each field, authorized sources, etc. Analogous rules for catalogers of works are called **cataloging rules.**

end user
In the context of this book, usually the searcher, client, or patron who retrieves, views, and uses the data in a vocabulary or work record, as distinguished from the editors or catalogers. In the context of systems design, the term refers to any client for whom a database system is designed and used; from that perspective, it could include the editors or catalogers for whom an editorial or cataloging system has been designed.

end-user thesaurus
A thesaurus designed for direct access by searchers rather than for use by indexers. Instead of controlling the terminology, the purpose of an end-user thesaurus is to help searchers find useful terminology for improving, narrowing, and broadening their queries. *See also* **indexer thesaurus.**

entity
In the context of computer science, a self-contained piece of data that can be referenced as a unit. In a more general sense, the term is used in this book to refer to a distinct person, place, or concept in a vocabulary.

entity-relationship model
A type of conceptual data model that represents structured data in terms of entities and relationships. An **entity-relationship diagram** can be used to visually represent information objects and their relationships. Because the constructs used in the entity-relationship model can easily be transformed into relational tables, this type of model is often used in database design.

entry array
A type of display, often used for headings, in which any two or more entries that have the same broader heading (e.g., *Religious art—Ancient Egyptian, Religious art—Christian, Religious art—Hindu,* etc.) are grouped together vertically under the broader heading. While this is not a true hierarchical display, it may resemble a hierarchical display through use of indentation.

equivalence relationship
In a thesaurus, the relationship between synonymous terms or names for the same concept, typically distinguishing **preferred terms** (descriptors) and **nonpreferred terms** (variants or UFs). *See also* **associative relationship** and **hierarchical relationship.**

equivalent term
A term that is considered an equivalent in search-and-retrieval, including not only true synonyms but possibly also near-synonyms and any other terms that are considered closely enough related to be useful in broadening a query; to narrow a query, exact equivalents could be used instead.

exact equivalence
The relationship between synonyms in one language and terms in different languages that have the same usage and meaning. *See also* **inexact equivalence** and **nonequivalence.**

exact match
Electronic term-matching that produces a result that precisely matches the user's query term and does not implement automatic Boolean operators, truncation, proximity ranges, or stemming. In a strictly applied exact match, **normalization** is not used, so that differences in punctuation, spacing, and diacritics are maintained in the match. *See also* **best match.**

exhaustivity
In the context of cataloging and indexing, the degree of depth and breadth that the cataloger uses in assigning indexing terms or writing a description. Measures of greater exhaustivity include the use of a greater number of optional fields and the assignment of a greater number of indexing terms for each field. *See also* **specificity.**

expansion
See **query expansion.**

explode a hierarchy
To retrieve and display all the descendants of any given node, typically in a graphic display.

extension vocabulary
A thesaurus that is created with the intention of, or is later adapted for, linking to another vocabulary that is larger, broader, or more generic; the extension vocabulary is typically linked through node linking, rather than being integrated at many points in the original vocabulary. *See also* **microcontrolled vocabulary, node linking,** and **satellite vocabulary.**

external node
See **leaf node.**

facet
Also called a **faceted display.** A fundamental, homogeneous, and mutually exclusive category of information in a thesaurus (e.g., the *AAT* has seven facets: Associated Concepts, Physical Attributes, Styles and Periods, Agents, Materials, Activities, and Objects).

facet indicator
A **node label** that designates a **facet.**

false hit
Also called a **false drop.** In search and retrieval, an entry in a list of results that does not comply with the user's intended results.

federated searching
Also called **broadcast searching, cross-database searching, metasearching,** and **parallel searching.** Performing queries simultaneously across resources that are in different domains and created by different communities. Federated searching may involve searching across multiple databases, different platforms, and varying protocols, thus requiring the application of **interoperability** between resources and vocabularies.

field
In the context of this book, an area (often mapping to a metadata element in a metadata element set) in the user interface of a system where a discrete unit of information is displayed or the cataloger can enter information. Note: In this context, *field* is not necessarily equivalent to a **database field.**

filing rules
A set of guidelines that determine how letters, numbers, spaces, and special characters should be processed when assembling an alphabetical or other listing. *See also* **sorting.**

first name
Also called a **given name.** In Western tradition, the name of a person that identifies that individual, typically unique in the immediate family and used with a last name (e.g., *Richard* in *Richard Meier*). *See also* **last name** and **middle name.**

flat-file database
A database with a data model designed around a single table, often a single file containing many records that all have exactly the same fields. It is a simpler model than the more highly structured relational and object-oriented models.

flat format
In the context of a thesaurus, an alphabetical display in which only one level of broader contexts and one level of narrower contexts are displayed for each focus record. *See also* **generic structure.**

focus
Also known as a **head noun** for terms and a **trunk name** for proper names. In the context of a compound term, the noun component that identifies the class of concepts to which the term as a whole refers (e.g., *buttresses* in the term *flying buttresses*). In the context of a modified name such as a place name, the part of the name that is not a modifier (e.g., *Etna* in *Mount Etna*). *See also* **modifier.**

folksonomy
A neologism referring to an assemblage of concepts, which are represented by terms and names (called *tags*) that are compiled through **social tagging,** generally on the Web. A folksonomy differs from a **taxonomy** in that it is not structured hierarchically, and the authors of the folksonomy are typically the casual users of the content rather than professional indexers following standard protocols and using standardized controlled vocabularies.

format
Used in two senses in this book. In the context of cataloging art, the configuration of a work—including technical formats—or the conventional designation for the dimensions or proportion of a work (e.g., *cabinet photograph* or *IMAX*). In the context of computer science, the physical layout of a data storage device or the logical structure or composition of a file.

format control
See **controlled format.**

free-text field
A field that may contain data entered without any vocabulary control or system-defined structure. It may be used to express ambiguity, uncertainty, and nuance in a note. *See also* **controlled field** and **text.**

generic concept
In the context of this book, a concept in a vocabulary that is described by terms other than proper nouns or names (e.g., the type of artwork, such as *amphora*, or a material, such as *terracotta*). Generic concepts do not include proper names of persons, organizations, geographic places, named subjects, or named events.

generic posting
In controlled vocabularies, the use of narrower terms as *used for* terms for a descriptor that is really a broader term in the same vocabulary record. A generic posting is typically used as a time-saving strategy rather than making separate records for all the terms and linking them hierarchically. *See also* **up-posting.**

generic structure
A display format for a thesaurus in which all hierarchical levels are displayed by using indentation, codes, or punctuation marks. *See also* **flat format.**

genus/species relationship
Also called a **generic relationship.** A hierarchical relationship in which all

children must be a *kind of, type of, or manifestation of* the parent. The genus/species relationship is the most common hierarchical relationship in thesauri and taxonomies, because it is applicable to a wide range of topics. *See also* **instance relationship** and **whole/part relationship.**

given name
See **first name.**

gloss
See **qualifier.**

grandparent
In a thesaurus, the level immediately above the parent of the focus record (e.g., in the following example, *Indiana* is the grandparent of *Columbus: Columbus, Bartholomew county, Indiana, United States*).

granularity
See **specificity.**

group
Also called an **archival group** or **record group.** In the context of cataloging works, refers to an aggregate of items that share a common provenance. *See also* **component** and **item.**

group-level cataloging
Describing and assigning indexing terms for a group of works as a whole, typically focusing on the most important or most frequently occurring characteristics in the items of the group. *See also* **item-level cataloging.**

guide term
A **node label** that is not a **facet,** but is created as a hierarchical level to provide order and structure to thesauri by grouping narrower terms according to a given logic. Guide terms are not used for indexing and are often enclosed in angled brackets or otherwise distinguished from other terms in displays (e.g., *<photographs by form>*).

hardware
The physical components of a computer system, including those that are mechanical, electronic, magnetic, and electrical such as disks, disk drives, chips, electronic circuitry, keyboards, monitors, modems, and printers. *See also* **software.**

harmonization
In the context of vocabularies and standards, the process of preventing, minimizing, or eliminating technical and content differences and contradictions between standards or vocabularies that have the same or similar scope or that must work interchangeably or in concert.

heading
Also called a **label.** A string of words comprising a term combined with other information that serves to modify, disambiguate, amplify, or create a context for the main term in displays. Examples include the listing of qualifiers and/or broader contexts for terms (e.g., *rhyta (<vessels for serving and consuming food>, containers)*), place types and administrative broader contexts for place names (e.g., *Dayr al-Bahri (deserted settlement) (Qinā governorate, Egypt)*), or biographical information for people's names (e.g., *Francesco Aliunno (Italian calligrapher, active 15th century)*). *See also* **authority heading, name authority,** and **subject heading list.**

head noun
See **focus.**

hidden Web
Also called the **deep Web** or **invisible Web.** The sum of the Web pages that are not accessible to Web crawlers or robots, usually because they are either dynamically generated by a user querying a database or are password protected or subscription based.

hierarchical display
Also called a **classified display** or **systematic display.** In a thesaurus, a graphic arrangement of terms showing broader/narrower relationships through the use of indentation, codes, or another method.

hierarchical relationship
The broader and narrower (parent/child) relationship between two entities

in a thesaurus, namely whole/part (e.g., *Montréal* is part of *Québec*), genus/species (e.g., *bronze* is a type of *metal*), or instance relationships (e.g., *Montréal* is an instance of a *city*). It is the basic structure that creates a **hierarchy.**

hierarchy
An organization of records related by levels of superordination and subordination. Each record in the hierarchy, except the root, is a narrower context of the record above it. *See also* **monohierarchy, polyhierarchy,** and **subfacet.**

historical term
Also called a **historical name.** In the context of the vocabularies discussed in this book, a term or name that was used to refer to a person, place, subject, or concept in the past, but in current usage has been replaced with a different term or name (e.g., historical names for *St. Petersburg, Russia,* are *Leningrad* and *Petrograd*).

hits
See **results list.**

homograph
A term that is spelled the same as another term, but the meanings of the terms are different (e.g., *drums* can have at least three meanings: components of columns, membranophones, or walls that support a dome). Homographs exist whether or not the terms are pronounced alike. Terms are generally considered homographs despite differences in capitalization, punctuation, or diacritics. *See also* **qualifier.**

homophone
A term that is pronounced like another term but spelled differently (e.g., *bows* and *boughs*). Homophones are not typically labeled in traditional controlled vocabularies.

human indexing
See **indexing.**

hyperlink
Also called a **hypertext link.** In the context of online information, an embedded link that connects different parts of an online document or data set to other parts of the document or to other documents. It is usually indicated by color or other emphasis applied to a word, phrase, icon, or symbol.

hypertext database
A dataset that resides as a collection of online documents with links joining various parts to each other, with access provided via an interactive browser.

Hypertext Markup Language (HTML)
A markup language used to create the layout and presentation of documents for World Wide Web applications.

image
In the context of cataloging art, a visual representation of a *work,* usually existing in a photomechanical, photographic, or digital format. In a typical visual resources collection, an *image* is a slide, photograph, or digital file.

indentation
Also called **indention.** In the context of printing or other displays of typed words or texts, refers to the white or blank space of a fixed width on a row along the right or left margin of a display, as commonly used to indicate the first line in a new paragraph of text. Graduated indentation is used to indicate relationships between parents and their descendants in hierarchical displays of thesauri.

indexer
A person who assigns indexing terms for a work or image, typically the same person as the cataloger. *See also* **cataloger.**

indexer thesaurus
A thesaurus designed to control terminology and guide indexers in the choice of terms. *See also* **end-user thesaurus.**

indexing
Also called **human indexing** and **manual indexing.** In the context of this book, the process of evaluating information and designating indexing terms by using controlled vocabulary that aids in finding and accessing the cultural work record. Refers to indexing done by human

labor, not to the automatic parsing of data into a database index (**automatic indexing**), which is used by a system to speed up search and retrieval.

inexact equivalence
The relationship between synonyms in one language or terms in different languages that have similar or overlapping meaning and usage but are not true synonyms (e.g., *floating* and *flying*). *See also* **exact equivalence, nonequivalence,** and **partial equivalence.**

information object
A digital unit or group of units, regardless of type or format, that a computer can address or manipulate as a single discrete object. *See also* **content object.**

information processing
See **processing.**

information retrieval database
Also called an **IR database.** Any database designed primarily for discovering and retrieving information. The systems that work with IR databases provide the following: a search interface to permit users to compose queries, methods for searching through the target data, viewable or behind-the-scenes indexes, and results displays.

initialism
A set of initials that stand for the full form of a name (e.g., *MFA*, for *Museum of Fine Arts*). *See also* **abbreviation** and **acronym.**

instance relationship
A hierarchical relationship in which all children must be an example of a broader context, most commonly seen in vocabularies where proper names are organized by general categories of things or events (e.g., if the proper names of mountains and rivers are organized under the general categories *mountains* and *rivers*). *See also* **genus/species relationship** and **whole/part relationship.**

interactive processing
See **processing.**

internal node
See **nonleaf node.**

interoperability
In the context of controlled vocabularies, the ability of two or more vocabularies and their systems or components of their systems to map to each other's data, with the goal of exchanging information or enhancing discovery.

inverse document frequency (IDF)
An automatic ranking method often used in a formula with **term frequency** in information retrieval and text mining to estimate how important a term is to a set of data and how useful it will be in retrieval.

inverted form
Also called an **inverted index.** In the context of a controlled vocabulary, the indexing form of a multiple-word name or term, where the last name or trunk portion of the term is listed first, followed by a comma and the descriptive word (e.g., *Wren, Christopher,* or *buttresses, flying*). *See also* **natural order form** and **permuted index.**

invisible Web
See **hidden Web.**

ISO (International Organization for Standardization)
A worldwide voluntary, nontreaty network of national standards institutes of approximately 160 countries. The standards bodies work in partnership with international organizations, governments, industry, business, and consumer representatives to reach consensus, set standards, and promote their use with the goal of facilitating trade and meeting the broader needs of society.

item
In the context of cataloging art, an individual object or work. *See also* **component** and **group.**

item-level cataloging
Describing and assigning indexing terms for individual items in a collection of works. *See also* **group-level cataloging.**

jargon
A characteristic terminology of a particular group or discipline that is typically not understood by a more general audience.

keyword
In the context of vocabularies, a **verbal unit** or word of a term that may be used in a search expression (e.g., for the place name *Sena Julia, Sena* is one keyword and *Julia* is another). In the broader context of online retrieval, any significant word or phrase in the title, subject headings, or text associated with an information object.

Keyword in Context (KWIC)
A type of automatic indexing in which each word in a text, title, subject heading, string of words, or term becomes an entry word in the index, with the exception of words in **stop lists.** Variations on KWICs are KWOCs (Keyword Out of Context) and KWACs (Keyword Alongside Context).

keyword index
An index based on individual words (keywords) found in a vocabulary term, text, or other content object.

label
See **heading.**

language model
A type of automatic indexing based on term weighting and relevance prediction that attempts to predict probable query search terms based on term frequencies within documents and the inverse document frequency of terms across the target data. It is similar to the **probabilistic model.**

last name
Also called a **surname.** In Western tradition, the family name used with a first name to identify a person (e.g., *Meier* in *Richard Meier*). *See also* **first name** and **middle name.**

latent semantic indexing (LSI)
A form of automatic indexing based on the co-occurrence clustering of terms in combination with content that is associated with these clusters; it attempts to partially address the problem of the variety of terms that can be used to express similar concepts.

Latin 1
A character set (consisting of 191 characters) that is part of a series of ASCII-based character encodings defined in *ISO/IEC 8859-1:1998: 8-Bit Single-Byte Coded Graphic Character Sets—Part 1.*

latinization
See **romanization.**

lead-in term
See ***used for*** **term.**

leaf linking
See **node linking.**

leaf node
Also called an **external node.** In a thesaurus, a node that has no children, as with the ends or tips of hierarchical trees.

lexeme
A fundamental unit of the words of a language, around which may be clustered a set of words that are different forms of the same word (e.g., *paint* is the lexeme for *paints, painted*).

lexical unit
Also called a **lexical item.** One or more words that refer to a single concept (e.g., *flying buttresses* or *bills of sale*). *See also* **bound term** and **compound term.**

lexical variant
A term that is a different word form for another term, caused by spelling differences, grammatical variation, or abbreviations (e.g., *watercolor* and *water-colour*). Lexical variants are considered as and grouped with synonyms in a vocabulary record, but they technically differ from synonyms in that synonyms are different terms for the same concept. *See also* **synonym.**

link
In the context of this book, any relationship between two vocabulary records, two works, a work and image, or a work or image and an authority. Compare to **hyperlink.**

literary warrant
Justification for the inclusion of a term in a vocabulary based on published evidence that is sufficient to prove that the form, spelling, usage, and meaning of the term are widely agreed upon in authoritative sources. *See also* **organizational warrant, source,** and **user warrant.**

load
The process of moving or transferring files or software from one disk, computer, or server to another disk, computer, or server. To **upload** means to transfer from a local computer to a remote computer; to **download** means to transfer from a remote computer to a local one.

loan word
In the context of a given language, a word that is taken directly from another language (e.g., *sotto in su,* an Italian phrase used in English to mean painted in correct perspective as if viewed from below).

local authority
An authority developed for local use. Although often compiled from one or more standard authoritative published vocabularies, a local authority enforces preferences and usage pertinent for the local setting. *See also* **authority file** and **derivation.**

locator
In a bibliographic index, the part of an index entry that indicates the location of the book, page, or other resource. In an online index, it may be a hyperlink to the source.

logical data model
A data model that includes all entities and the relationships among them based on the structures identified in a conceptual data model, and that specifies all attributes for each entity. The data is described in as much detail as possible, without regard to how it will be implemented in a specific database. *See also* **conceptual data model.**

logical record
See **record.**

main term
See **descriptor.**

manual indexing
See **indexing.**

mapping
A set of correspondences between terms, fields, or element names used for translating data from one standard or vocabulary into another, or as a means of combining terms or data for search and retrieval. *See also* **crosswalk.**

markup language
A formal way of annotating a document or collection of digital data using embedded encoding tags to indicate the structure of the document or data file and the contents of its data elements. This markup also provides a computer with information about how to process and display marked-up documents. HTML, XML, and SGML are examples of standardized markup languages.

material culture
A term referring to art together with the broad realm of physical objects and edifices produced by a culture. *See also* **cultural heritage.**

metadata
A structured set of descriptive elements used to describe a definable entity. This data may include one or more pieces of information, which can exist as separate physical forms. In the context of art information, metadata includes data associated with information about the creation, physical characteristics, history, location, administration, or preservation of the work.

Metaphone
A phonetic algorithm for matching terms and names by sound, as pronounced in English, by translating words into a standard code or representation. It was developed by Lawrence Philips to address the perceived deficiencies in the Soundex algorithm. Metaphone and its later improvements are available as built-in operators in a number of systems. *See also* **Soundex.**

metasearching
See **federated searching.**

microcontrolled vocabulary
Also called a **microthesaurus.** A controlled vocabulary that is limited in the range of topics covered but fits within the domain of a larger, broader, or more generic controlled vocabulary. It typically contains highly specialized terms that are not necessarily in the broader controlled vocabulary but that map to the hierarchical structure of the broader controlled vocabulary. *See also* **derivation, extension vocabulary,** and **satellite vocabulary.**

middle name
In Western tradition, any name for a person placed before the last name (surname) but after the first name (e.g., *Alan* in *Richard Alan Meier*). *See also* **first name** and **last name.**

minimal description
In the context of cataloging art, a record containing the minimum amount of information in the minimum number of fields or metadata elements.

modeling
See **derivation.**

modifier
In a compound term or name, the adjectival component that modifies the noun (e.g., *flying* in *flying buttresses; Mount* in *Mount Etna*). *See also* **focus.**

monohierarchy
A hierarchy in which each child has only one immediate parent. Distinguished from a **polyhierarchy.**

monolingual
Expressed in a single language, as distinguished from **multilingual.** In a monolingual thesaurus, the terms and names are expressed in only one language.

movable work
In the context of cataloging art, any tangible object capable of being moved or conveyed from one place to another, as opposed to real estate or other buildings. Distinguished from **built work.**

multilingual
Expressed in more than one language, as distinguished from **monolingual.** In a *multilingual thesaurus,* terms and other information may be expressed in more than one language.

name authority
An authority containing proper names, most often personal names. *See also* **subject heading list.**

narrower term (NT)
Also called **narrower context** or **child.** A record to which another record or multiple records are superordinate in a hierarchy (e.g., *Brewster chair* is a narrower term to *armchair*). In thesauri, the relationship indicator for this type of term is NT. Variations on the notation include NTG (narrower term generic), NTP (narrower term partitive), NTI (narrower term instance), NT1 (narrower term level 1), NT2 (narrower term level 2), etc.

narrow results
To adjust criteria in a search in order to retrieve a smaller number of more precise results that better match the intention of the searcher. *See also* **broaden results.**

natural language
Spoken or written texts, as distinguished from fielded data and **controlled vocabulary.**

natural order form
In the context of a controlled vocabulary, the form of a multiple-word name or term, where the name or term appears in the form that would be used in speech or a written text (e.g., *Christopher Wren* or *flying buttresses*), rather than inverted (as may be appropriate for an index). *See also* **inverted form.**

navigation
In the context of search and retrieval, the facility that allows users to move through a controlled vocabulary or other content

object by using preestablished links or relationships.

near synonymy
Also called **quasi-synonymy.** The characteristic of a term with meaning that is regarded as different from another term, but both the terms are treated as equivalents for the purposes of broadening retrieval. *See also* **synonym** and **true synonymy.**

neologism
A term that has been newly invented, or an existing term to which a new meaning is applied, often arising in the professional literature of a discipline.

nickname
A familiar, affectionate, derogatory, or humorous name that is used to refer to a person, place, or corporate body as a replacement for, or in addition to, the real or official name (e.g., *Masaccio,* meaning "big Tom," is a nickname for the painter *Tommaso Guidi*). (In the case of *Masaccio,* in the *ULAN* it is the preferred name based on literary warrant.) *See also* **pseudonym.**

NISO (National Information Standards Organization)
A nonprofit association that is accredited by the American National Standards Institute (ANSI) and identifies, develops, maintains, and publishes technical standards to manage information.

node
In the context of a thesaurus, any point or record in the hierarchy that is a location at which a branch or individual record (leaf) is attached; thus, the basic conceptual unit used to build hierarchies.

node label
A word or phrase inserted into a hierarchy to indicate the logical classification of the terms beneath it. *See also* **facet indicator** and **guide term.**

node linking
Also called **leaf linking.** In the context of combining multiple vocabularies, a method that uses various nodes in the hierarchical structure of a source controlled vocabulary to link to more detailed controlled vocabularies that are applicable to a single node of the parent hierarchy. The vocabulary linked to a broader vocabulary in this way is often called an **extension vocabulary.**

nondisplayed index
A machine-readable index that is not displayed for browsing or other direct access of end users, but is used behind the scenes to improve accuracy or speed in search and retrieval. Such indexes may be created beforehand or on the fly at the time of the query. *See also* **displayed index.**

nonequivalence
In mapping one vocabulary to another, the situation where there is no exact match, no term in the second language has partial or inexact equivalence, and there is no combination of descriptors in the second language that would approximate a match. *See also* **exact equivalence** and **inexact equivalence.**

nonleaf node
Also called an **internal node.** In a hierarchy, a node that links to one or more narrower contexts. *See also* **leaf node.**

nonpreferred parent
In a polyhierarchical thesaurus, any parent that is not flagged as preferred for use as a default in displays. *See also* **preferred parent.**

nonpreferred term
Also called a **nonpreferred name.** Any term in a vocabulary record that is not the **preferred term,** which is the term flagged as preferred for use as default in displays.

normalization
In the context of vocabulary retrieval, normalizing terms through a process of converting a term to its simplest form by removing case sensitivity, spaces, punctuation, and diacritics. It differs from **database normalization,** which is the process of reducing a complex data structure into its simplest structure, a technique used to eliminate data redundancy by

converting Unicode text into a standardized form, among other things.

notation
For a thesaurus, the alphabetic code used to express term types (D, AD, UF), associative relationship (RT), hierarchical relationships (BT, NT, BTG, NTG, BTP, NTP, BTI, NTI, BT1, BT2, NT1, NT2), and scope notes (SN), among others. *See also* **classification notation.**

object
See **work.**

object-oriented database
A data model where the universe is divided into a framework of classes, with each class containing instances or members (called "objects"). Classes can contain subclasses, members of which inherit the properties of the parent or "superclass." Rules and algorithms for processing the data are integrated with the data.

online catalog
In the context of art information, a type of system used by end users to search for and view data and images.

ontology
A formal, machine-readable specification of a conceptual model, in which concepts, properties, relationships, functions, constraints, and axioms are all explicitly defined. While an ontology is not technically a controlled vocabulary, it uses one or more controlled vocabularies for a defined domain and expresses the vocabulary in a representative language that has a grammar for using vocabulary terms in an automated way to express something meaningful.

operating system
Also called an **operating system program.** A software program that runs a computer, as distinguished from an **application** program, which is designed to accomplish a task for an end user (e.g., word processing).

operational specificity
Also called **postings specificity.** An automated method that attempts to predict the specificity of terms in a domain based on the number of postings or links to that term in a content object (e.g., a term that is linked to very few content objects is predicted to be highly specific).

organizational warrant
Justification for the inclusion of a term in a vocabulary based on the specialized requirements or jargon of the group or organization that is creating or sponsoring the vocabulary. *See also* **literary warrant** and **user warrant.**

orphan term
In a thesaurus, a record that has no associative or hierarchical relationship to any other term in the thesaurus.

orthography
Correct or proper spelling and form of a word or words, including capitalization, diacritics, and punctuation, based on standard usage or convention.

paradigmatic relationship
Also called a **semantic relationship.** A relationship between terms or concepts that is permanent and based on a known definition.

parallel searching
See **federated searching.**

parent
See **broader term (BT).**

parenthetical qualifier
A **qualifier** placed in parentheses for display.

parent string
The display of hierarchical parents in a horizontal string, as distinguished from vertical indented displays or displays using **notation.**

parsing
In processing data, a process where data is broken or filtered into smaller, more distinct units.

partial equivalence
The relationship between terms in two vocabularies where one term has a broader

scope but is partially synonymous with the other term. *See also* **exact equivalence** and **inexact equivalence.**

partitive relationship
See **whole/part relationship.**

patronymic
Also called a **patronym.** A word or words used with a given name to identify a person; common in early Western personal names when last names were uncommon (e.g., *Bartolo di Fredi* means "Bartolo, son of Fredi"); may also refer to a surname derived from a paternal ancestor (e.g., *Robinson* means "son of Robin").

permuted index
A type of index where individual words of a term are rotated to bring each word of the term into alphabetical order in the term list. *See also* **inverted form.**

phonetic matching
A process by which terms are matched to other terms that are presumed to sound like the original term, in an attempt to compensate for users' misspellings or general variation in spelling of names or terms (e.g., *Meier* and *Meyer* are pronounced alike). **Phonetic algorithms**—such as Soundex, Metaphone, and others—are used for indexing words by their pronunciation.

physical feature
In the context of geographic information, a characteristic of the earth's surface that has been shaped by natural forces, including continents, mountains, forests, rivers, and oceans. *See also* **administrative entity.**

pick list
A user interface feature that allows the user to select from a preset list of terms and is typically used to control vocabulary for indexing or to provide options in a query. A pick list is generally populated with a controlled list.

polyhierarchy
A thesaurus in which any record may be linked to multiple parent records. *See also* **hierarchy.**

polyseme
A word or lexical unit (e.g., a compound term) with multiple meanings; known as a **homograph** in written language and a **homophone** in spoken language.

postable term
See **descriptor.**

postcoordination
The process of combining two or more terms at the time of retrieval rather than at the indexing stage; usually uses the Boolean operators AND, OR, or NOT (*Baroque* AND *cathedral*) in formulating a query. *See also* **precoordination.**

posting
In the context of indexing, any instance of a given indexing term having been assigned to records, documents, or other content objects. Formulas used for predicting the usefulness of terms or methods of retrieval may count the number of postings relative to the target content objects or use the numbers of postings in other statistics.

postings specificity
See **operational specificity.**

precision
A measure of a search system's effectiveness in terms of retrieving only relevant results; expressed as the ratio of relevant records or documents retrieved from a database to the total number retrieved in response to the query. A high-precision search means that most of the results retrieved will be relevant; however, a high-precision search will not necessarily retrieve all relevant results. Recall and precision are inverse ratios (when one goes up, the other goes down). *See also* **recall.**

precoordination
The formulation of a compound term or multiword heading at the time of indexing, rather than at the time of retrieval. An example of a precoordinated term is *Baroque cathedrals;* an example of a precoordinated heading is *United States—History—Civil War, 1861–1865. See also* **postcoordination.**

predefined report
A report for which the query and the output have been written and made available for repeated use by users; users may be allowed to enter variables that are plugged into the report. *See also* **ad hoc query.**

preferred flag
A designation indicating that a term or other data instance is preferred over others of the same type in a record. In addition to a preferred term for the record overall, there may be a **preferred indexing name flag** for the inverted order version of the term, a **preferred display name** for the natural order form of the name, a **preferred role** or **preferred place type** flagged among a list of roles or place types, and so on.

preferred parent
In a polyhierarchical thesaurus, the broader context that is chosen as conceptually preferred; or, to serve as the default in hierarchical displays. *See also* **nonpreferred parent.**

preferred term
Also called a **preferred name.** The term designated among all synonyms or lexical variants for a concept to be used as the default term to represent the concept in displays and other situations. In a monolingual thesaurus, the preferred term is also the only descriptor in the record. In a multilingual thesaurus, there may be a descriptor for every language, but there is often only one preferred term for the record as a whole. *See also* **descriptor.**

preprocessing
Also called **data preprocessing.** Preliminary processing or transformation of data in order to facilitate further processing, parsing, etc.

probabilistic model
An automatic relevance and weighting method in which terms in a text or other content object are modeled as random variables so that term frequency and distribution are used to predict the probability of relevance. *See also* **language model.**

procedure
Also called a **subprogram** or **subroutine.** A relatively independent portion of computer code within a larger computer program that performs a specific task in a series of steps.

processing
Also called **data processing** or **information processing.** The manipulation or transformation of data through a series of operations. In **batch processing,** the operations are grouped together in batches and performed automatically; in **interactive processing,** the operations are prompted by input from a human programmer or user. *See also* **computer program.**

program
See **computer program.**

programming language
A formal language defined by syntactic and semantic rules and used to write instructions that can be translated into machine language and then executed by a computer (e.g., SQL, C++, C#, Java, Perl).

provisional term
See **candidate term.**

pseudonym
A false or fictitious name, especially one assumed by an artist, author, or other person to maintain anonymity or to designate an identity for a particular activity, among other reasons (e.g., *Le Corbusier* is a pseudonym assumed by the architect *Charles Édouard Jeanneret*). *See also* **nickname.**

punctuation
In the context of vocabulary terms, the marks from standard written communication used to clarify, organize, or indicate how a word or words should be read (e.g., hyphen, comma, period, quotation marks, parentheses).

qualifier
A word or phrase used to distinguish a term in a vocabulary from otherwise identical terms that have different meanings. A

qualifier is separated from the term, usually by parentheses. It is also called a **gloss;** although, strictly speaking, a qualifier should be used only with homographs, and a gloss has a more general meaning in the field of linguistics. *See also* **homograph.**

quasi-synonymy
See **near synonymy.**

query
Also called a **search.** In the context of retrieval, a command to look in a database and find records or other information that meet a specified set of criteria (e.g., *select subject_id from term where normalized_term like 'A%' and historic_flag = 'H';*). The most precise queries are those that return the fewest false hits.

query expansion (QE)
Reformulating a query in order to return a broader or more comprehensive set of results (e.g., adding synonyms to the user's search term).

recall
A measure of a search system's effectiveness in terms of retrieving all results that are possibly relevant, expressed as the ratio of the number of relevant records or documents retrieved over all the relevant records or documents. A high recall search retrieves a comprehensive set of relevant results; however, it also increases the likelihood that marginally relevant content objects will also be retrieved. Recall and precision are inverse ratios. *See also* **precision.**

reciprocity
In reference to vocabulary records, the characteristic of a two-way relationship in which both entities have mutual dependence, action, or influence on each other. Semantic relationships in controlled vocabularies must be reciprocal, meaning each relationship from one record to another must also be represented by a reciprocal relationship in the other direction. Reciprocal relationships may be **symmetric** (e.g. RT/RT) or **asymmetric** (e.g. BT/NT).

record
Also called a **logical record.** In the context of this book, a conceptual arrangement of fields referring to a vocabulary concept or a work. This is different from a **database record,** which is one row in a database table or another set of related, contiguous data. *See also* **concept record.**

record group
See **group.**

related term (RT)
A concept that is associatively (not hierarchically) linked to another concept in a thesaurus. In thesauri, the relationship indicator for this type of term is RT. *See also* **associative relationship.**

relational table database
Also called a **relational database.** A database in which data is organized into columns and rows according to specific defined relationships (e.g., in a vocabulary database, a table of terms may be linked to a table for languages).

relationship
In the context of this book, a link between two types of data, records, files, or any two entities of the same or different types in a system or network. *See also* **link.**

relationship indicator
A word, code, or other device used in thesauri to identify the semantic relationship between terms (e.g., UF), other fields (e.g., SN), or records (e.g., BT).

relevance
The extent to which information retrieved in a search is judged by the user to meet the criteria of the query.

relevance ranking
Ranking and sorting of query results, typically estimated by an algorithm that calculates the number and weight of occurrences of the search term in the targeted data.

report
An organized set of data presented in a format suitable for viewing or printing,

typically produced by a preestablished query that may or may not have variables that are manipulated by the user.

repository
In the context of art and related disciplines, refers to an institution, agency, or individual that has physical or administrative responsibility for an art object, work of architecture, or cultural object.

required fields
Fields or data elements that are required to meet a standard or the requirements of a system's operations. *See also* **core fields.**

reserved characters
Letters, numbers, or symbols that have special uses or meanings in a programming or querying language.

results list
The records or other data retrieved in response to a query and presented online or in a system in an organized display.

retrieval
In the context of this book, the activity of using a search or other method to find records or other data in a database. *See also* **query.**

romanization
Also called **latinization.** The conversion of a character or word expressed in a non-Roman alphabet or writing system (e.g., Cyrillic or Korean) into the Roman alphabet by means of transcription, transliteration, or a combination of the two methods.

root
Also called **root node** or **top term.** The highest level of the hierarchy, from which all branches descend.

rotated listing
See **permuted index.**

satellite vocabulary
A thesaurus that is created with the intention of, or is later adapted for, linking to another vocabulary that is larger, broader, or more generic; it may be integrated at many points in the original vocabulary. *See also* **extension vocabulary, microcontrolled vocabulary,** and **node linking.**

schema
Also called a **scheme.** In the context of this book, the organization, structure, and rules for a set of data (e.g., the set of tables, views, indexes, and descriptions for columns in a database, or the organization and description of an XML document).

scope note (SN)
A note explaining the coverage, specialized usage, and meaning of terms. In thesauri, the relationship indicator for this note is SN.

search
See **query.**

searching
Operations or algorithms intended to determine if one or more data items meet defined criteria or possess a specified property.

***see also* reference**
A type of cross-reference, usually in a printed index, directing the reader to a related term or entry. A *see also* reference differs from a *see* reference in that the *see also* reference is not made between synonyms, but between terms or headings that are more peripherally related.

***see* reference**
A type of cross-reference, usually in a printed index, directing the reader from a nonpreferred term or subject heading to the preferred term or subject heading for the same concept. The term or subject heading at the *see* reference is a synonym for the preferred term or heading.

semantic linking
A method of linking terms in a vocabulary or larger database according to the meaning of the terms and relationships between terms.

semantic relationship
See **paradigmatic relationship.**

SGML (Standard Generalized Markup Language)
International Standards Organization standard *ISO/IEC 8879:1986;* a markup

language first used by the publishing industry, for defining, specifying, and creating digital documents that can be delivered, displayed, linked, and manipulated in a system-independent manner. XML and HTML are derived from SGML.

sibling
A concept that shares the same immediate broader context (one level higher) as other concepts. Siblings are subordinate to the same broader concept and are at the same hierarchical level.

single-to-multiple term equivalence
In the context of mapping terms from different vocabularies to each other, the situation that occurs when a term in one vocabulary has no direct match in the second vocabulary, but instead must be mapped to a combination of terms.

social tagging
The decentralized practice and method by which individuals and groups create, manage, and share tags (terms, names, etc.) to annotate and categorize digital resources in an online "social" environment. *See also* **folksonomy.**

software
The components of a computer system that are not physical, including programs, procedures, algorithms, and documentation pertaining to the operation of a system and the performance of specific tasks, such as word processing, Web browsers, photo editing, and art cataloging or vocabulary editing. *See also* **hardware.**

sorting
In the context of this book, the automated process of organizing a results list, data elements in a record, or other data in a particular sequence based on established criteria or attributes of the data—for example, alphabetically, by parent string, or by an associated date. There may be primary sort criteria and secondary sort criteria (e.g., an algorithm can be formulated to first sort place names in a results list alphabetically, and then—for homographs in the list—to sort by the parent string). *See also* **filing rules.**

Soundex
A phonetic algorithm for matching terms and names by sound, as pronounced in English, by translating words into a standard code or representation. It was developed by Robert Russell and Margaret Odell and patented in 1918 and 1922. The National Archives and Records Administration (NARA) maintains the current rule set for the official implementation of Soundex used by the U.S. Government. *See also* **Metaphone.**

source
In the context of building vocabularies, a citable reference to a term in the literature that helps establish its form, spelling, usage, and meaning. *See also* **literary warrant.**

source authority
In the context of this book, a bibliographic authority file used to control the citations providing warrant for terms in a vocabulary or information in a work record.

source language
In the context of translating or mapping one vocabulary to a vocabulary in another language, the language of the original vocabulary. *See also* **target language.**

specialized vocabulary
See **microcontrolled vocabulary.**

specifications
In the context of designing an information system, the formal, detailed description of user and technical requirements, including specific descriptions of procedures, functions, screens, reports, materials, other features, and hardware. *See also* **user requirements.**

specificity
In the context of indexing, the degree of precision or **granularity** used in assigning terms. Measures of greater specificity include the use of the narrowest applicable indexing term rather than a broader, more generic term. *See also* **exhaustivity.**

SQL (Structured Query Language)
A standard command language used with relational databases to perform queries and other tasks.

standard
A vocabulary, set of rules, code of practice, or description of characteristics and parameters that is documented, established by experts, or approved by an authoritative body and widely recognized or employed as an authoritative exemplar of correctness or best practice; used within a discipline or domain in order to promote interoperability and efficiency.

statistical specificity
See **operational specificity.**

stemming
In the context of mapping terms for search and retrieval, the alteration of a term by automatically truncating or removing common suffixes, word endings, or prefixes in order to find a match, usually applied to sets of related words that are derived from a common root and appear in a variety of grammatical forms (e.g., *paint, painting, painted*).

stop list
In the context of search and retrieval, words in a vocabulary or target data that are ignored in searching or matching because they occur too frequently or are otherwise of little value in retrieval for a given domain. Common stop lists for a text contain articles, conjunctions, and prepositions, although these words are typically not included in a stop list for a vocabulary.

string syntax
Also called **string indexing.** The creation of headings by computer algorithm, characterized by headings that are more consistent than the typically idiosyncratic headings created by hand (e.g., the automatic concatenation of a parent string in a heading for a geographic place, such as *San Gimignano (Siena province, Tuscany, Italy)*).

structure
See **data structure.**

subfacet
A major conceptual division of a thesaurus that is located near the top of the tree but under a facet. *Also* called a **hierarchy** in the *AAT*, although *hierarchy* has a more general meaning as well.

subject
In the context of this book, the focus concept of a vocabulary record (e.g., the subject of a ULAN record is a person). Also used to refer to the subject matter (often iconographical content) of what is depicted in or by a work of art or the content of a text.

subject heading list
An alphabetical list of words or phrases used to indicate the content of a text or other thing; characterized by **precoordination** of terminology, meaning that several unique concepts are combined in a string (e.g., *Archaeology and art—China—History—20th century*). A type of controlled vocabulary. *See also* **authority heading** and **heading.**

subject indexing
A term typically used in the context of bibliographic cataloging but also applicable to cataloging art; refers to the application of indexing terms to the content of the document, as contrasted to a description of its physical characteristics.

subprogram
See **procedure.**

subroutine
See **procedure.**

surface Web
See **visible Web.**

surname
See **last name.**

switching
In the context of mapping one vocabulary to another, refers to the use of a third vocabulary (a **switching vocabulary**) that itself can link to terms in each of the two original controlled vocabularies; useful when the original two vocabularies do not map well

directly to each other. *See also* **direct mapping.**

symmetric relationship
In the context of a thesaurus, a reciprocal relationship that is the same in both directions (e.g., RT/RT). *See also* **asymmetric relationship** and **reciprocity.**

syndetic structure
Also called **cross-reference links.** In the context of a vocabulary, refers to the linking of equivalent, broader, narrower, and other related terms so that they can be used as cross-references to each other and to related headings for the purpose of access.

synonym
A term having a different form but exactly or very nearly the same meaning as another term. *See also* **near synonymy** and **true synonymy.** Compare **lexical variant.**

synonym ring list
A type of controlled vocabulary containing terms that are considered equivalent for the purposes of retrieval but do not necessarily have true synonymy.

synonymy
A type of semantic relation in which two words or terms have the same or very similar meaning. *See also* **near synonymy** and **true synonymy.**

syntax
In the context of this book, the structure of elements in a compound term or name (e.g., last name first, comma, first name, middle initial) or heading; also used to refer to the structure of elements in a search query (e.g., rules for the placement of the Boolean operators OR, AND, or NOT between terms); and analogous to the linguistic structure of elements in a sentence.

synthesis note
A brief preliminary finding, example, or recommendation. This expression was used in the original print publication of the *AAT* to refer to bottom-of-page notes throughout each subfacet (or hierarchy) that suggested ways in which descriptors from that subfacet could be combined in post-coordination with other descriptors (these recommendations are now found in the *AAT Editorial Manual*).

system
Also called a **computer system.** A number of interrelated hardware and software components that work together to store and convert data into information by using electronic processing. In the context of this book, a system for building and maintaining vocabularies, cataloging art, or performing search and retrieval. *See also* **database.**

systematic display
See **hierarchical display.**

table
See **data table.**

target language
In the context of translating or mapping one vocabulary to a vocabulary in another language, the language into which the original vocabulary is being translated. *See also* **source language.**

taxonomy
A classification organized into a hierarchical structure and applicable to a defined domain. Often used to refer to the classification of living organisms according to physical characteristics, but the term and principles can be applied to classification in any discipline. Unlike thesauri, taxonomies do not typically include synonyms and associative relationships. *See also* **folksonomy.**

term
A word or group of words representing a single concept; a vocabulary record comprises terms and other information, including relationships, scope notes, sources, etc. Additionally, in the jargon of thesaurus construction, the word *term* is often used as shorthand to refer to the concept that is represented by that *term* (e.g., BT and NT actually refer to the relationships between concepts). The distinction between a *term* in the strict sense and *term* meaning a *record* must often be inferred from the context of the discussion.

term frequency (TF)
An automatic ranking method often used in a formula with **inverse document frequency** in information retrieval and text mining to measure how important a term is to a set of data and how useful it will be in retrieval.

term record
In the jargon of thesaurus construction, the collection of information associated with a descriptor, including the history of the term, its relationships to other terms and records, etc. In this book, it is referred to as a **record** (or a **concept record**) in order to distinguish it from the information that is actually associated only with the term table in a relational database model (e.g., language of the term, contributor of the term).

text
In the context of this book, data that is not vocabulary controlled and generally unstructured beyond the common structure of standard language expressions of characters, words, sentences, or paragraphs. *See also* **free-text field.**

thesaurus
A controlled vocabulary arranged in a specific order and characterized by three relationships: equivalence, hierarchical, and associative. Thesauri may be monolingual or multilingual. Their purposes are to promote consistency in the indexing of content and to facilitate searching and browsing.

top term (TT)
See **root.** In thesauri, the relationship indicator for this type of term is TT.

transcription
In the context of cataloging art, the process of recording a term or text word-for-word and letter-for-letter, including accurately copying capitalization, punctuation, spacing, line breaks, illegible passages, and all other possible aspects of the original (e.g., to accurately express the nuances of an artist's signature or an ancient architectural inscription). Transcriptions in this context are typically semidiplomatic or seminormalized transcriptions, meaning both substantive and accidental features of the original are retained, but abbreviations are spelled out using brackets or other punctuation to distinguish the original from the editorial content.

translation
The process of changing a term or text from one language into another by interpreting the meaning of the original (source) term and expressing it as an equivalent in the second (target) term (e.g., *copper mines* in English is translated as *mines de cuivre* in French).

transliteration
The process of rendering the letters or characters of one alphabet or writing system into the corresponding letters or characters of another alphabet or writing system, generally based on phonetic equivalencies. While a common noun will often be translated, a proper name in a non-Roman alphabet is more often transliterated. There are often multiple standards for transliterating from one writing system to another, thus producing multiple variant names.

tree structure
A controlled vocabulary display format in which the complete hierarchy of records is shown or accessible by clicking. The tree structure may be constructed by assigning a tree number or line number to each record, or by another method. *See also* **hierarchical display.**

true synonymy
The characteristic of terms or names that have meanings that are identical or as nearly identical as is possible with language. The purpose of enforcing true synonymy in a vocabulary is to increase precision in indexing and retrieval. *See also* **near synonymy and synonym.**

truncation
In searching and matching, the action of cutting off characters in a search term in order to find all terms with a certain common string of characters; typically involves the user employing a wildcard

symbol to search for a string of characters no matter what other characters follow (or sometimes, precede) that string (e.g., searching for *arch** will retrieve *arch, arches, architrave, architecture, architectural history,* etc.).

trunk name
See **focus.**

typography
The font style and size, and arrangement, appearance, and layout of words and texts on a page; in the context of this book, one of the critical elements in designing an end-user display of vocabulary records.

Unicode
A 16-bit character encoding scheme and standard for representing letters, characters, and diacritical marks in most of the world's modern scripts.

unique identifier
A number or other string that is associated with a record or piece of data, exists only once in a database, and is used to uniquely identify and disambiguate that record or piece of data from all others in the database.

upload
See **load.**

up-posting
Also known as **autoposting.** The automatic generation of search terms or indexing terms by adding broader terms to the specific term requested by a searcher or used by the indexer. *See also* **generic posting.**

***used for* term**
Also called a **UF.** In thesaurus jargon, a term that is not a descriptor and not an alternate descriptor. If the thesaurus is being used as an authority, a *used for* term is not authorized for indexing. *Used for* terms typically comprise spelling or grammatical variants of the descriptor or have true synonymy with the descriptor.

user
See **end user.**

user interface (UI)
The portion of the design and functionality of a cataloging, editorial, search and retrieval, or other system or Web site with which end users interact, including the arrangement of displays, menus, clickable text or images, pagination, etc. A user interface that is easy for users to utilize is called **user friendly.**

user requirements
In system design, the initial formal explanation of functionalities, displays, and reports expressed from the point of view of the users' needs and expectations. *See also* **specifications.**

user warrant
Justification for a term in a controlled vocabulary based on the frequency of user queries that employ the term. User warrant may be used for terms intended for retrieval but is typically not sufficient warrant for posting a term in a thesaurus used for indexing. *See also* **literary warrant** and **organizational warrant.**

variable
In a query, criteria or factors that may be changed to produce different results (e.g., as may be expressed in a *where* clause, as the relationship type code in this query: *select distinct subjecta_id from associative_rels where rel_type_code = '2110';*). *See also* **criteria.**

variant term
In a vocabulary, a term that is not the preferred term but refers to the same concept, including *used for* terms and alternate descriptors.

vector-space model
A method of automatic weighting in retrieval where an algebraic model is used for term frequency and distribution, creating representative vectors in multiple dimensional space; when compared to the vectors of an incoming query, the relevance of results may be predicted.

verbal units (VU)
In linguistics and computer science, the phonemic, morphemic, or grammatical

clauses or units of language or texts, corresponding in part to syllables, letters, or words.

visible Web
The subset of the World Wide Web that is visible to Web browsers and can be indexed by search engines' Web crawlers or robots, in contrast to pages that are impenetrable by search engines or to data that is generated dynamically.

visual arts
See **art.**

vocabulary
See **controlled vocabulary.**

vocabulary control
The process of enforcing the use of certain terminology with the goal of providing consistency and improving retrieval.

warrant
In the context of vocabularies, sources that provide justification for the spelling and usage of a term to refer to a particular usage for a concept, including warrant of publications, common usage by experts of a discipline, or other sources.

Web browser
A software application that enables users to view and interact with information and media files on the Web (e.g., Internet Explorer, Mozilla Firefox, and Safari).

Web site
A collection of related electronic pages (**Web pages**), generally formatted in HTML and found at a single address where the server computer is identified by a given host name.

weighted term ranking
See **best match.**

whole/part relationship
Also called a **partitive relationship.** A hierarchical relationship between a larger entity and a part or component. In the context of cataloging art, it typically refers to a relationship between two work records or two records in a thesaurus (e.g., *Florence* is part of *Tuscany*). *See also* **genus/species relationship** and **instance relationship.**

wildcard
Also called a **wildcard character** or **wildcard symbol.** In searching, a character or symbol, such as an asterisk or percent sign, that is used to represent any other character or characters in a Boolean query or other string (e.g., the asterisk in *Buonar**).

word sense disambiguation (WSD)
In automatic search and retrieval, the problem of determining in which sense a homograph is intended in a given data set or text. *See also* **disambiguation.**

work
In the context of this book, a creative product, including architecture; artworks such as paintings, drawings, graphic arts, sculpture, decorative arts, and photographs that are considered to be art; and other cultural artifacts. A work may be a single item or may be made up of many physical parts.

XML (Extensible Markup Language)
A simple, flexible markup language derived from SGML. Originally designed for large-scale electronic publishing, but now playing an increasingly important role in the publication and exchange of a wide variety of data on the Web.

Selected Bibliography

Agirre, Eneko, and Philip Edmonds, eds. *Word Sense Disambiguation: Algorithms and Applications.* New York: Springer, 2007.

Ahronheim, Judith R. "Descriptive Metadata: Emerging Standards." *Journal of Academic Librarianship* 24 (1998): 395–404.

Aitchison, Jean, Alan Gilchrist, and David Bawden. *Thesaurus Construction and Use: A Practical Manual.* 4th ed. New York: Fitzroy Dearborn, 2002.

American Library Association. *ALA Filing Rules.* Chicago: American Library Association, 1980.

Anderson, James D. *Guidelines for Indexes and Related Information Retrieval Devices: A Technical Report.* Bethesda: National Information Standards Organization, 1997.

ANSI/NISO Z39.19-2005: Guidelines for the Construction, Format, and Management of Monolingual Controlled Vocabularies. Bethesda: National Information Standards Organization, 2005.

ANSI/NISO Z39.50-2003: Information Retrieval: Application Service Definition and Protocol Specification. Bethesda: National Information Standards Organization, 2003.

ANSI/NISO Z39.85-2001: Dublin Core Metadata Element Set. Bethesda: National Information Standards Organization, 2001.

Association for Library Collections and Technical Services, Association of College and Research Libraries, and American Library Association. *Gearing Up for the Future: The "Art & Architecture Thesaurus" Model for Subject Access.* Chicago: American Library Association, 1992.

Baca, Murtha. "Making Sense of the Tower of Babel: A Demonstration Project in Multilingual Equivalency Work." *Terminology* 4, no. 1 (1997): 105–16.

———. "Practical Issues in Applying Metadata Schemas and Controlled Vocabularies to Cultural Heritage Information." *Cataloging and Classification Quarterly* 36, nos. 3–4 (2003): 47–55.

Baca, Murtha, ed. *Introduction to Art Image Access: Issues, Tools, Standards, Strategies.* Los Angeles: Getty Research Institute, 2002.

———. *Introduction to Metadata.* 2nd ed. Los Angeles: Getty Research Institute, 2008. http://www.getty.edu/research/conducting_research/standards/intrometadata/.

Baca, Murtha, and Patricia Harpring. *Categories for the Description of Works of Art.* Rev. ed. Los Angeles: J. Paul Getty Trust, 2009. http://www.getty.edu/research/conducting_research/standards/cdwa/.

———. "The Getty Vocabularies and Standards: Describing, Cataloging, and Accessing Information about

Architecture and Architectural Documents." *COMMA: International Journal on Archives* (forthcoming).

Baca, Murtha, Patricia Harpring, Elisa Lanzi, Linda McRae, and Ann Baird Whiteside. *Cataloging Cultural Objects: A Guide to Describing Cultural Works and Their Images.* Chicago: American Library Association, 2006.

Baker, Thomas. "A Grammar of Dublin Core." *D-Lib Magazine* 6, no. 10 (2000). http://www.dlib.org/dlib/october00/baker/10baker.html.

Bales, Kathleen. "The USMARC Formats and Visual Materials." *Art Documentation* 8, no. 4 (1989): 183–85.

Barry, Randall K., ed. *ALA-LC Romanization Tables: Transliteration Schemes for Non-Roman Scripts.* Washington, D.C.: Library of Congress, 1997.

Bates, Marcia J. "Indexing and Access for Digital Libraries and the Internet: Human, Database, and Domain Factors." *Journal of the American Society for Information Science* 49 (1998): 1185–1205.

Beebe, Caroline. "Image Indexing for Multiple Needs." *Art Documentation* 19, no. 2 (2000): 16–21.

Bell, Lesley Ann. "Gaining Access to Visual Information: Theory, Analysis and Practice of Determining Subjects—A Review of the Literature with Descriptive Abstracts." *Art Documentation* 13, no. 2 (1994): 89–94.

Benedetti, Joan M. "Words, Words, Words: Folk Art Terminology—Why It (Still) Matters." *Art Documentation* 19, no. 1 (2000): 14–21.

Besser, Howard. *Introduction to Imaging.* 2nd ed. Edited by Sally Hubbard and Deborah Lenert. Los Angeles: Getty Research Institute, 2003. http://www.getty.edu/research/conducting_research/standards/introimages/.

Blum, F. *"Art & Architecture Thesaurus."* Book review. *Choice* 28 (1990): 603.

Bold, John, and Robin Thornes. *Documenting the Cultural Heritage.* Los Angeles: J. Paul Getty Trust, 1998.

Borgman, Christine L. *From Gutenberg to the Global Information Infrastructure: Access to Information in the Networked World.* Cambridge: MIT Press, 2000.

BS 1749:1985: British Standard Alphabetical Arrangement Filing Order of Numerals and Symbols. London: BSI Group, 1985.

BS 8723-1:2005, BS 8723-2:2005, BS 8723-3:2007, BS 8723-4:2007: Structured Vocabularies for Information Retrieval. London: BSI Group, 2005–7.

Canow, Joanne, David Kerr, and Patricia Whittaker. *Faceted Classification, A Group Perspective: History, Current and Future Applications.* Vancouver: Univ. of British Columbia, 2002.

CDWA Lite: XML Schema Content for Contributing Records via the OAI Harvesting Protocol. Los Angeles: J. Paul Getty Trust, 2005. http://www.getty.edu/research/conducting_research/standards/cdwa/cdwalite.html.

Chen, Hsin-Liang, and Edie M. Rasmussen. "Intellectual Access to Images." *Library Trends* 48 (1999): 291–302.

Craven, Tim. *Thesaurus Construction: An Introductory Tutorial.* London, Ont.: Univ. of Western Ontario, 2002.

Dewey, Melvil. *Dewey Decimal Classification and Relative Index.* Edited by Joan S. Mitchell et al. 4 vols. Albany, N.Y.: Forest, 1996.

Getty Vocabulary Program. *Editorial Guidelines.* Los Angeles: J. Paul Getty Trust, 2003–. http://www.getty.edu/research/conducting_research/vocabularies/editorial_guidelines.html.

Greenberg, Jane. "Intellectual Control of Visual Archives: A Comparison between the *Art & Architecture Thesaurus* and the Library of Congress *Thesaurus for Graphic Materials.*" *Cataloging and Classification Quarterly* 16, no. 1 (1993): 85–117.

Harpring, Patricia. "The Architectural Subject Authority of the Foundation for Documents of Architecture." *Visual Resources* 7 (1990): 55–63.

———. *Brief Rules: Training Manual for Contributors.* Los Angeles: J. Paul Getty Trust, 2007. http://www.getty.edu/research/conducting_research/vocabularies/brief_vocab_training_manual.pdf.

———. "Can Flexibility and Consistency Coexist? Issues in Indexing, Mapping, and Displaying Museum Information." *Spectra (The Journal of the Museum Computer Network)* 26, no. 1 (1999): 33–35.

———. "Contributing to the Getty Vocabularies." *VRA Bulletin* (forthcoming).

———. "The Getty *Cultural Objects Name Authority (CONA).*" *Art Documentation* (forthcoming).

———. "How Forcible Are Right Words!: Overview of Applications and Interfaces Incorporating the Getty Vocabularies." *Museums and the Web 1999: Selected Papers.* Pittsburgh: Archives & Museum Informatics, 1999. http://www.archimuse.com/mw99/papers/harpring/harpring.html.

———. "The Limits of the World: Theoretical and Practical Issues in the Construction of the *Getty Thesaurus of Geographic Names.*" In *ICHIM 97: Fourth International Conference on Hypermedia and Interactivity in Museums: Proceedings,* 237–51. Paris: Archives & Museum Informatics, 1997.

———. "Proper Words in Proper Places: The *Thesaurus of Geographic Names.*" *MDA Information* 2, no. 3 (1997): 5–12.

———. "Resistance Is Futile: Inaccessible Networked Information Made Accessible Using the Getty Vocabularies." In *ASIS Annual Conference Proceedings*, 838. Silver Spring, Md.: American Society for Information Science, 1999.

———. "The Role of Metadata Standards in Mapping Art Information: The Visual Resources Perspective." *VRA Bulletin* 27, no. 4 (2000): 71–76.

Helmer, John F. *"Art & Architecture Thesaurus."* Book review. *Art Documentation* 10, no. 1 (1991): 41–42.

Hourihane, Colum. *Subject Classification for Visual Collections: An Inventory of Some of the Principal Systems Applied to Content Description in Images. VRA Special Bulletin* 12. Columbus: Visual Resources Association, 1999.

International Terminology Working Group, sponsored by the Getty Information Institute. *Guidelines for Forming Language Equivalents: A Model Based on the "Art & Architecture Thesaurus."* Los Angeles: J. Paul Getty Trust, 1998.

ISO 2788:1986: Documentation—Guidelines for the Establishment and Development of Monolingual Thesauri. Geneva: International Organization for Standardization, 1986.

ISO 8879:1986: Information Processing—Text and Office Systems—Standard Generalized Markup Language

(SGML). Geneva: International Organization for Standardization, 1986.

ISO 5964:1985: Documentation—Guidelines for the Establishment and Development of Multilingual Thesauri. Geneva: International Organization for Standardization, 1985.

ISO/CD 25964-1: Information and Documentation—Thesauri and Interoperability with Other Vocabularies—Part 1: Thesauri for Information Retrieval. Geneva: International Organization for Standardization, forthcoming.

ISO/IEC 8859-1:1998: Information Technology—8-Bit Single-Byte Coded Graphic Character Sets—Part 1: Latin Alphabet No. 1. Geneva: International Organization for Standardization, 1986.

ISO/IEC 10646:2003: Information Technology—Universal Multiple-Octet Coded Character Set (UCS). Geneva: International Organization for Standardization, 2003.

Jackman-Schuller, Carol E. "Words, Words, Words: Managing the Wealth of the AAT—Early Efforts at Implementation." *Art Documentation* 9, no. 2 (1990): 75–76.

Joint Steering Committee for Development of RDA. *RDA: Resource Description and Access*, forthcoming.

Joint Steering Committee for Revision of AACR et al. *Anglo-American Cataloguing Rules*. 2nd ed. Chicago: American Library Association, 2004.

Lancaster, F. Wilfrid. *Vocabulary Control for Information Retrieval*. 2nd ed. Arlington: Information Resources, 1986.

Lanzi, Elisa. "The Linguistic Challenge of a Multilingual AAT." *Art Documentation* 14, no. 2 (1995): 19.

Lanzi, Elisa, ed. *Introduction to Vocabularies: Enhancing Access to Cultural Heritage Information*. 2nd ed. Edited by Patricia Harpring. Los Angeles: Getty Research Institute, 2000. http://www.getty.edu/research/conducting_research/vocabularies/introvocabs/.

Lee-Smeltzer, Kuang-Hwei (Janet). "Finding the Needle: Controlled Vocabularies, Resource Discovery, and Dublin Core." *Library Collections, Acquisitions and Technical Services* 24 (2000): 205–15.

Leise, Fred, Karl Fast, and Mike Steckel. "All about Facets and Controlled Vocabularies." *Boxes and Arrows* (9 December 2002). http://www.boxesandarrows.com/view/all_about_facets_controlled_vocabularies.

———. "Synonym Rings and Authority Files." *Boxes and Arrows* (26 August 2003). http://www.boxesandarrows.com/view/synonym_rings_and_authority_files.

Library of Congress. *Library of Congress Filing Rules*. Washington, D.C.: Library of Congress, 1980.

———. *Library of Congress Subject Headings: Principles of Structure and Policies for Application*. Washington, D.C.: Library of Congress, 1990–2001. http://www.itsmarc.com/crs/shed0014.htm.

Lider, Brett, and Anca Mosoiu. "Building a Metadata-Based Website: Ontologies." *Boxes and Arrows* (21 April 2003). http://www.boxesandarrows.com/view/building_a_metadata_based_website.

McCulloch, Emma, and George Macgregor. "Analysis of Equivalence Mapping for Terminology Services." *Journal of Information Science* 34 (2008): 70–92.

Miller, Uri. "Thesaurus Construction: Problems and Their Roots." *Information*

Processing and Management 33 (1997): 481–93.

Molholt, Patricia, and Toni Petersen. "The Role of the *Art & Architecture Thesaurus* in Communicating about Visual Art." *Knowledge Organization* 20 (1993): 30–34.

Nagel, Lina. "The Spanish-Language Version of the *Art & Architecture Thesaurus:* History, Current Status, Implementation, and Dissemination." *VRA Bulletin* 32, no. 2 (2005): 30–34.

National Center for Biotechnology Information. NCBI Taxonomy Homepage. National Library of Medicine. http://www.ncbi.nlm.nih.gov/Taxonomy/.

Olson, Tony, and Gary Strawn. "Mapping the LCSH and MeSH Systems." *Information Technology and Libraries* 16 (1997): 5–19.

Panofsky, Erwin. *Meaning in the Visual Arts: Papers In and On Art History.* Garden City, N.Y.: Doubleday, 1955.

Petersen, Toni. "Developing a New Thesaurus for Art and Architecture." *Library Trends* 38 (1990): 644–58.

Porter, Vicki, and Robin Thornes. *Guide to the Description of Architectural Drawings.* Revised by Patricia Harpring. Los Angeles: J. Paul Getty Trust, 2005. http://www.getty.edu/research/conducting_research/standards/fda/.

RBMS Bibliographic Standards Committee. *Thesaurus Construction and Maintenance Guidelines.* Chicago: Association of College and Research Libraries, 1998.

Roberts, Helene E. "Do You Have Any Pictures of . . . ?: Subject Access to Works of Art in Visual Collections and Book Reproductions." *Art Documentation* 7, no. 3 (1988): 87–90.

———. "A Picture Is Worth a Thousand Words: Art Indexing in Electronic Databases." *Journal of the American Society for Information Science and Technology* 52 (2001): 911–16.

Rowley, Jennifer, and John Farrow. *Organizing Knowledge: An Introduction to Managing Access to Information.* 3rd ed. Burlington: Gower, 2000.

Smits, Jan. "Metadata: An Introduction." *Cataloging and Classification Quarterly* 27, nos. 3–4 (1999): 303–19.

Soergel, Dagobert. "SemWeb. Proposal for an Open, Multifunctional, Multilingual System for Integrated Access to a Knowledge Base about Concepts and Terminology." In *Proceedings of the Fourth International ISKO Conference, 15–18 July 1996, Washington DC,* 165–73. Frankurt am Main: Indeks Verlag, 1996.

Spiteri, Louise F. "The Use of Facet Analysis in Information Retrieval Thesauri: An Examination of Selected Guidelines for Thesaurus Construction." *Cataloging and Classification Quarterly* 25, no. 1 (1997): 21–37.

Stanley, Janet L. "African Art and the *Art & Architecture Thesaurus.*" *Museum Studies Journal* 2, no. 2 (1986): 42–52.

Straten, Roelof van. *An Introduction to Iconography.* Revised English ed. Translated from the German by Patricia de Man. Yverdon, Switzerland: Gordon & Breach, 1994.

Svenonius, Elaine. *The Intellectual Foundation of Information Organization.* Cambridge: MIT Press, 2000.

Taylor, Arlene G., and Daniel N. Joudrey. *The Organization of Information.* 3rd ed. Westport, Conn.: Libraries Unlimited, 2009.

Taylor, Bradley L. "Chenhall's *Nomenclature,* the *Art & Architecture*

Thesaurus, and Issues of Access in America's Artifact Collections." *Art Documentation* 15, no. 2 (1996): 17–23.

Thornes, Robin, with Peter Dorrell and Henry Lie. *Introduction to Object ID: Guidelines for Making Records That Describe Art, Antiques, and Antiquities.* Los Angeles: J. Paul Getty Trust, 1999.

Tillett, Barbara. *What is FRBR? A Conceptual Model for the Bibliographic Universe.* Washington, D.C.: Library of Congress, 2004. Originally published in *Technicalities* 25, no. 5 (2003). http://www.loc.gov/catdir/cpso/whatfrbr.html.

Tudhope, Douglas et al. "Query Expansion via Conceptual Distance in Thesaurus Indexed Collections." *Journal of Documentation* 62 (2006): 509–33.

Turner, James M. "Subject Access to Pictures: Considerations in the Surrogation and Indexing of Visual Documents for Storage and Retrieval." *Visual Resources* 9 (1993): 241–71.

Vellucci, Sherry L. "Metadata and Authority Control." *Library Resources and Technical Services* 44 (2000): 33–43.

Vizine-Goetz, Diane et al. "Vocabulary Mapping for Terminology Services." *Journal of Digital Information* 4, no. 4 (2004).

Warner, Amy J. *A Taxonomy Primer.* Ann Arbor: Lexonomy, 2002.

Warren, Susanne. "Workshop: Using the *AAT Art & Architecture Thesaurus:* Practical Applications." *Art Documentation* 11, no. 2 (1992): 63.

Whitehead, Cathleen. "Faceted Classification in the *Art & Architecture Thesaurus.*" *Art Documentation* 8, no. 4 (1989): 175–77.

Wielinga, B. J., et al. "From Thesaurus to Ontology." *Proceedings of the First International Conference on Knowledge Capture,* 194–201. New York: Association for Computing Machinery, 2001.

Willer, Mirna. "Modeling Authority Data: FRAD." In *LIDA: Libraries in the Digital Age, 25–30 May 2009, Dubrovnik-Zadar* [proceedings], 207. Dubrovnik: Inter-University Center, 2009.

Zeng, Marcia Lei, and Lois Mai Chan. "Trends and Issues in Establishing Interoperability among Knowledge Organization Systems." *Journal of the American Society for Information Science and Technology* 55, no. 5 (2004): 377–95.

Note: All Web sites were accessed on 1 May 2009.

Introduction to Controlled Vocabularies: Terminology for Art, Architecture, and Other Cultural Works

Patricia Harpring

Patricia Harpring is managing editor of the Getty Vocabulary Program, where she supervises the contributions and editorial work for the *Art & Architecture Thesaurus* (*AAT*), *Union List of Artist Names* (*ULAN*), *Getty Thesaurus of Geographic Names* (*TGN*), and *Cultural Objects Name Authority* (*CONA*). She is coeditor, with Murtha Baca, of *Cataloging Cultural Objects: A Guide to Describing Cultural Works and Their Images* (2006), *Categories for the Description of Works of Art* (*CDWA*), and the *CDWA Lite* XML schema for art and architectural records. She is the author of editorial rules for building vocabularies and numerous papers and presentations on cataloging art, controlled vocabularies, data standards, and building information systems for art, architecture, and other cultural objects. She holds a PhD in art history from Indiana University and is author of *The Sienese Trecento Painter Bartolo di Fredi* (1993).